Eastern Destiny

Eastern Destiny

Russia in Asia and the North Pacific

G. Patrick March

PRAEGER

Westport, Connecticut
London

Library of Congress Cataloging-in-Publication Data

March, G. Patrick, 1924–
    Eastern destiny : Russia in Asia and the North Pacific / G.
Patrick March.
      p. cm.
    Includes bibliographical references and index.
    ISBN 0–275–95566–4 (alk. paper).—ISBN 0–275–95648–2 (pb : alk.
paper)
    1. Russia—Territorial expansion. 2. Russia—Relations—Asia.
3. Asia—Relations—Russia. 4. Soviet Union—Relations—Asia.
5. Asia—Relations—Soviet Union. 6. Russia—Relations—Pacific
Area. 7. Pacific Area—Relations—Russia. 8. Soviet Union—
Relations—Pacific Area. 9. Pacific Area—Relations—Soviet Union.
I. Title.
DK43.M34   1996
303.48'24705—dc20   96–2199

British Library Cataloguing in Publication Data is available.

Library of Congress Catalog Card Number: 96–2199
ISBN: 0–275–95566–4
    0–275–95648–2 (pb)

First published in 1996

Praeger Publishers, 88 Post Road West, Westport, CT 06881
An imprint of Greenwood Publishing Group, Inc.

Printed in the United States of America

The paper used in this book complies with the
Permanent Paper Standard issued by the National
Information Standards Organization (Z39.48–1984).

10 9 8 7 6 5 4 3 2 1

Contents

Illustrations

Maps

1. Eastward the Russians thrust, from the icy waters of the Arctic

to the deserts and mountains of Central Asia.

Maps

1. Eastward the Russians thrust, from the icy waters of the Arctic

to the deserts and mountains of Central Asia.

Preface

This work is essentially an effort to present, in one volume, a coherent story of Russian eastward expansion. The desirability of such a book became apparent to the author while teaching a course for several years on the history of Russia in Asia and the North Pacific. Whereas many published works are available on certain facets of the subject, such as Siberia, Central Asia, Sino-Russian relations, or Russian Alaska, no offerings furnish any sort of wide perspective of the overall saga. This volume should properly be viewed as an outline history. In one volume, one could pretend to do no more on such a vast subject.

What is set forth herein is no attempt at original analysis but rather a rational narrative based on well-known works by a wide variety of experts in the field. That is not to say that in many instances primary sources in Russian and English have not been regularly consulted. However, since the subject is so broad in scope and the general facts are reasonably well known, the story presented does not require meticulous footnoting for attribution. For further perusal, a suggested reading list including the works of many of these experts is provided in lieu of a more formal bibliography. On the assumption that the readership will be primarily American, only English titles of reasonably available books have been included.

In recounting the tale of Russian expansion in this volume, a special effort has been made to describe the setting for the geographical areas of expansion. Brief historical background is provided not only for the Russians but also for the Mongols and other Central Asians, the Chinese, the Japanese, and the Koreans. At the same time, care is taken to ensure a feel for the conflicting aims of other European powers in East Asia and the North Pacific, including the shores of North America, whose interests were seen as threatened by Russian expansion.

The focus throughout the book is directed primarily at events taking place on the perimeter of the Russian state rather than at colonization and development of the lands once they come under the dominion of tsar or commissar. That is to say, primary concentration is on the expansion (and occasional contraction) of the nation's borders as well as on the attendant international politics.

The standard transliteration of Russian words is used with certain exceptions such as the letter *y* to represent the final vowel sound of the masculine adjectival endings in such names as Rozhestvensky. Also, the "soft sign" is generally omitted in most Russian words unless direct quotes are involved. The Russian form of the name is usually given, such as "Aleksandr" for "Alexander" except in the case of rulers, whose names are so familiar in their anglicized form.

In the case of Chinese words and names, the Wade-Giles system of transliteration is used except for those familiar place names from the Postal Atlas, such as "Peking" and "Sian." Since the popular media now mostly employ the Pinyin system of transliteration, this version of the name is given in parentheses in the index, and cross-indexing of the two (or three) forms is provided. Japanese personal names are given in the Japanese fashion: the surname precedes the given name. The same practice, of course, applies to the names of Chinese and Korean persons.

The author is especially indebted to Professor John Stephan whose consuming interest and aggressive pursuit of the subject inspired in all his students a fascination with the remarkable march of Muscovy across the Eurasian continent. Gratefully acknowledged is his personal encouragement in researching and teaching about Russian expansion to the farthest east. The support of two successive directors of the Center for Russia in Asia at the University of Hawaii, or CeRA, Pat Polansky and Bob Valliant, is happily recognized. The quality of the maps is owed to the talents of Jane Eckelman of Manoa Mapworks, Honolulu.

Introduction

When dealing with Russian territorial expansion one encounters a succession of superlatives, such as the greatest expanse of steppe, the most extensive coniferous forest, the longest coastline, and the coldest climate of the Northern Hemisphere, to name just a few. When the nation achieved its maximum extent of area as the Russian Empire or the Soviet Union, it was the largest country in the world, holding dominion over more than 40 percent of Eurasia, the most capacious landmass on this earth. In addition, for the better part of a century, Russia controlled—or laid claim to—a half million square miles of land in North America.

Whereas Muscovy would push its borders deep into Europe, its most dramatic expansion was to the east and southeast into Asia. Two centuries ere a youthful United States was driven across the North American continent by "Manifest Destiny," the Muscovites had traversed an even wider continent under much harsher conditions of climate and terrain. They then pushed on to Alaska where they arrived a half century before the British George Vancouver or the American Robert Gray first appeared in the North Pacific.

The story of Russian eastward expansion has its roots in the very origin of the first real polity of Eastern Europe. This was Kievan Russia, which resulted from the melding of indigenous eastern Slavs with invading Scandinavian Vikings known as Varangians (or *Rus'*) in the ninth century. The people of this new collection of principalities were converted to Orthodox Christianity about a hundred years later, a significant event which granted them a legacy from Byzantium of concepts such as autocracy and caesaropapism. Kievan Russia fought constantly against migratory steppe peoples, with more or less success, until they were submerged by the Mongol onslaught in the mid-thirteenth century. For the next 240 years, the eastern Slavs suffered the humiliation of subjection to the Mongol—or Tatar—Yoke. It was small wonder that Muscovy, which rose from the ashes of Kievan Russia as the strongest of the Russian principalities, was autocratic and paranoid concerning the security of its borders.

A succession of astute great princes of Muscovy succeeded in territorial expansion at the expense of their neighbors. Particularly effective was Ivan III (ruled 1462–1505) who defeated Novgorod, thereby extending Muscovite control to the Ural Mountains. It was he, as well, who actually shed the Mongol Yoke in 1480. Further, through his marriage to Zoe, niece of the last emperor of the eastern Roman Empire, Byzantine autocratic concepts were reenforced, even to the introduction of the title "tsar"—the Slavic version of "caesar."

Despite these achievements, Muscovy was still hemmed in. It was denied access to the Black Sea by Turks and Tatars and to the Baltic by Swedes, Poles, Lithuanians, and the Hanseatic League. Ivan the Terrible (ruled 1553–1584) controlled only one coastline—in the far north, a dubious asset until enterprising English and Dutch navigators arrived in search of a northeast passage to the Orient. It was during Ivan's reign that Muscovite expansionist energies were effectively directed eastward. First, defeat of the Kazan Tatars in 1552 afforded easy access into the Urals via the Kama River, a tributary of the Volga. Then, just four years later, victories over the Astrakhan Tatars opened the lower Volga all the way to the Caspian, thus bringing the shores of Persia within ready reach. It was late in Ivan's rule that the first major step was taken in the conquest of Siberia when the redoubtable Cossack Yermak Timofeevich and his desperate followers subdued the khanate of Sibir in the basin of the Irtysh River. Such was the momentum of the advance that Russians stood on the shores of the Sea of Okhotsk in 1639, only fifty-seven years later.

The Time of Troubles, which followed the death of Boris Godunov (ruled 1598–1605), gave clear illustration to the Muscovites of the chaos that could result from a weak and faction-ridden leadership in their capital. Thus, in 1613, after suffering the indignities heaped on them by Swedes, Poles, Lithuanians, and Cossacks, the people of Moscow rose up and installed Michael Romanov as their new autocrat. It was Michael's grandson, Peter the Great (ruled 1682–1725), who transformed himself from the tsar of Muscovy into the emperor of Russia and who finally pushed Russian authority to the shores of the Baltic. It was he who also provided the stimulus for three major thrusts to Russia's east: delineation of an agreed Russo-Chinese border stretching from the Altai Mountains of western Mongolia to the Sea of Okhotsk; explorations from Kamchatka, which reached the shores of Japan; and the expedition of Vitus Bering and Aleksei Chirikov, which brought the first Europeans to the northwestern reaches of the North American continent.

Later in the eighteenth century, Catherine the Great presided over the conquest of southern and western Ukraine through decisive military victories over the Ottoman Turks. She was also a major player in the partitions of Poland which eliminated that state from the map of Europe. At the same time, entrepreneurs, such as Grigori Shelikhov, were extending the hunt for sea otter pelts to the

Aleutians and Alaska while others were trying unsuccessfully to open trade with Japan, a nation that had isolated itself from the Western powers by means of its exclusion policy.

The advent of the nineteenth century witnessed the efforts of the newly chartered Russian American Company to control the destiny of Russia's possessions in the Pacific. One of the overriding problems facing company operations, which had frustrated the people in the fur trade during the preceding two centuries, was the provision of adequate sustenance. The tough and resourceful Alexander Baranov, chief manager for the Russian American Company in Alaska during a tumultuous twenty years, attempted to solve the problem in various ways. One way was by purchase from the British and Americans; another was by the establishment of a company site at Fort Ross near Bodega Bay in California. These efforts would lead to just some of his many disappointments. Dr. Georg Schaffer's vision of Hawaii as a provisioning source likewise would not materialize. Ultimately the Russian American Company's very raison d'être came into question as the sea otter population of the North Pacific precipitately declined. Lessons learned from the Crimean War clearly revealed the inability of the empire to defend Alaska and led to Alexander II's decision to sell it to the United States in 1867.

By the middle of the nineteenth century, Japan's exclusion policy could no longer resist the naval power of the Western nations. Just a year after American Commodore Matthew Perry forced the Japanese to open their country, Russian Vice Admiral Evfimi Putiatin signed a treaty (1855) with Japan which sought to draw a boundary between that nation and his. Not until after the lapse of twenty years would the border be clearly delineated whereby Russia received the island of Sakhalin and Japan all the Kuril Islands, which stretched from Kamchatka to Hokkaido.

Meanwhile, as China grew weaker, and the maritime powers of the West dramatically increased their presence in the western Pacific, Saint Petersburg sought to consolidate its holdings by taking deep bites into Chinese territory along the Amur River and the western shores of the Sea of Japan. The climax of this evolution in 1860 was the cession of Amuria and Ussuria from China, to the extent of one-third of a million square miles of land.

Now deeply concerned about retention of its far-flung Asiatic possessions, the Russian Empire commenced, in the last decade of the nineteenth century, the construction of the Transsiberian Railway. In order to alleviate somewhat the extraordinary engineering problems inherent in such an undertaking, Russian Finance Minister Sergei Witte was able to convince the Chinese to permit routing of a key segment of the railroad across the middle of Manchuria, thus linking up, in the shortest distance, Vladivostok and Transbaikalia by a line called the Chinese Eastern Railway. This was the beginning of a gradual growth of Russian influence in Manchuria, a process that would only be stopped by ill fortune suffered in the Russo-Japanese War of 1904–1905. The result of this conflict was a division of Manchuria into Russian north and Japanese south. Further,

Russia was deprived of any influence in Korea and was forced to cede the southern half of Sakhalin to the Japanese Empire.

The nineteenth century saw, as well, Russian expansion across the Caucasus Mountains and into Central Asia. The kingdom of Georgia sought protection of the Russian tsar in 1804, and the next half century witnessed a very gradual but bloody Russian advance at the expense of the Ottoman Turks and the Persians in Transcaucasia. At the same time that Saint Petersburg was selling Alaska and encountering the limits of its expansion in East Asia, it began to focus its attention on western Turkestan. By the seventh decade of the century, the era known on the world stage as the Late Imperial Period began to set in, during which vast territories in Africa, Asia, and the Pacific came under European control. The principal Russian push during this time would be in Central Asia where eager army officers precipitated the rapid expansion of Russian authority to the borders of Afghanistan and Persia—which the British viewed as their own client states and buffers in the defense of India. This confrontation was but one aspect of the Anglo-Russian ''great game'' of imperial politics whose arena stretched from the Ottoman Empire in the west to the northeastern seaboard of the Chinese Empire.

The Russian Empire at this stage, except the loss of Alaska, had expanded to its fullest, having come up against the stops of German, British, and Japanese power. This condition continued into World War I and all the cataclysmic events associated with it. The autocratic authority of the tsar and the devoted servants of the state had heretofore provided the centripetal force required to hold the empire together. Unfortunately, Tsar Nicholas II's tenuous exercise of this authority could not withstand the buffeting of total war. Following his abdication and the ensuing period of chaos engendered by a provisional government, a revolution, and a civil war, a strong central authority was finally restored by the Bolsheviks, but only after the loss of western and Baltic border lands. A clever innovation was then instituted—the Union of Soviet Socialist Republics—which paid lip service to the various non-Russian ethnic groups along the perimeter from Belorussia to the Transcaucasus and Central Asia but which at the same time retained supreme power in Moscow, now the center in place of Saint Petersburg.

China likewise was given over to revolution, one that differed from the Russian revolution in that it resulted in fragmentation into provinces ruled by autonomous warlords. Into these seeming Russian and Chinese political vacuums came the Japanese with dreams of mainland empire. After being frustrated by the Great Powers in their early attempts to capitalize on the situation, the Japanese did succeed in establishing a puppet regime in Manchuria in 1932 and eradicating, for the time being, the Russian presence therein. However, by the end of the decade, Soviet power in the Far East had grown to the point where Japanese attempts to broaden their sphere of influence at the expense of the Soviet Union or the first Soviet client state—Mongolia—were decisively repulsed. Tokyo then turned south and commenced the conquest of China.

In World War II, the survival of the Soviet Union was owed in no small measure to the Soviet-Japanese Neutrality Treaty which permitted wholesale movement of Soviet troops from the Far East to the European battle front against Germany and which made possible the delivery of the majority of American Lend-Lease through Vladivostok all during the war. After the tide of war turned against the Germans in 1943 and 1944, Soviet forces recovered great stretches of land in Eastern Europe. As the result of the Yalta agreements of February 1945, Soviet authority was extended over European territory lost to Russia in 1920—and more. In the Far East, having received territorial promises at Yalta and having renounced the Neutrality Treaty with Japan, the Soviet Union joined the war on the side of the United States and occupied southern Sakhalin and all the Kuril Islands.

Although Yosif Stalin reluctantly agreed to coexist amicably with the Republic of China, his concern was eased by the victory of the People's Liberation Army in China in 1949. This event was fortuitous as well for China since the Soviet Union dealt rather generously with a sister communist state by renouncing its claims to the Chinese Eastern Railway, Port Arthur, and Talien. The Sino-Soviet honeymoon outlived Stalin's death in 1953 only by about half a decade, and war between the two behemoths of the communist world seems to have been narrowly averted at the end of the seventh decade of the century.

After the death of Stalin, although the Soviet Union had built up a huge war machine—including the largest navy in peacetime history—and space program, the country was governed by men who were products of the bureaucracy of the all-powerful Communist party. They therefore were not in position to implement the changes in the nation required to meet the dynamic challenges from the rest of the world. Mikhail Gorbachev, perhaps the most perceptive of the leaders following Stalin, was powerless to effect the changes required, and he fell from power in the attempt and saw the fragmentation of the Soviet Union itself.

The purpose of this volume is simply to present a brief but coherent account of Russian expansion into Asia and the North Pacific and the occasional withdrawal from some segments thereof. This work is intended, as well, to provide some sense of the historical forces that brought about such events and the reactions they elicited from those border states and the Great Powers most affected.

Eastern Destiny

1

Geography:
A Colossal and Chilling
Expanse

Despite the intimacy afforded by modern television, the name "Russia" still conjures up only a vague mental image of a very remote land. Few Americans, unless they are Russian or Soviet specialists, realize just how far north on our globe that nation is positioned. Most are cognizant that on our continent the greatest length of the Canadian/U.S. border is along the 49th parallel of north latitude, but very few realize that in Eurasia the great bulk of the Russian Republic lies north of the 50th parallel. Indeed, casual examination of a good map reveals that only two relatively small salients of the country extend south of 50 degrees: the segment between Ukraine and Kazakhstan which reaches to the Caucasus Mountains; and the Maritime District in the Far East which abuts ultimately on the northeastern border of North Korea.

In spite of the remoteness of the Russian homeland, it is closer to us than most Americans are aware. Next to Mexico and Canada, which have land borders with the United States, Russia is our closest neighbor. Only 2.5 miles separate the islands of Big Diomede (Russian) and Little Diomede (American) in the Bering Strait. Another common misconception is that the Nile is the only major river in the world that flows northward. A quick glance at a map of Siberia shows that three of the world's great rivers—the Ob/Irtysh, the Yenisei, and the Lena, each of which drains a basin essentially as large as that of the Nile—all flow northward into the Arctic Ocean.

Viewing Russia along a line from west to east, one is struck immediately by the fact that it extends across 170 degrees of longitude, almost halfway around the world. Although frequently excluded by scholars as part of the Far East, the Russian Federation continues eastward beyond all other Asian countries by 45 degrees of longitude. In proceeding from the Baltic to Cape Dezhnev, one traverses eleven time zones.

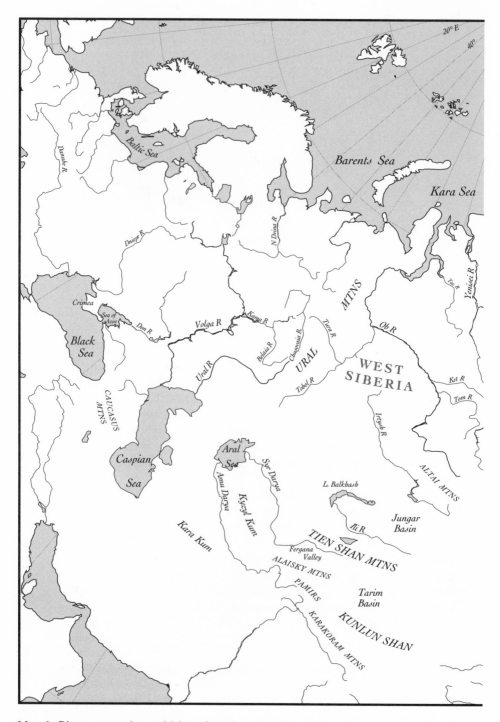

Map 1. Rivers, mountains, and lakes of northern Eurasia.

2

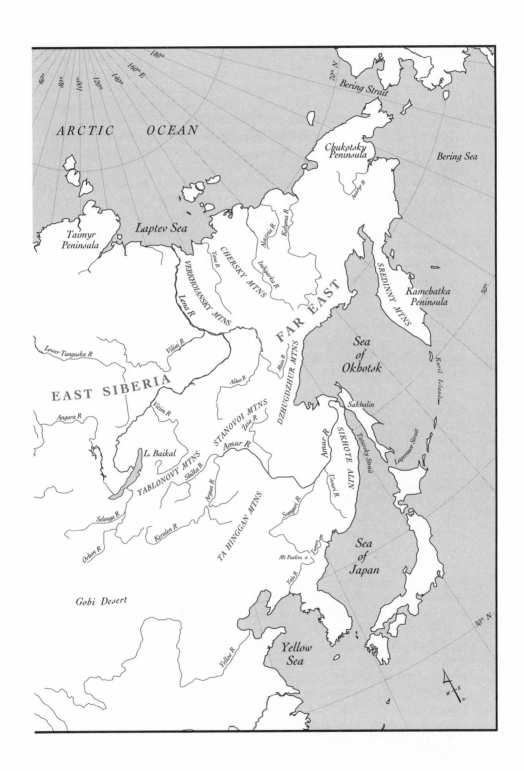

ARCTIC OCEAN

60° 80° 100° 120° 140° 160° E 180°

70° N.

Bering Strait

Bering Sea

Chukotsky
Peninsula

Taimyr
Peninsula

Laptev Sea

CHERSKY MTNS

Alazeia R.

Kolyma R.

Indigarka R.

Anadyr R.

Yana R.

VERKHOIANSKY MTNS

Lena R.

FAR EAST

SREDINNY MTNS

Kamchatka
Peninsula

50°

Lower Tunguska R.

Vilui R.

Maia R.

Sea
of
Okhotsk

Kuril Islands

EAST SIBERIA

Aldan R.

Angara R.

Vitim R.

STANOVOI MTNS

Zeia R.

DZHUGDZHUR MTNS

Sakhalin

Tatarsky Strait

Laperouse Strait

L. Baikal

Amur R.

Amur R.

SIKHOTE ALIN

YABLONOVY MTNS

Shilka R.

Argun R.

Ussuri R.

Selenga R.

Kerulen R.

TA HINGGAN MTNS

Sungari R.

Sea
of
Japan

Orbon R.

Mt Paektu ×

Tumen R.

30° N.

Gobi Desert

Yalu R.

Yellow R.

Yellow
Sea

N
W E
S

3

As one moves eastward inside Russia from Europe into Asia, he or she is made aware of such transition, by definition, when traversing the Ural Mountains or crossing the Ural River. The imaginary intercontinental dividing line then extends south of the Ural River, through the Caspian Sea, along the Caucasus Mountains, across the Black Sea, and finally out the Turkish Straits.

The Asiatic part of Russia is divided into three huge segments. The western-most of these, known as West Siberia, is roughly defined as that land lying between the Urals and the Yenisei River. It comprises a low-lying plain, very marshy in places, which is principally drained by the Ob/Irtysh river system. Beneath this 800,000–square-mile chunk of territory lies a veritable sea of oil and gas. Next, the land lying east of the Yenisei and west of the Lena River is called East Siberia and consists mostly of a plateau area. Third, the territory stretching from the Lena River to the Pacific Ocean is known as the Far East, usually preceded by the word ''Russian'' or ''Soviet.'' This huge area exceeds two million square miles in size and includes a wide variety of terrain and range of climate which attains survival extremes in its northeastern reaches.

One can, as well, divide Asiatic Russia (together with the Central Asian re-publics that were part of the Soviet Union) into startlingly different regions proceeding from north to south. The northernmost of these, stretching from the Arctic Ocean to approximately the Arctic Circle, is the tundra. This is a land bereft of trees and covered mostly by moss and lichens. In the summer the frozen surface melts and dissolves into a slush called muskeg. Also in the sum-mer, great swarms of giant mosquitoes materialize. Although the tundra is vir-tually uninhabited, kernels of population have gradually grown at the mouths of the great rivers. These extremely remote sites are provisioned by the intrepid ships of the Northern Sea Route's annual convoy through the icy waters of the Arctic Ocean.

To the south of the tundra lies the world's greatest coniferous forest, the taiga. This vast belt, which ranges from the Baltic to the Pacific, boasts a north-south width varying from 600 to 1,200 miles. Within this forest land of firs, pines, and larches have lived scattered tribes of primitive peoples and some of the world's most valuable furbearing animals.

As the taiga stretches to the south, it very gradually gives way (roughly around 50° north latitude) to the third distinct geographic land belt. This is the steppe, the world's most extensive grassland. Reaching from the Hungarian plain in the west through Ukraine, the northern Caucasus region of Russia, Kazakh-stan, and Mongolia to Manchuria in the east, the steppe lands have for millennia been the home of wandering herdsmen whose migrations have regularly chal-lenged the sedentary populations of China, India, Persia, and Europe. The great length of the steppe is constricted or divided at certain points along the way. The Gobi Desert, for example, divides the steppe into that belonging to Inner Mongolia and that belonging to Outer Mongolia. The steppe also is tightly squeezed by the T'ien Shan Mountains in Turkestan.

To the south of the steppe, in Central Asia, lie desert regions of varying degrees of climatic hostility such as the Kara Kum and Kyzyl Kum. Thus, since the taiga is not conducive to grazing and the desert is inhospitable, the steppe has been the historic highway of Eurasia.

Asiatic Russia, which often is casually dubbed "Siberia," earns its reputation as a giant icebox. Indeed, the lowest temperatures recorded in the Northern Hemisphere have occurred at Verkhoiansk, near the lower Lena River, reaching to within five degrees of $-100°$ F. This is in contrast to the coldest North American temperature of not quite $-80°$ F observed in Alaska. The weather is so cold that Russians use not only double- but also triple-paned windows as insulation in their buildings. Concentric double-tubing is required to give adequate protection against the freezing of water pipes. Work and school generally continue until the weather reaches $-50°$ F, for not only does the body suffer, but machinery is difficult to operate; rubber tires and even iron become brittle. It is relatively easy to determine when it is $-50°$ F: spittle bounces.

A brutal fact of life is that 40 percent of Asiatic Russia and virtually all of the Russian Far East is covered by permafrost, that is, by permanently frozen ground. Only West Siberia is relatively free of this challenge. Permafrost adds significantly to the costs of construction since all structures must be built on pilings sunk deep into the frozen earth. The only other major country faced by this problem, Canada, has had to build only towns of modest size on permafrost. In Russia, significantly larger centers such as Irkutsk, Chita, and Yakutsk have been constructed at great cost. In contrast to the bitter cold winters in Asiatic Russia, certain areas of the Far East can become quite hot and humid in July and August. Examples are Khabarovsk and Vladivostok. As a result, rapid temperature changes of as much as $75°$ F can occur in a period as brief as five hours.

The faunae are highly diverse, especially in the Far East where the taiga tiger, the largest of all cats, still exists—at least at this writing. Throughout the taiga live all kinds of furbearing animals. Thanks to the bitter winters, the pelts of these creatures are the finest in the world. The most famous is the sable, but top quality is also provided by fox, squirrel, ermine, ferret, and beaver. This rich supply of furs has throughout the centuries been a vitally important asset to the state and indeed was the principal lure that drew the Russians ever eastward beyond the Urals until they finally reached the Pacific Ocean in the seventeenth century. While speaking of animals, it might be mentioned that the mosquitoes are fierce not only in the tundra but throughout the region, especially in areas of permafrost.

A number of mountain ranges ring the region. In the west, so low as to be more accurately described as hills, are the Ural Mountains. Although they might not provide spectacular vistas (it is the rare peak which projects above 5,000 feet), they are a treasure house of mineral wealth. In addition to gold and precious stones, including diamonds, there are ores of many commercial metals, such as chromium, iron, copper, aluminum, and nickel. The Urals also are a rich source of coal, and oil and natural gas are found in copious quantities on either side of the range. The Caucasus Mountains, which are disposed along a north-west/southeast line between the Caspian and Black seas, are Europe's highest peaks. Mount Elbruz, at 18,510 feet, towers almost 3,000 feet above the topmost heights of the Alps.

Three dominant mountain ranges compress the steppe in Central Asia and divide that vast land into eastern and western Turkestan (sometimes referred to, respectively, as Chinese and Russian Turkestan). The southwesternmost of these are the Pamirs which lie just north of the modern state of Afghanistan. These towering peaks, which reach to more than 24,000 feet in height, form the western wall of the Tarim basin. Just to the northeast is another range, almost as high, which extends some 1,500 miles generally on a northeast/southwest axis. This is the T'ien Shan ("Mountains of Heaven") which divides Chinese Turkestan into the Tarim basin to the south and the Jungar basin to the north. Then, to the northeast of the T'ien Shan, in what is now the southwestern part of the Mongolian People's Republic (Outer Mongolia), are located the Altai Mountains. These peaks, while not as spectacular as the others, still rise to over 15,000 feet. They form the northern barrier of the Jungar basin and extend eastward along the northern edge of the steppe.

In the northeastern part of Mongolia commences a series of ranges, essentially southwest to northeast in orientation, which comprise the watersheds between the Lena and Amur rivers. The more famous of these are the Yablonovy and Stanovoi mountains. It was over these barriers that intrepid Russian adventurers came in the seventeenth century and first made contact with tribes tributary to the Manchus. A third range, the Dzhugdzhur, is a spine reaching northward from the east end of the Stanovoi and rising abruptly from the western shore of the Sea of Okhotsk.

Two other mountain ranges require our attention: the Sikhote Alin and Sredinny. The former, which dominates the Maritime District (the part of Russia that lies to the east of Manchuria), is of moderate height (to about 6,000 feet), is heavily forested, and contains unusual faunae, including the taiga tiger. The Sredinny Range, constituting the backbone of the Kamchatka Peninsula, reaches elevations in excess of 15,000 feet and contains numerous volcanoes, situated as it is on the "ring of fire" of the Pacific basin.

The remote part of the Far East that lies east of the Lena basin and north of both the Sea of Okhotsk and Kamchatka Peninsula features two mountain systems running north and south. The one nearest the Lena is named the Verkhoiansky Range, and the one just to the east, the Chersky. These two spines, together with high plateaus extending on to the Bering Strait, form the watersheds of three not inconsequential river systems which flow into the Arctic Ocean and one whose waters drain into the Bering Sea.

The largest Russian island in the Far East is Sakhalin. To the north of the Japanese island of Hokkaido and separated from it by the La Perouse Strait, this narrow piece of land parallels the eastern coast of mainland Asia for more than 500 miles. At its northwestern corner, it is very close to and opposite the mouth of the Amur River. An island chain whose history is entwined with that of Sakhalin is called the Kurils. These islands, which stretch from the southern tip of the Kamchatka Peninsula to the northeast corner of Hokkaido, a distance of over 600 miles, form a barrier between the Sea of Okhotsk and the open waters of the Pacific Ocean. Like Sakhalin, the Kurils are washed by waters which provide some of the richest fishing grounds in the world.

Whereas Sakhalin has been blessed with land resources, such as timber, oil, and coal, the Kurils provide precious little other than what is contained in the surrounding sea. Indeed, they are among the most inhospitable pieces of land anywhere on the globe. They are an ocean navigator's nightmare. They are shrouded in mists for a large portion of the year, largely owing to the sharp temperature gradient between the waters on either side of the chain. The tides and currents are complex and confusing, and for two months out of the year (January and February) floating ice is much in evidence. A further danger is the volcanic nature of the area which frequently is manifested in earthquakes and tsunamis.

The rivers of Asiatic Russia have played a significant role in the history of the region. The Ural River flows from the Ural Mountains into the Caspian Sea. Itself considered part of the imaginary line separating Asia from Europe, the Ural, for all its lack of familiarity to nonspecialists, is the third longest river of Europe (after the Volga and the Danube). The Caspian Sea, which is land-locked and so more correctly a lake, receives the waters of the Volga, the Ural, and other smaller rivers such as the Terek. Since it has no outlet, it loses its water through evaporation and thus becomes ever saltier.

To the east lies a similar hydraulic system comprising the Aral Sea and two rivers which have seen the struggle of civilizations for some 2,500 years. These are the Amu Darya and Syr Darya (the Oxus and Jaxartes in texts on ancient history). These two great streams originate in the heights of the Pamir and western T'ien Shan mountain ranges respectively and empty, finally, into the Aral Sea. The upper Syr Darya gives life to the Fergana Valley which is bordered on the north by the western spines of the T'ien Shan and on the south by the Alaisky Range. Like the Caspian, the Aral has no outlets and, in an even more arid environment than the Caspian, loses its water to evaporation. Today this land-locked body of water is an ecological disaster, occasioned primarily by the massive drain on the two rivers for irrigation, so that what was one of the largest lakes in the world is rapidly disappearing. A third similar system, but smaller in scale, is the Ili River, which rises in the eastern T'ien Shan (in China) and flows westward into Lake Balkhash (in Kazakhstan).

Much mightier in scale than the foregoing are the four major rivers in the Asiatic part of Russia. These are the Ob/Irtysh, the Yenisei, the Lena, and the Amur. The Ob/Irtysh river system is similar to the Mississippi/Missouri in that one great river is the tributary of another. The Irtysh rises in the Altai Mountains of southwestern Mongolia. As it flows north and west, it begins to gather the output of rivers flowing generally eastward from the Urals before joining the

Ob some 600 miles before that stream enters the huge Ob estuary and then the Arctic Ocean. The Ob itself originates on the north slopes of the Altai Mountains at the northwestern corner of Mongolia. As noted previously, this system drains virtually all of the flatlands of West Siberia.

The Yenisei River, which finds its source in the northern reaches of Mongolia, roughly 200 miles west of Lake Baikal, proceeds northward to the Arctic in a remarkably straight line. Since its course is along the western edge of the plateau that comprises East Siberia, it stands to reason that the bulk of its waters drain from the plateau, and its principal tributary is the Angara which is the outlet from Lake Baikal.

The third of the great rivers draining northward is the Lena. It finds its sources in the mountain ranges near Lake Baikal and those farther east such as the Yablonovy and Stanovoi; tributaries drain as well from the Verkhoiansky Range farther to the north. The principal city of the Lena is Yakutsk, located roughly halfway from Lake Baikal to the Arctic Ocean, in an area not far removed from the coldest spot in the Northern Hemisphere.

The fourth of the major river systems is the Amur, the only one that proceeds essentially in a west to east direction. It is formed by the confluence of the Shilka (rising just to the southeast of Lake Baikal) and the Argun (whose principal source is the Hailar which rises in the Ta Hinggan Mountains of northwestern Manchuria). The Amur River—or Heilungchiang (Chinese for ''Black Dragon River'')—serves as the Sino-Russian border until joined downstream by the Ussuri River near the modern city of Khabarovsk. The Amur proceeds, thence, inside Russian territory to its mouth on the Tatarsky Strait just opposite the island of Sakhalin. One of the most important tributaries of the Amur is the Sungari, the largest river inside Manchuria. Indeed, the earlier Chinese viewed the Sungari as the major river with the Amur as its tributary.

Other major streams worthy of note at this time would include those to the east of the Lena, all of which flow into the Arctic Ocean and drain very cold, bleak territories: the Yana, Indigarka, and Kolyma. Finally, the Anadyr empties into the bay of the same name and thence into the Bering Sea.

Some of the lakes in what was Soviet Asia have already been mentioned. The Caspian Sea, in reality the largest lake, also happens to be, technically, the lowest point in Europe. The Aral Sea, ranked fourth in size as recently as 1981, now is a fraction of its former surface area. Lake Balkhash, like the Aral Sea, is very shallow and has no outlet. Lake Baikal receives the water of numerous small rivers and streams and is drained by the Angara River. Although only rated eighth in area, it is the world's deepest. It is the largest single repository of fresh water, holding more than all the Great Lakes combined. It contains more water than any other lake except the Caspian, the waters of which are salt laden. It has an ecology with unique fish and mammals, even including a separate species of seal.

Soviet—or Russian—Asia is regularly described as a treasure house of riches. It contains 90 percent of the natural resources of the former Soviet Union. The timber supply is represented by the vast coniferous forests of the taiga, something beyond compare elsewhere in the world. We have mentioned the oil and gas reserves in West Siberia and the general region of the Urals. In addition to the minerals mentioned as occurring in the Urals, gold and ores of virtually every metal are found in the Russian Far East, along with huge deposits of graphite and coal. The second most profitable diamond fields anywhere are located in Yakutia in East Siberia. The power potential of the great rivers is impressive, and some of the world's most gigantic hydroelectric complexes have been constructed on the Yenisei River and its major tributaries. In addition to all these riches of the earth and rivers may be added the incredible fish resources in waters off the coasts of the Russian Far East.

The peoples of the former Soviet Union and Russian Empire are of an extraordinary variety. In the European part, except for the Finno-Ugric tongues of Estonia and Finland, virtually all the languages are of the Indo-European family. This includes, in addition to the Slavic languages which prevail in Russia, Ukraine, and Belarus, the Baltic languages of Latvia and Lithuania and the Romance language of Moldova. In the Transcaucasus, Armenian is of the Indo-European family, but the tongues spoken in the general area of Georgia constitute a family all their own. East of the Urals, except in the more heavily populated centers and along the major lines of communication, where Russian is dominant, mostly varieties of the Finno-Ugric or Altaic languages are encountered. The former survive in the taiga region of West Siberia, and are spoken by the rather scattered groupings of such peoples as the Komi, Khanty, and Selkup.

The Altaic language family is represented by three main groupings: Turkic, Mongolic, and Tungusic. The most widely spoken are versions of the Turkic in Central Asia, stretching from Azerbaijan in the Transcaucasus, through Turkmenistan, Uzbekistan, Kazakhstan, and Kyrgyzstan; in these countries, the speakers are numbered in the tens of millions. Also included among the Turkic speakers, within the Russian Federation, are large segments of the population in the republics of Tatarstan and Bashkortostan. Another important Turkic tongue, somewhat removed from the others, is Yakut, spoken by the inhabitants of the "freezing unit" of the "Siberian icebox." Their home stretches from the middle of East Siberia far to the north and east. Indeed, Yakutia—at over a million square miles of territory—constitutes the largest autonomous republic in the Russian Federation. If an independent country, it would rank eighth in size in the world.

Mongolic representatives of the Altaic family of languages are concentrated at two spots: the Kalmyks, just west of the lower Volga River, and the Buriats, who inhabit the areas to the west, south, and east of Lake Baikal. The Tungusic speakers (probably the most famous in history were the Manchus, rulers of China for 268 years), like the Finno-Ugrians of West Siberia, are now scattered in rather small concentrations throughout Siberia and the Far East in communities such as the Even, Evenk, and Orok.

Another language group, designated Paleo-Siberian, is represented on the Kamchatka Peninsula by the Koryak tongue and on the eastern end of the continent, the Chukotsky Peninsula, by the Chukchi language. The Nivkh of northern Sakhalin also are of this group. Small numbers, as well, of Eskimos, Aleuts, and Ainu are found in the more remote reaches of the continent and island groups to the east. One tongue found in former Soviet Asia of the Indo-European family, besides Russian, is Tadjiki, spoken by the people of Tajikistan, located just to the north of eastern Afghanistan.

A term regularly encountered in the history of Asia which can cause confusion is "Tatar." There is an ethnic concentration in the Russian republic named Tatarstan, centered in the city of Kazan, whose population speaks a Turkic language, designated Tatar. Throughout Russian history, there have been other peoples designated Tatars, such as the Nogai Tatars and, more recently, the Crimean Tatars. In historical usage, however, the word "Tatar" has not been accorded such specificity in its meaning. A Turkic word, it denotes a Turkic-speaking Sunni Moslem. In Europe the term acquired a fearful connotation about the time of the Mongol conquest in the thirteenth century. Many of Jenghis Khan's military units, which included just such Tatars, struck terror into the hearts of the Europeans. The name "Tatar" understandably became confused with the word "Tartar," which derives from the Greek word "Tartaros" (that segment of Hell reserved for special punishment). The term was used by the Romans centuries before to describe the fierce Parthian warriors of the east.

It was the Asian environment we have discussed in this chapter into which the Russians would expand, commencing in the waning years of the sixteenth century. It was a land grandiose in scope with vast natural resources. It was a land of extraordinary diversity in its human resources, from the Eskimos in the tundra to the primitive tribes of the taiga, and on to the more violent and vibrant peoples of the steppe whose polities were many and varied, ephemeral, and kaleidoscopic. The steppe was at once a unifier and a separator. Its peoples would wash in waves upon the sedentary populations of the peripheral states. Tribes of Inner Asia would be formed and reformed into a variety of nations which were greatly influenced by the nearest civilization center. But no single power would dominate the entire range of the steppe until the advent of the Mongol conquest, nor come close again until the later growth and expansion of the Russian and Chinese empires. The Russians, when they came, would first move quickly across the taiga to the Pacific Ocean. Then, much more slowly and carefully, would they expand into the more dangerous steppe and across the daunting waters of the North Pacific toward North America.

2

Early Russian Experiences with Asia and Asians

By the ninth century A.D., the eastern Slavs, who regularly experienced frictions with the Balts in the northwest and Finno-Ugrians to the north, for centuries had also to contend with a parade of migrants gravitating continuously westward across the steppe to their south. This included the Huns in the fifth century, followed by the Avars in the sixth. The Khazars established an imposing polity north and west of the Caspian during the seventh and eighth centuries, and the Magyars appeared in the ninth. Later would come the Pechenegs and Cumans.

It was one of the three great Viking surges of the ninth century that would forever change the political environment of the eastern Slavs. These Scandinavian invaders, known in history as the Varangians, thrust up the rivers that empty into the eastern and northern Baltic. The source of these streams, the Valdai Hills in the vicinity of modern-day Moscow, afforded easy portages to major rivers flowing to the east and south, notably the Volga to the Caspian and the Dniepr to the Black Sea. At the logical ends of their water voyages, the Varangians would encounter, in the east, the lands of the Abbasid Caliphate and, to the south, the power of the Byzantine Empire.

Rurik, the legendary leader of the Varangians (who called themselves *Rus'*), is supposed to have established Novgorod as the base of his power in 862. Some twenty years later the center of Varangian (Russian) activity was moved south to the north edge of the steppe on the Dniepr River at a spot named Kiev. This provided a more efficient base for trade to the south and defense against steppe migrants from the east. In two generations the Vikings lost their identity and language. Indeed, the grandson of Rurik was named Sviatoslav, although his military qualities and successes were worthy of his Viking antecedents. The polity or nation that resulted from the synthesis of eastern Slav and Viking is generally referred to as "Kievan Russia." This became a loose federation of

Map 2. Mongol Empire, late thirteenth century.

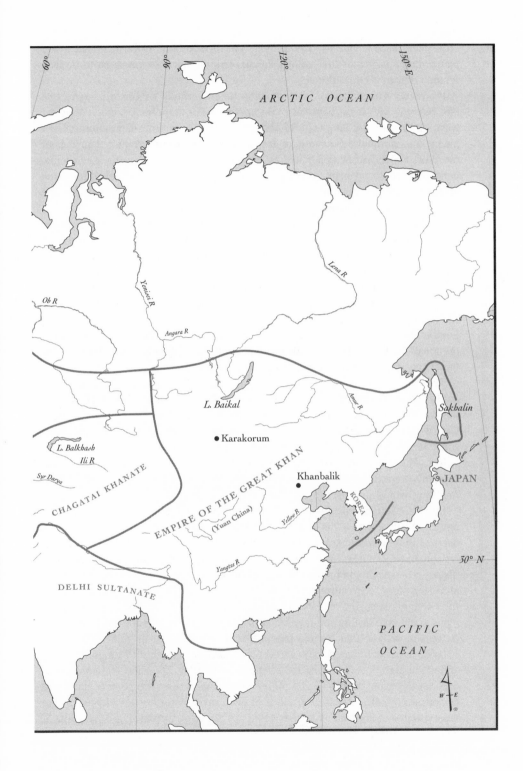

ARCTIC OCEAN

60°   90°   120°   150° E

Ob R

Yenisei R

Lena R

Angara R

L. Baikal

Amur R

Sakhalin

● Karakorum

L. Balkhash
Ili R

Syr Darya

CHAGATAI KHANATE

EMPIRE OF THE GREAT KHAN

Khanbalik
●

(Yuan China)

Yellow R

KOREA

JAPAN

30° N

DELHI SULTANATE

Yangtze R

PACIFIC

OCEAN

W   E

city-states, each under its own prince. The prince holding forth in Kiev was *primus inter pares*, or first among equals. In time his position came to be designated that of "Great Prince."

It was the Great Prince Vladimir who opted in favor of Christianity in 988 and oversaw the mass baptism of his people. The important point is that the form of Christianity adopted was that of the Orthodox from Constantinople. It meant the introduction of culture from the Eastern Church rather than that of the West which had been adopted by the western Slavs. As a result, the Oriental concept of caesaropapism, practiced by Byzantium—that the arbiter of temporal affairs serves also as arbiter for religious affairs (he who is Caesar is also the Pope)—would become not at all an alien idea.

Vladimir, who has been accorded the soubriquet "the Saint," was a leader who knew well how to exercise power, as did his son Yaroslav the Wise (ruled 1015–1054). Following Yaroslav, however, the line of succession became thoroughly muddled so that Kievan Russia evolved into a sort of crazy quilt of small principalities where each prince boasting descent from the conqueror Rurik could lay claim to the office of Great Prince. None was powerful enough, with rare exceptions, to amass the political and military authority essential to make good on his claim. The princes would lack the energy and cohesion to withstand the great challenge of the mid-thirteenth century presented by the Mongol forces under the leadership of a grandson of Jenghis Khan.

The Mongol conquest is considered by some to be the most traumatic manmade shock on earth prior to the carnage of World War I. The warriors from the Mongolian steppe would create, in three generations, the most extensive land empire the world has ever seen. This mighty phenomenon resembled in some ways the vigor and irresistibility of the Arab conquest of six centuries before. But the Arabs were propelled by a new, vibrant religion whereas the Mongols were driven by a conviction, arrived at by a few scattered steppe tribes, that they would just rise up and conquer the world.

Into the Mongol world was born the boy Temuchin in the year, it is generally agreed, 1162. Despite his status as the son of an important tribal leader, fate decreed that he would suffer years of privation and misfortune before surmounting all his difficulties and becoming one of the most charismatic leaders in history. His success in battle lent a magic to his name, and his own steadfastness and deep sense of loyalty were requited by his early followers. His message to the Mongols was that the "unity of the tents" was necessary if the Mongols were to achieve lasting military success against their neighbors and beyond. So successful was he that, by the year 1203, he could count on the obedience of 130,000 mounted archers. His force was based on the sturdy Mongolian pony and the superb horsemanship and strength of its rider. The short composite bow used by the Mongols required a pull weight of well over 100 pounds and could be remarkably effective to a distance of 300 yards. A further advantage was the nonexistent bathing habits of the Mongols which contributed a dimension of chemical warfare.

While an excellent tactician (the Mongols maneuvered at high speeds and were experts at feints and false retreats), Temuchin was also a shrewd and thorough strategist and psychologist. His campaigns were preceded by the careful gathering of intelligence, and his forces made conscious use of terrorism as a weapon of warfare. This was a calculated measure, just as was his decision to reduce the language of the Mongols to written form to record the achievements of his people.

A landmark year of Mongol expansion was 1206 when the first Great *Kurultai* (assembly) was held. On this memorable occasion, Temuchin was recognized as the supreme leader of the Mongols and granted the title of Jenghis ("Illustrious") Khan. Perhaps the most important action taken was the confirmation of the goal of these steppe warriors: the conquest of the world. As a result of their decision, Russians and the peoples of East Asia would, for the first time, come into close contact with each other.

Jenghis Khan's first move was to seize control of a key segment of the famous Silk Road, that slender thread connecting China with the rest of the Eurasian continent. He then focused his efforts on the conquest of northern China, but his attention was drawn to the Khwarizmian Empire in Central Asia where members of a Mongol caravan had been murdered. This action could not go unanswered. The Mongol leader therefore left his general, Mukali, to prosecute the war in the east as best he could while the greater part of the Mongol army followed their khan into western Turkestan. The bulk of his force negotiated the passes of the T'ien Shan in the late summer of 1219, but a detachment of 20,000, under the general Jebe, proceeded directly through the Pamirs in the dead of the winter of 1219–1220. As a result, the forces of Shah Muhammed of Khwarizm, arrayed along the Syr Darya River to meet the main Mongol onslaught, found the forces of Jebe at their back, descending from the Pamirs. The empire of Khwarizm was overwhelmed in an orgy of massacres in the course of the next year and a half.

Jenghis Khan then returned to the war in northern China, but before he departed eastward in 1221, he sent his redoubtable generals, Subotei and Jebe, to reconnoiter to the west. Accordingly, a force of 25,000 horsemen swept every human obstacle in its way through northern Iran, Azerbaijan, and Georgia, arriving finally in the steppes to the west of the Caspian in 1222. Here the Mongols encountered the Cumans (known as well as the Kipchak Turks and, by the Russians, as the *Polovtsy*). They then investigated as far as the Dniepr River where for the first time Mongols and Russians met, much to the misfortune of the latter.

Subotei suggested that the Russians join him in a common cause against the Cumans. In answer, the Russians executed the Mongol envoys and joined the Cumans to form a force of some 80,000 to fight Subotei's army. It was the spring of 1223 when the Russo-Cuman force attacked. The Mongols steadily fell back to the east for an entire week, stringing out the columns of their enemy. Then, on the eighth day, by which time they had retreated to the Kalka River, just north of the Sea of Azov, the Mongols suddenly and savagely turned and routed the entire allied army. Subotei and Jebe, their mission completed, turned and led their force back to the Mongol homeland.

In 1235, eight years after the death of Jenghis Khan, a major decision was taken by his successors to extend Mongol authority in two major directions, each under the leadership of one of Jenghis Khan's grandsons. One campaign, under Kubilai, was to complete the conquest of east Asia. The other was to proceed into Europe under Batu.

Batu's chief of staff was the experienced general Subotei, who by now was in his sixties. The army moved rapidly across the mainland of Asia (3,000 miles just to begin a campaign) and by late 1237 had subdued the Cumans and the Bulgars in the Volga region. They then unleashed an invasion into the north-eastern Russian principalities in the taiga, including Rostov, Suzdal, and Vladimir (Moscow, in the same region, was of very little significance in that age). The Russians were unable to pose a viable defense and were soundly defeated in a battle on the Sit River on the fourth day of March in 1238. The road now was indefensible northwest to the rich prize of Novgorod. The Mongols, however, experienced fighters in cold climates that they were (and as a result much wiser than such later conquerors as Charles XII of Sweden, Napoleon, and Hitler), feared the possibility of early spring thaws and resisted the temptation. Instead, they withdrew to the great pasture land in the steppe east of the Don River and commenced careful preparations for further conquest.

By the autumn of 1240, Batu's emissaries to Kiev were unceremoniously thrown to their deaths from the city walls. The next series of events could be easily anticipated. After the quick capture of Chernigov and Pereiaslavl, the Mongols directed their full fury against Kiev, which was taken on December 6, 1240. The city was virtually destroyed, and the bulk of the inhabitants were massacred to the point that papal legates two years later would comment on the small number of houses left standing and the quantity of skulls and bones littering the countryside.

Batu's goal had been the Hungarian plain as a base for operations against the rest of Europe, but the first need was to protect the army's right flank. Thus a wheeling movement was effected through Poland. After taking and burning Cracow, the Mongols met and demolished a combined Polish/German army at Liegnitz (modern Legnica) in April 1241. After plundering Silesia, they swept down into Hungary. King Bela IV fled toward the Adriatic with the Mongols in hot pursuit. Thus it was that Mongol patrols were in Zagreb and along the Dalmatian coast when word reached Batu that his uncle Ogodei, the Great Khan, had died. Europe lay virtually defenseless before the victorious Mongols. The Holy Roman Empire was on the verge of a fragmentation that was being staved off by the brilliant Frederick II. England was undergoing an important political metamorphosis under the ineffectual rule of Henry III, son of King John of Magna Carta fame, and the saintly Louis IX of France was more interested in building magnificent Gothic churches. It is most probable, therefore, that Ogodei's death spared Western Europe the terror and devastation of a Mongol invasion.

Batu's presence was required in Karakorum for the selection of a new great khan, but on the way east he took the time to establish a capital, Sarai, on the lower Volga River. Here he and his successors would hold forth as lords of the lands of Eastern Europe for the next two and a half centuries. This huge portion of the Mongol Empire would be known variously as the Kipchak Khanate, the Western Horde, the White Horde, or, ultimately, as the Golden Horde. The period of Russian subjugation under the rulers in Sarai would be known in Russian history as the time of the Mongol Yoke or Tatar Yoke.

In the east, meanwhile, Kubilai's armies had not been restricted to the conquest of China and the establishment of the Mongol—or Yuan—dynasty in that country. His forces penetrated northeast into the Amur valley, all the way to its mouth. By the 1280s they had subdued the indigenous Ainu on Sakhalin and had established garrisons on the island. Mongol horsemen overwhelmed the kingdom of Korea, but two attempted invasions of Japan, the first in 1274 and the second in 1281, were both fated to be frustrated by the fury of typhoons.

The last of Jenghis Khan's grandsons to add extensive territories to the empire was Kubilai's younger brother Hulegu. In 1256 he descended from west Turkestan across the Amu Darya River to invade the Iranian plateau, including Afghanistan, Parthia, Persia, and Media. He established his capital in Tabriz and prepared his army for the invasion of Mesopotamia two years later. Hulegu destroyed the power of the Old Man of the Mountain and his Assassins, a fanatical and militant arm of Shi'ite Islam, and his campaign into Mesopotamia overwhelmed the Abbasid Caliphate which was the outward symbol of Sunni greatness in Baghdad. He was finally halted just to the north of Jerusalem by Mameluke troops from Egypt. The territories conquered by Hulegu would be known by the name of the Il Khanate, and his successors would be converted to Islam. By the early fourteenth century, they would adopt the Shi'ite version of the religion.

The Mongol Empire therefore, by the year 1280, comprised four major segments. To the east lay the vast domains under the direct rule of Kubilai, known as the Great Khanate, which included Yuan China. In southwest Asia was the Il Khanate which had been carved out by Hulegu. In Eastern Europe and Western Asia, the descendants of Batu were ruling the Kipchak Khanate (Golden Horde). The fourth major portion of the empire was that in the middle, comprising essentially East and West Turkestan, down to and including Sogdiana, the land between the Syr Darya and Amu Darya rivers. This was the *ulus* which was assigned by Jenghis Khan to his second son Chagatai.

The Il Khanate would endure under Hulegu's successors until about 1350. The Yuan dynasty in China would be replaced by the Ming in the year 1368. Power in Chagatai would be usurped by a Turkish leader, Tamerlane, in the middle of the fourteenth century, and his son would continue to rule until 1447. In Eastern Europe, the overlordship of the khans of the Golden Horde would be acknowledged by the Russians until the Tatar Yoke would finally be thrown off in 1480 during the reign of Ivan III.

Although rifts in the "unity of the tents" had appeared by the time of Kubilai, the Mongol conquest created a political continuum that existed for many decades, stretching from the Pacific Ocean to the Mediterranean and through the steppe to the west of the Dniepr River. For the first and only time in history, a single political authority ruled the Chinese, the Koreans, and the Russians. Fighting men were drawn from all parts of the empire to serve where most needed. This was particularly true when the power bloc dominated by Batu, Kubilai, and Hulegu would provide warriors for each other's operational needs. Representatives of the pope and the king of France would make the trek to Karakorum, the capital of the Great Khan, seeking favors against their enemies in the Holy Land. The wonders of Sung Chinese genius, such as gunpowder, the rudder post, and the navigational use of that marvelous lodestone, the compass, would find their way west, thanks to the *Pax Mongolica*.

The Mongol Yoke, of such long duration, would leave an indelible impression on the peoples of Eastern Europe. In the first place, the Russians were forcibly brought into contact with the rest of the Eurasian continent, all the way to the Pacific Ocean. A second consideration was that the Russians were cut off from their cultural umbilicus, Constantinople, and indeed from the Black Sea altogether. As a matter of fact, the steppe lands of Eastern Europe became known, appropriately, as the "Wild Fields" and would not become permanently repeopled for half a millennium. Under the Mongol Yoke, there would be more cruel punishments and more illiterate princes. Women would be placed in seclusion in an Oriental way, designed to protect them from predation, a status that would not be altered until the time of Peter the Great in the early years of the eighteenth century.

As the result of the Mongol Yoke, the autocratic and military elements of the Russian system were strengthened. A greater tolerance of tyranny was instilled along with enhanced receptivity of the concept of an infallible *vozhd'* (charismatic leader). The populace became inured to privation and conditioned to obedience and respect for power and authority. A greater emphasis came to be placed on security, and a paranoid fear of invasion was inculcated into the eastern Slavs. This in turn would lead to a compulsion to expand over their neighbors, lest they themselves be expanded over. Interestingly, one result of the centuries under the thumb of the Golden Horde would be an absence of discrimination on the basis of race or color when dealing with the peoples of Asia. Intermarriage was not unusual, at the highest levels, and religious differences were more important than racial ones.

After the Mongol conquest, the Russians quickly learned the depths of degradation to which they had been reduced. No longer were the Russian princes able to entertain the idea that they would determine who should succeed to the title of Great Prince. It would be decided for them by their conquerors. He who was designated Great Prince by the Great Khan in Karakorum and, later, by the khan of the Golden Horde, had to suffer the indignity of trekking to his master and obsequiously performing the kowtow. Further, and of most immediate hurt, there was the payment of tribute to the masters at Sarai. At first, Mongol troops were the tax collectors, but later the task would be delegated to certain Russian princes. As stated earlier, the tributary Russians were required, as well, to provide troops to fight wherever the khan in Sarai might dictate. Onerous as this status might be, it became even more so in the fourteenth century when the khans of the Golden Horde adopted the Islamic religion. (By that time, the Mongol blood flowing in the veins of those in the thin upper veneer of Golden Horde authority had become greatly diluted by the regular infusion of Turkic.)

The city-state of Novgorod was blessed with a very wise member of the Rurikid house in the critical years of the mid-thirteenth century: Alexander (1219–1263), who became prince of Novgorod in 1236. He therefore was resident in the city at the time of the Mongol decision not to attack. Although Novgorod was spared the full brunt of the Mongol invasion, its wise young Prince Alexander (who became known as Alexander Nevsky after a victory over the Swedes on the Neva River in 1240) convinced the city elders that the only feasible attitude for the city to adopt toward the Mongols was that of submission. Not coincidentally, it was Alexander who was designated Great Prince by the Mongol khan.

In the Russian lands of the northeast, centered on the cities of Vladimir, Suzdal, Rostov, and a gradually emerging Moscow, princely power was more in the ascendancy than in the rest of Russia, and very gradually the authority of Moscow would surpass that of the others. Moscow, earliest mentioned in 1147, was first surrounded by protective wooden walls at the direction of Yuri Dolgoruki in 1156. More than a hundred years later, it would be Daniel, a son of Alexander Nevsky, who became the first permanently resident prince of the Rurikid line. Daniel's clever son Ivan I (ruled 1328–1341), known as *Kalita*, or "money bags," would leave a deep imprint on the still embryonic state of Moscow—or Muscovy. Very obsequious to the khan at Sarai, he secured appointment not only as Great Prince but also as tribute collector for the Golden Horde. This latter role gave Ivan a strong arm to wield over the other Russian city-states. As is the case historically with tax collectors, a percentage of the collected revenues were his, thus enriching him at the expense of the other princes. He was in a position to call in Mongol troops to punish those neighbors who resisted his demands. He could force some into bankruptcy and pressure others into submission, thereby expanding his principality. A further enhancement of his prestige occurred when he persuaded the Metropolitan of Kiev to move to Moscow where he would be known as the "Metropolitan of Kiev and All Russia." Now, for the first time in generations, the Great Prince and Metropolitan were resident in the same center.

Ivan's grandson Dmitri, who ruled as Great Prince from 1359–1389, experienced his finest hour when his forces defeated an army of the Golden Horde at Kulikovo on the banks of the Don River in 1380. For this achievement he became known as Dmitri Donskoi. However, Khan Tokhtamish raised a new army and captured, looted, and burned Moscow just two years later. The Mongol Yoke was once again in place and would remain for yet a hundred years.

A major player in the fortunes of Moscow was the charismatic Tatar leader Tamerlane. In 1391 he delivered a sharp defeat to the forces of the Golden Horde under Tokhtamish near the Yaik (Ural) River, and four years later he destroyed another Golden Horde army on the banks of the Terek River near the western shore of the Caspian. Thus seriously weakened, the Golden Horde began to fragment. The western portion, centered in the Crimean Peninsula, broke away under its independent khan by 1433 (a fleeting independence since the Crimean khan would become vassal to the Ottoman sultan some forty years later). A separate khanate divorced itself from Sarai and set up its center at Kazan, near the confluence of the Kama and Volga rivers in 1445.

Commencing in 1462, the throne of Moscow was encumbered by Dmitri Donskoi's great-grandson Ivan III (the Great). Ivan III was never known as a great warrior or a leader who asserted an impetuous charisma. Rather, he was patient and calculating, willing to rely on diplomacy to achieve his ends and taking sharp action only when, in his view, the timing was exactly right and the risk was minimal. His reign of forty-three years would be considered eminently successful and, since the territory of Muscovy was increased by several times, would be referred to as "the gathering of Russia."

Ivan's careful perceptiveness was evident in the choice of his second wife in 1472. This was Zoe Paleologina, niece of the last Byzantine emperor, Constantine XI. The wedding took place only nineteen years after the fall of Constantinople to the Turks, and Zoe's brothers were the claimants to the now defunct Byzantine throne. Her presence would have considerable effect on life in Moscow. Foreign architects were brought in to build the new red walls of the Kremlin. The Byzantine imperial symbol of the double-headed eagle was adopted, as were more sophisticated and complex court ceremonies. The original influence of Byzantium, incurred at the time Christianity was adopted in the tenth century, would be reinforced, including the concept of caesaropapism and an accent on autocracy. A further intensification of this trend would result in the heady, ambitious development of a new delusion of grandeur known as the "Moscow the Third Rome" idea. This perspective of history saw Rome as the first, Constantinople as the second, and Moscow as the third great leader of the Christian struggle to stem the Asiatic hordes that threatened Europe. Not surprisingly at this time, Ivan III came gradually to be addressed and referred to as "tsar," the Slavic form of "caesar." This was not at the time adopted as an official title, however, nor would it be for more than half a century.

Both Novgorod and Moscow entertained thoughts of a union of all the Russian peoples, but they differed widely as to the form such a union should assume. The Novgorodians envisioned a loose association whereas the Muscovites saw unity in the subordination of all to the political and military authority of a great prince: federation versus autocracy. Although Novgorod was an affluent city-state, it did not possess the human resources required to field a military force comparable to that of Moscow. Therefore, the Muscovites were able to deliver a military coup de grâce to the city in 1478. Ivan had earlier incorporated the lands of Viatka (to the northeast of Moscow). These, together with the new vast holdings absorbed from Novgorod, now provided the great principality of Moscow with lands reaching to the Ural Mountains.

Another major achievement realized by Muscovy during the long reign of Ivan III was the formal rejection of the Tatar Yoke. In 1480 Khan Ahmad failed in his military attempt to reassert the supremacy of the now seriously weakened Golden Horde. Thus, 240 years after the invasion of the Mongols under Batu, an uncontested sovereignty was exercised from Moscow. By the end of the fifteenth century, Muscovy had become a major power in the affairs of Eastern Europe. It had developed into a strongly organized, centralized state capable of resolute decisions and possessed of a military tradition that could take the action necessary to implement such decisions. A heightened sense of purpose had been inherited from the late Byzantine Empire as defender of the Orthodox faith. In the early sixteenth century, the Muscovite state seemed poised and ready to handle the manifold threats arrayed against it. To the northwest, beyond former Novgorod were the Swedes and, to the south of them, the Germanic Knights. To the west lay Poland/Lithuania which controlled many former Russian lands, including what is now Belarus and northwestern Ukraine. To the east and south lay the Tatar lands under three separate khans in Kazan, Sarai, and Bahcesaray (in the Crimea).

The expansive and acquisitive energies of Muscovy would seem to be directed at the recovery of lands peopled by eastern Slavs, but, in fact, as we shall see, the Muscovite compulsion to expand would first be accommodated by the vast territories to the east.

3

Ivan IV and
Muscovite *Drang nach Osten*

Ivan IV (usually identified by the sobriquet "The Terrible" or "The Dread"),
grandson of Ivan III, was only three years old when he ascended the throne in
1533. A regency was obviously necessary, and the resulting environment was a
veritable hell for the young sovereign. Violence, including murders, executions,
and torture, was a norm surrounding the life of the developing Great Prince.
Perhaps the sole positive aspect of the situation was that Ivan was given ample
time and opportunity to become a competent and avid reader. He became one
of the best-read rulers of the sixteenth century. Like Henry VIII of England, he
became very well informed on religious matters.

Of particular importance to our story were the military undertakings launched
by Ivan IV after he had taken the reins of power into his own hands. In 1552
he conducted a successful campaign against the Kazan Tatars. His capture of
the town of Kazan was particularly auspicious by virtue of its location near the
confluence of the Volga and its important eastern tributary, the Kama. Ready
access by water into the middle Urals was now feasible. Four years later he was
equally successful in subjugating the heart of the old Golden Horde, by then
known as the Astrakhan Tatars, on the lower Volga. This gain provided, for the
first time since the Mongol conquest, ready access for the Russians to the Caspian Sea. As a result, an important route was now open for trade with Persia,
unhampered by Tatar interference. These conquests meant that two of the three
principal offshoots of the Golden Horde were now in Muscovite hands. The
third, the Crimean Tatars, under the suzerainty of the Ottoman Turks since the
late fifteenth century, would not be subjected to Russian control for another 220
years.

Ivan's warfare in the west, designed to open an outlet on the Baltic, was
doomed to failure. The money and naval power of the Hanseatic League,

Map 3. Area of Eurasia expanded into by Moscovy/Russia, 1500–1900.

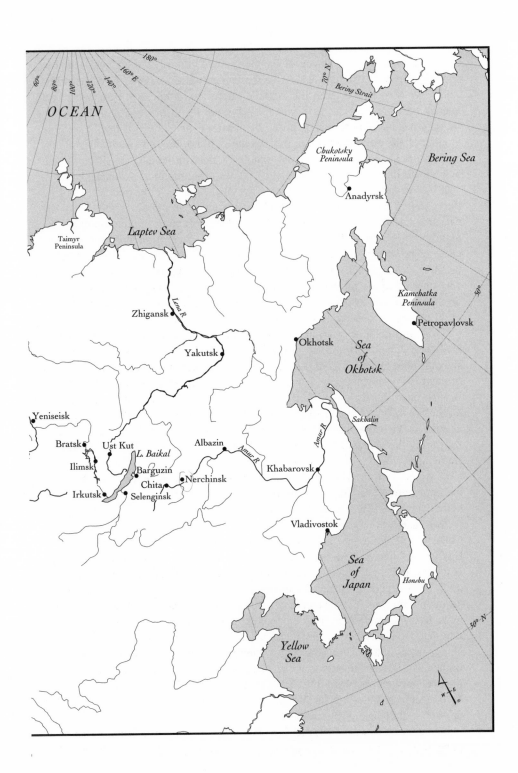

OCEAN

180°

160° E

140°

120°

100°

80°

60°

70° N

Bering Strait

*Chukotsky
Peninsula*

Bering Sea

Anadyrsk

Laptev Sea

Taimyr
Peninsula

*Kamchatka
Peninsula*

50°

Petropavlovsk

Zhigansk

Lena R.

Okhotsk

*Sea
of
Okhotsk*

Yakutsk

Yeniseisk

Sakhalin

Bratsk

Ust Kut

Albazin

Amur R.

L. Baikal

Khabarovsk

Ilimsk

Barguzin

Amur R.

Nerchinsk

Irkutsk

Chita

Selenginsk

Vladivostok

*Sea
of
Japan*

Honshu

30° N

*Yellow
Sea*

N

W   E

S

25

combined with the land power of the Germanic Order of Livonia, succeeded in shutting Moscow off from access to the technological exports of Western Europe. The Muscovy of Ivan the Terrible, therefore, although it now had direct contact with the Middle East, was cut off from the Black Sea and the Baltic. Its only oceanic coastline was in the far north on the shores of the White Sea, an inlet of the Arctic Ocean. In this desolate setting, the only semblance of any real sovereign presence was at the mouth of the Northern Dvina River which boasted the tiny village of Kholmogory (later to be renamed Arkhangelsk).

It was to this unpretentious site that the British came in the year 1553 during the so-called Age of Discovery, which had been set in motion at the end of the fifteenth century by the voyages of Christopher Columbus and the intrepid Portuguese navigators such as Vasco da Gama. The route around Africa to India came to be known as the southeast passage to the Orient from Europe. From the time of Magellan's voyage (1519–1522), the route to Asia via Cape Horn was referred to as the southwest passage. There was therefore a rush to find northeast and northwest passages to the Far East, the former presumably to the north of Europe and Asia and the latter to the north of North America.

It was in pursuit of a northeast passage that the English under the leadership of Richard Chancellor arrived in Kholmogory in 1553. They obviously fell well short of their intended goal, but they did find a port that was a source of rich furs and, to a lesser degree, Eastern goods which could find their way from the Persian lands bordering the Caspian Sea. Kholmogory thus became a window on the West for Ivan the Terrible, although a rather inconvenient one. However, in spite of the navigational hazards of Arctic voyages, such a trade route was free from the threats of Sweden, the Hanseatic League, and other predators rimming the Baltic. Within two years, the Royal Muscovy Company was chartered (the first of the English chartered companies) to handle the trade. By 1565 the arrangement was improved, in Muscovite eyes, with the arrival of the Dutch to challenge the English monopoly of trade.

Two factors now came into play which would begin to focus the attention of Muscovy on the Asian lands to the east, both related to the presence of the English and Dutch. One was the greater demand for furs occasioned by this new trade and a consequent need to find new sources. What little the Muscovites did know of the land (generally referred to as Mangazeia) just to the east of the northern Urals was that it reputedly was teeming with valuable furbearing mammals. The second factor was the perpetual impatience of the Westerners to seek a northern route to the Far East. Fearful that they might succeed and thus reach new sources of furs, the Muscovites attempted to dissuade them from probing farther east along the northern seacoast.[1] All things considered, Ivan had the impetus to move eastward into Asia. He had, as well, the ready avenue provided by the Kama tributary of the Volga. He was not, however, in a position to take on such a challenge at the moment.

Ivan's attention was riveted on internal affairs of state, wherein he was struggling to assert his autocratic authority over the hereditary boyar nobility. He was, as well, challenging the powers to the west in the Livonian War, which would last from 1557 until 1582. As a result, the responsibilities for Muscovite interests to the east were borne increasingly by a remarkable family: the Stroganovs. First mentioned around the end of the fourteenth century, the family Stroganov was at that time already involved in trading activity in the basin of the Northern Dvina River. This entrepreneurial activity was gradually expanded to the production and marketing of salt. Although under the authority of the Novgorodian government at that time, the Stroganovs also leased lands nearby which belonged to the princes of Moscow. They were careful to maintain good relations with this rising power to the south. Indeed, when Vasili II, father of Ivan III, was captured by the Kazan Tatars in 1445, the Stroganovs contributed handsomely to the ransom payment.

By virtue of their eastern location and enterprising nature, the Stroganovs soon began to send trading agents eastward over the Ural Mountains. They were very alert to opportunities and early on came to know not only of the wealth of furbearing animals east of the Urals but also the natural assets of the area of Perm (on the Kama just west of the Urals), such as salt, iron ore, and soil fit for growing grain. A major problem, however, was one of access. For this reason, as early as 1557, Anikei Stroganov approached Ivan IV with a request for exploitation rights. Largely as the result of the presentation of lavish gifts, talk of the resources in the Urals, and discussion of the need for the more accessible route up the Kama River, Ivan granted the Stroganovs a charter to some 5 million acres by a decree of April 4, 1558. In essence, the Stroganovs became viceroys in the region with full responsibility for its colonization. This private empire would be expanded by another 3 million square miles in a further charter on January 2, 1564, and yet another 1.5 million acres in 1568.

The Stroganovs set to work in almost frenzied fashion to exploit their new resources in the Kama River basin, especially along the Chusovaia, a major tributary whose flow originated in the Urals. The salt works took priority, followed closely by the smelting of iron ore. As the works were begun and land cleared, the indigenous population had to make way. The felling of the forests for fuel (great quantities were required for the salt works) and the spread of agriculture deprived the native population of prime hunting areas. The Stroganovs were reasonably fair in their dealings but also very hardheaded businessmen who could understand best their own priorities. Thus the native population, made up largely of Ostiaks, Cheremis, and Voguls, became increasingly restless. These peoples, in frustration, began periodically to conduct raids against the Stroganov installations. Such attacks were not well coordinated, and the situation was not considered critical. But activity east of the Urals would intensify the threat.

Once Ivan IV had absorbed the realm of the Kazan Tatars, the next polity worthy of the name lying to the east was that of the khanate of Sibir with its center at Isker on the Tobol River. The Tobol, fed by its tributary the Tura, flowed east and north until it merged with the Irtysh, the principal branch of the Ob River. The population of Sibir was made up of a mixture of Ostiaks, Voguls, and others. The people therefore were overwhelmingly of pagan stock. The relationship between Sibir and Muscovy originally was rather proper and friendly, and the khan of Sibir acknowledged himself a vassal to the tsar. This comfortable arrangement came to a halt as the result of the conquest of Sibir in 1563 by Kuchum, leader of an Islamic horde from the south and east.

Attacks on the lands of the Stroganovs thereafter gradually intensified and were often conducted under the leadership of Makhmetkul, a nephew of Kuchum. Conditions deteriorated to the point where, in 1574, Ivan granted a new charter to the Stroganovs. They now were granted authority to control the situation by any means necessary, including the building and manning of forts on both slopes of the Urals, as far as the Irtysh and Ob rivers. In other words, a private war with Sibir was now authorized. Since the Stroganovs needed most of their population as labor in their enterprises, their main problem was one of manpower. The solution would be a remarkable marriage of Cossack and entrepreneur.

By the later years of the sixteenth century, cossackdom had become an established institution in southeastern Europe. It was largely the product of two factors: (1) harsh conditions for peasants and serfs on the estates of Poland, Lithuania, and Muscovy and (2) the "Wild Fields" of the Ukrainian steppes, a heritage of the Mongol conquest. Particularly in the fifteenth and sixteenth centuries, the steppe Tatars regularly conducted slaving raids to the north and northwest, carrying off hundreds of thousands of Slavs and Balts to the slave market at Kaffa in the Crimea. At the same time, on the estates of the great landowners in the north, the hardier and more independent serfs began to flee southward to seek a freer, albeit much more dangerous, life in the Wild Fields. Gradually, their services were contracted for by the states to the north as an effective border guard. Thus the Cossacks came to be free men who owed their freedom to their service in defense of the Polish, Lithuanian, and Muscovite southern borders. Their settlements—or *stanitsy*—grew up along the rivers, notably the Dniepr and Don.

The man known in history as the "Conqueror of Siberia" was Yermak Timofeevich. He is also usually identified as a Cossack. He grew up in the north, actually near the Chusovaia tributary, so that he was familiar with the taiga in the Kama basin. After he grew to manhood, it seems that for reasons not quite clear he spent time with the Don Cossacks. By the year 1580, as luck would have it, several Cossacks were being sought by Muscovy as the result of an attack on "friendly" Tatars east of the Volga. Through fortuitous circumstances, these Cossacks, the Stroganovs, and Yermak would team up in the year 1581 to handle the problem posed by Sibir.

The force put together for the campaign totaled some 840 men, including 540 Cossacks, many of whom were considered criminals by the government in Moscow. The rest, from various sources and nationalities, had wandered into the Stroganovs' domains. The Stroganov brothers supplied the arms, dry victuals,

and other equipments required by the troops, and Yermak provided the leadership necessary to forge some semblance of military discipline in the motley
group.

Yermak and his band ascended the Chusovaia River and one of its branches
into the Urals. They wintered over in the mountains where they augmented their
own supplies of food by looting the possessions of the local tribes. The following spring, when the ice melted, they descended the Tura River toward the
Tobol. The principal military advantage of Yermak's men was that of muskets
(they had no cannon), but the advantage of mobility lay with Kuchum and his
mounted warriors. The first action occurred at Tiumen where the defenders were
frightened off, leaving valuable food supplies behind. The Russians continued
to float downstream into the Tobol River and thence toward its confluence with
the Irtysh where Isker, capital of Sibir, was being frantically fortified by Kuchum. The Moscovites were harried regularly during the descent but successfully
fought off every attempt to inhibit their progress.

Finally, as the autumn wore on, Yermak and his band were faced with another
winter. The decision was made to stake all on a frontal assault on Isker. The
first attempt failed, but a few days later, on October 25, 1582, the final all-out
attack against the defenders, who were commanded by Makhmetkul, was
launched. Although the Cossacks were outnumbered by as many as twenty to
one, not all the forces in the town were inspired to fight for their Muslim leaders.
Still, the defense held until Makhmetkul was seriously wounded and spirited
away across the Irtysh where Kuchum was observing the battle. The defenders
now broke, and the day was won by Yermak and his desperate men. From that
day forward, it was certain that Siberia would become part of the principality
of Muscovy.

Yermak immediately took advantage of the situation to collect tribute from
all the tribes in the immediate region in order to assert his mastery on behalf
of the tsar. He then wisely sent one of his lieutenants, the Cossack leader Koltso,
with 2,400 choice sable pelts, back across the Urals toward Moscow. The timing
was exquisite, for the mood of Ivan was dark indeed. The Livonian War had
just been terminated to the disadvantage of Moscow, and news had been received that local tribesmen were conducting raids into Perm, west of the Urals.
Ivan was so distressed that he had sent a menacing letter to the Stroganovs
accusing them of misusing their authority in sending traitors such as Yermak
and his men to stir up a hornet's nest in the east Ural area. Into this unhappy
environment came Koltso, a man with a Muscovite price on his head. His news
of the conquest of Sibir, together with the gift of 2,400 sable pelts, quickly
dissolved the gloom. In fact, Ivan forgave all the Cossacks their earlier transgressions and ordered that two suits of armor and his own fur stole be sent to
Yermak for his personal wear. He later would direct that government troops
under *Voevoda* Bolkhovsky be sent to Isker.

Such troops, however, would not arrive until 1584, after the death of Ivan.
In the meantime, Yermak successfully continued as the satrap of Sibir. One of

his successes was the capture of Makhmetkul, the nephew of Kuchum. The young warrior was treated well and was sent to Moscow where he joined the Muscovite service and saw action against the Swedes and Crimean Tatars. But continuing actions against the native troops of all sorts, especially those in support of Kuchum, drained Yermak's limited resources. Even the arrival of Bolkhovsky's troops in 1584 was no help since they were inadequately provisioned, and Bolkhovsky himself died soon after their arrival. Still, the iron will of Yermak ensured the survival of the Russians until he himself fell victim to a Tatar ruse in the early autumn of 1585. In trying to escape ambush, he plunged into the Irtysh and, weighed down by the splendid armor given him by Ivan the Terrible, perished.

The remaining garrison at Isker, now down to 150 souls, decided to return to Moscow, and the former khan of Sibir, who had been unseated by Kuchum more than two decades before, was now once again in Isker. This disappearance of the Muscovites from the Ob/Irtysh basin proved to be of very short duration, however, thanks in large part to the fascinating figure of Boris Godunov. Ivan the Terrible had murdered his son Ivan in a fit of rage and was therefore succeeded in March 1584 by another son, Fedor, who unfortunately was mentally incompetent. This, as it turned out, was not greatly to the disadvantage of Muscovy since the real power in government was Boris Godunov, Fedor's brother-in-law. Godunov, of a noble Mongol family which had become Russified and converted to Christianity, would prove to have a paranoid concern with security. This trait manifested itself with even greater force when he became the elected tsar after Fedor died childless in 1598. Godunov's cautiousness drove him to ensure the security of Moscow by constructing major fortresses, exemplified by the one at Smolensk in the west. In the east as well, he realized the need for a strong position to defend the state *and* to ensure Muscovite control of the Asian taiga with its precious population of furbearing mammals.

By late summer 1586, 300 government troops under two Muscovite *voevody* had established the first permanent fort east of the Urals at Tiumen on the Tura River not far from the Tobol. At the same time, to protect the right flank of this salient, the town of Ufa was established on the Belaia River, which is another tributary of the Kama well to the south of the Chusovaia. The following year, government troops were sent to the confluence of the Tobol and Irtysh rivers to establish a new fortress, not far from the old capital (Isker) of Sibir. This new center, named Tobolsk, would become for more than two centuries the principal stronghold and administrative center of Russian authority in Asia.

From this point, the momentum for the eastern push of Muscovy into Siberia was provided by the *promyshlenniki* or entrepreneurs seeking fortunes from the furry creatures of the taiga. They were drawn ever eastward by the magnet of even more and finer pelts until, in the unbelievably short time of fifty years, they reached the Pacific Ocean some 4,000 miles away. They were not the elite of society but rather desperate adventurers who would brave the harshest climatic conditions in the Northern Hemisphere in their passionate attempts to reap the riches of the wild environment. Some were trappers, but the normal practice of acquisition was to demand furs from the intimidated native population and enforce compliance as necessary by the taking of hostages.

Following the *promyshlenniki* came the representatives of the Muscovite crown, the serving men, to ensure that the tsar received his fair share (the best one-tenth) of the fur harvest. These people built *ostrogi* or forts, very similar to the stockades in the American West two and a half centuries later. In order to control the fur trade, these *ostrogi* were positioned at strategic points along the route eastward, notably at the confluence of major streams and at key portages. The forts were manned by a combination of Cossacks and regular troops. Free-booters were granted the status of Cossacks so that, in the tradition of the frontier, they were free men in return for their military service. The Cossacks outnumbered regular troops, and this imbalance increased the farther into the wilderness, away from Moscow, the fort was located. By 1594, in order to have a defense against such Tatars as those still following Kuchum, a fort named Tara was built at the confluence of the Tara and Irtysh rivers where the taiga begins to meld into the steppe. There would be no movement farther up the Irtysh into the steppe for a very long time. In the same year, the spread of Muscovite authority was symbolized by a fort at Obdorsk in the lower Ob and at Surgut on the upper Ob well above the confluence of the Ob and Irtysh.

The Muscovite presence methodically moved into the eastern tributaries of the Ob. In the far north, a body of men descended into the Ob estuary and ascended thence into the Taz River where they established themselves at a site called Mangazeia. Only six years later they had negotiated a short portage from a Taz tributary to the Yenisei River where a fort named Turukhansk was built near the confluence of the Yenisei and its eastern tributary, the Lower Tunguska. At the same time, others moved up the Ob. A fort was established at Ketsk, on the Ket—an eastern tributary—in 1602, and Tomsk was built on the Tom, another eastern tributary, in 1604.

In the Muscovite capital, the death of Boris Godunov in 1605 led to chaos in the government. For the next eight years, the so-called Time of Troubles rocked Moscow. Order would not be restored until 1613 when the *Zemski Sobor* chose as tsar and autocrat Michael Romanov, whose grandfather was brother to the first wife, Anastasia, of Ivan IV. During the Time of Troubles, the *promyshlenniki* continued to press eastward, but the systematic building of government forts came to a standstill. Once the new dynasty was in place, however, the process quickly resumed. In 1618 Makovsk was built on the upper reaches of the Ket River. The following year saw the founding, across a short portage, of Yeniseisk on the Yenisei River.

For the next decade, the Yenisei basin provided sufficient challenge for the *promyshlenniki*, but already stories were rife of even richer fur sources to the east where an even mightier river flowed—the Lena. Indeed, two probes into the basin had been made by 1628. Then, in 1630, a southern route was established by ascending the Angara and thence into the Ilim tributary where a fort was established and named Ilimsk. In the same year, across a short portage, another fort, Ust Kut, was built on the Lena itself. In just two years, a major milestone was achieved when an *ostrog* was set up at Yakutsk about 100 miles upstream from the point where the Aldan River flows into the Lena from the east. A northern route was also negotiated up the Lower Tunguska from the Yenisei to a short portage to the Viliui which, in turn, joined the Lena well downstream from Yakutsk. In this cold, remote wilderness just above the Arctic Circle, a fort was established at Zhigansk in 1632.

From the Lena basin, the Pacific Ocean would be approached via an eastern tributary of the Lena—the Aldan. In 1639 Ivan Moskvitin and a party of twenty ascended the river. They branched left into the Maia, tracing it to its source in the Dzhugdzhur Mountains. After a very brief portage, they were able to descend the short Ulia River to the Sea of Okhotsk. Thus, just fifty-three years after the founding of the town of Tiumen, the waters of the Pacific had been reached.

It should be noted that the trek to the east was confined to the taiga region, well to the north of the steppe. The reasons were essentially three. The first was that the animals being sought lived in the forest. A second reason was that the rivers afforded the most convenient means of transportation through the taiga. In the warmer part of the year, they provided an easily navigable waterway. From Moscow to the Sea of Okhotsk, the trip could be managed with only four portages. In wintertime, the frozen rivers were the most efficient route for the passage of sledges. The third reason for confining expansion to the taiga had to do with demographics. In the forests lived relatively primitive tribes whose populations were sparse and, therefore, easily subdued and controlled. The steppe, on the other hand, was peopled by much more warlike tribes, mostly Turkic and Islamic. Not for centuries would the Russian state be in a position to assert its will on the peoples to the south of the taiga, in what is most frequently referred to as Central Asia, such as the Bashkirs, Kazakhs, and Kirgiz.

An indication of the problems inherent in dealing with more populous groups is seen in the relations between the Muscovites and the Buriat Mongols. As described above, the eastward progress of conquest was rapid, with strategic points on the Lena established by the early 1630s, including Yakutsk in 1632. However, from the portage that connected the Yenisei and Lena (between Ilimsk and Ust Kut), the progress up the Angara to the south suddenly slowed. In the place of small Tungusic-speaking tribes, the more formidable Buriat Mongols now were encountered. The Buriats were distributed around Lake Baikal, extending both to the east and west of the lake. In 1631 a fort was built at Bratsk on the Angara by the Muscovites to serve as a base for a campaign against the Buriats—a campaign that would last for almost two decades. Not until 1643 were Russians able to travel to the source of the Angara—Lake Baikal. Finally, in 1648, Ivan Galkin successfully founded the *ostrog* Barguzin on the river of the same name on the east edge of the lake. From this strong position, in the midst of the Buriat population, the Muscovites were at last able to dominate and subjugate this stubborn people.

Muscovite activity was not nearly so inhibited in attempts to expand exploration to the east of the Buriats. This was the Amur River valley. The *voevoda* of Yakutsk had heard several rumors about tribes to the south and east which not only trapped valuable furs but also were engaged in farming and animal husbandry. Such stories had been encountered as early as 1639 by Ivan Moskvitin when he successfully reached the Sea of Okhotsk. Then, in the years from 1638 to 1640, the Cossack ataman Maxim Perfilev explored the tributary of the upper Lena known as the Vitim. He was unable to push over the Stanovoi Range, but he was informed by the various Tungusic tribes encountered that over the mountains lay the valley of the Shilka River (a major tributary of the Amur). Here, he was told, lived a tribe known as the Daurs, who were noted for their trapping and cultivation of grain.

Thus it was that in 1643 the *voevoda* of Yakutsk, Petr Golovin, dispatched a party of 133 men under the leadership of Vasili Poiarkov to explore the region. He ascended the Aldan tributary and one of its branches into the Stanovoi Range. After a short portage he descended the Zeia River system and, once he had encountered Daur villages, decided to winter over before reaching the confluence of the Zeia with the Amur. High-handed actions by the Russians quickly alienated the friendly Daurs, and Poiarkov's men were hard pressed to survive the winter. In the spring, they proceeded down the Zeia into the Amur and thence all the way to the river's mouth. Along the way, they encountered such people as the Duchers and Giliaks. After wintering over 1644 to 1645 near the mouth of the Amur, Poiarkov put to sea as soon as the weather permitted and made his way north along the coast to the spot where Moskvitin had reached the shore of the Sea of Okhotsk six years before. From that point, he followed the route of Moskvitin over the Dzhugdzhur Mountains into the Lena River system and thereby back to Yakutsk.

What Poiarkov did not know was that the tribes along the Amur he encountered were tributary to the Tungusic peoples centered in southern Manchuria known as the Manchus. At the very time that Poiarkov had made his historic trek, these same Manchus were busy, farther south and west, taking over control of China from the Ming dynasty and establishing their own dynasty—the Ch'ing.

A major part of the Asian continent still to be explored was the vast inhospitable area to the east of the Lena basin and north of the Sea of Okhotsk. This included the frozen Arctic coast and the rivers Indigarka, Kolyma, and Anadyr, which drained the massive Chukotsky Peninsula. The base for such activity was Yakutsk on the Lena. Two different expeditions descended the Lena in the 1630s. The first (1633–1638), under Ilia Perfirev and Ivan Rebrov, sailed eastward along the Arctic coast. The group discovered the mouth of the Yana River, negotiated the treacherous Laptev Strait, and found the estuary of the Indigarka River. The second undertaking (1636–1642), under the leadership of Elisei Buza, achieved essentially the same results. During the same period, a leader by the name of Poznik Ivanov blazed a different trail to the Indigarka. His expedition ascended a tributary of the lower Lena and effected a portage over the crest of the Verkhoiansky Range into the upper reaches of the Yana River. He then negotiated a portage over the Chersky Mountains into the Indigarka River system.

By the time Ivanov was returning to Yakutsk, another adventurer, Dmitri Zyrian, had pushed eastward along the Arctic coast to the Alazeia River (1640–1641) and would be the first of the explorers to encounter the Chukchi people. In 1642 Mikhail Stadukhin proceeded via the portage route from the Lena to the Indigarka. The following year, he descended the river and, two years later, arrived at the mouth of the Kolyma.

When Stadukhin arrived back at Yakutsk in 1646, plans were made for even more ambitious expeditions. These would result in the voyage of Semen Dezhnev, which began in the summer of 1648 from the mouth of the Kolyma River eastward. According to Dezhnev's account, he rounded the easternmost cape of the Asian landmass (now named Cape Dezhnev) in the month of August and then proceeded along the coast until forced to land and winter over near the Anadyr River. The following year, he ascended the river and built a small *ostrog* for himself and his remaining twelve men.[2] This *ostrog*, named Anadyrsk, would become the principal center in the farthest east of the Muscovite lands. The only major part of northeastern Asia not yet addressed is the Kamchatka Peninsula. A Russian presence there would have to wait for some decades and would be connected with the important events involving the Russians and Chinese in the Amur River valley. It will be dealt with in chapter 7.

Although the Muscovite state had asserted its control over virtually all of Asia north of the steppe regions by the middle of the seventeenth century, such control was via a slender and overextended umbilicus indeed. The many and various primitive tribes had been coerced into recognizing Russian overlordship by force of more modern weapons. Such recognition was acknowledged by the payment of *yasak*, or tribute, mostly in the form of furs, to this fearsome new presence in their lands. And it was not merely the conquest of new territory itself that drove the Muscovites to this remarkable expansion but rather the quest for fur pelts. Yet, as we have noted, there was indeed a governmental presence to ensure a share of the profits.

At the same time, as the lines of communication were stretched across the thousands of miles of Asia, Moscow was faced by a problem of mounting proportions: how to feed its people—how to feed the Russian fur traders. The Russians could not subsist on meat alone. Their constitutions required vegetables and, above all, grain. This matter we shall take up at greater length in chapter 8.

NOTES

1. Their concern would have been minimal had they themselves known of the daunting natural barriers challenging the sea route. Ships would have had to negotiate the icy

waters of the Kara Strait, the Kara Sea, and the passage north of the Yamal Peninsula just to attain the huge estuary of the Ob River. It would then have been necessary to penetrate up (south) the estuary a distance of some 400 miles before reaching the river proper.

2. It would be only fair to state here that some scholars have challenged the fact that Dezhnev actually made his way around the end of the continent. His achievement is to a great degree based on his letters and analysis thereof. The letters were lost for more than eighty years. The famed historian G. E. Muller discovered them in the Yakutsk archives in 1736.

4

Initial Sino-Muscovite Contacts

China is located in approximately the same range of latitude as is the United States, that is, on a tier just south of that of Russia and Canada. This means that the Eurasian steppe, which has for centuries been the source of threats to the security of southeastern Russia, has at the same time been constantly viewed by the Chinese as their dangerous northwest frontier. Since Russia and China were, until the seventeenth century, displaced from each other by thousands of east/west miles, the steppe served mostly as a buffer (except, in the age of Mongol domination, when it was a unifier). Only after the Muscovites spread across northern Asia to the Pacific coast would the two peoples first meet, clash, and try to delineate their respective spheres of interest and dominion.

"China proper" is that area occupying the central, eastern, and southern part of what is today the People's Republic of China (PRC). Amounting to 1.5 million square miles (or about 40 percent of the area of the PRC), it is essentially the region that has adequate natural rainfall for productive agriculture. Those areas to the west and north of China proper are much more arid and not readily adaptable to the large-scale raising of grain. These outer territories are, clockwise from the southwest, Tibet, Sinkiang, and Mongolia. A fourth peripheral area, to the northeast, is Manchuria. Aside from Tibet, these border areas have loomed large in Russo-Chinese relations.

From earliest time, the primary security concern of the Chinese has been the northwest frontier. This is one reason why the capital cities of strong dynasties were built on the Wei River, upstream from its confluence with the Huang-ho. Where rainfall is adequate to support agriculture, a sedentary Chinese population has developed. Where the rain is insufficient, grasslands have resulted, and nomadic herdsmen have held sway. A major problem of security for the Chinese, therefore, was how to cope with the nomadic barbarians of the steppe. One of

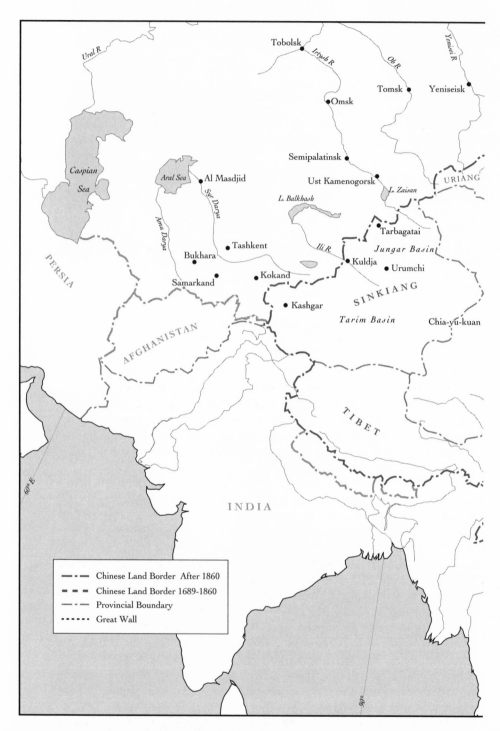

Map 4. Asiatic Russia and China, 1600–1900.

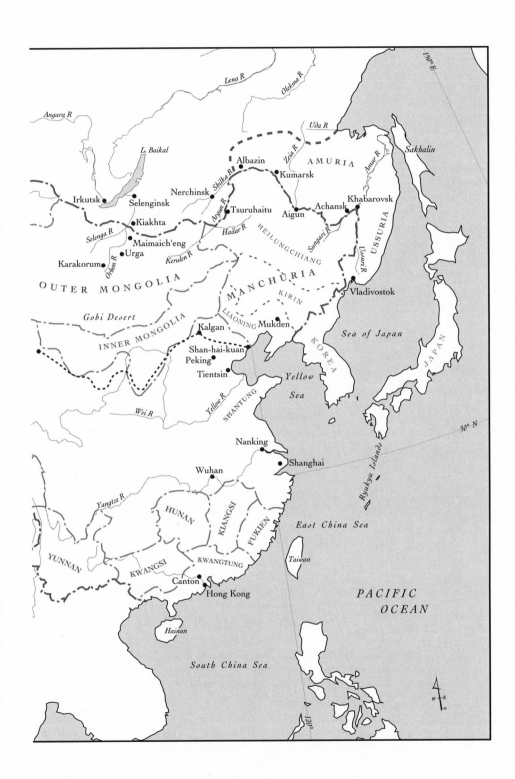

the earliest serious attempts was made by the use of walls. During the Warring States period (403–221 B.C.) of the Chou dynasty, those states nearest the frontier erected protective walls of varying design. When the Ch'in dynasty (221–206 B.C.) came into existence, the First Ch'in Emperor (Ch'in Shih Huang-ti) connected and extended the existing walls to produce what is known as the Great Wall of China.

During the Han (202 B.C.–A.D. 220) and the Tang (618–907) dynasties, the problem was solved by military domination of the northwest frontier. The Sung (960–1279) dynasty attempted, unsuccessfully, to cope with matters by paying for peace, and, as we have seen, the Yuan—or Mongol—dynasty established by Kubilai did not have a problem with the northwest or northern frontier since the Mongols dominated it all.

The power and authority of the Yuan dynasty quickly waned in the fourteenth century, and we see its demise in 1368. It was in turn replaced by the Ming. Now, for the first time since the T'ang, all of China proper was ruled by a truly Chinese dynasty. The Mongols were ousted from the country, and the Ming were in complete control of Inner Mongolia by 1370. The pursuit continued, past the Mongol capital of Karakorum, reaching as far as Lake Baikal by 1388. Ming armies moved to the northeast as well. They reached the Sungari River in Manchuria in 1387 and had taken over the guard posts on the lower Amur River by 1407.

The early Ming emperors were energetic and effective. Particularly the third, the Yung-lo emperor (ruled 1402–1424), was active in foreign affairs. Under his direction, relations (unsatisfactory though they were) were maintained with Tamerlane, then ruler of a vast empire stretching from Central Asia to the Mediterranean. He also ensured that the Great Wall was rebuilt and faced with stone. After he left the scene, however, China quickly sank into a state of xenophobia, reveling in its Chinese-ness after so many centuries of foreign domination. As to the northwest border, the principal concern was that there should never again be a coalition of Mongols such as Jenghis Khan had been able to structure. Thus, while the Great Wall had been refurbished as a measure of defense, the greater strategy was to ensure jealousy and alienation between the various Mongol tribes. This was achieved by more subtle means such as bribes, judicious marriages, misinformation, and incitement of one group against the other.

During the Ming dynasty, the so-called tributary system was greatly refined. The Chinese concept of world order was basically quite simple: he who is the emperor of China reigns supreme since China is deemed to be the only civilized society, surrounded by barbarians. The traditional name for China therefore is Chung-kuo, meaning ''Middle Kingdom.'' It follows that leaders of all barbarian countries are vassals and that communication between the emperor and such leaders must be on a tributary basis. Thus official contact between the Middle Kingdom and its tributaries could be accomplished only via tributary missions (i.e., representatives bearing gifts for the emperor). In actual fact, the gifts need not be of great intrinsic value; rather, it was the act of presenting them and performing the kowtow that had meaning. In fact, the foreigners usually received much more valuable gifts than they presented. Attached to such missions were serious traders who were able to do business in the shadow of the mission. Since strict Confucianist practice sanctioned only this system for the conduct of commerce, it became very important for neighboring countries to secure permission from the Chinese to launch such embassies. The frequency of the missions was a clear indication of the relative esteem in which any barbarian entity was held, and regulation of mission frequency was often used as a tool to influence Mongol behavior.

The proper ceremony attending the arrival, the stay, and the departure of the tributary embassies was of extreme importance. As a result, the element of the Chinese government responsible for them was the Board of Rites. That office, therefore, most nearly approximated a foreign ministry in its handling of the affairs concerning barbarian neighbors. The seriousness of the Chinese in viewing the embassies as tributary is indicated by the fact that the mission personnel were housed and fed by the Chinese government during their stay in the capital.

As the Ming dynasty declined, a Manchu leader named Nurhaci was building a remarkable totalitarian power in Manchuria. His innovation is known as the Banner System. The entire population under his control was divided into four, later eight, major groupings, each represented by a banner of a certain color or combination of colors. A banner was made up of many companies, each of 300 men. Each company included not just the 300 warriors but their families as well; thus, the entire nation was mobilized. As Nurhaci expanded the area under his control, a considerable Chinese population came to be included. In time they would be organized into eight Chinese banners. His government, near Mukden, was organized on Confucian principles and structured like that of the Chinese.

Soon after Nurhaci died in 1626, Manchu leadership was very capably assumed by his son Abahai. Under Abahai's direction, the Manchus would continue their dramatic rise and spread of dominance in East Asia. Under his leadership, the Manchus extended their sway over the Chahar Mongols in Inner Mongolia. A result was the formation of eight Mongol Banners to swell his military forces, and a special Manchu government institution called the Li-fan Yuan was established to handle Mongol affairs. Abahai's armies conquered Korea and would meet with success as well to the north. Commencing in 1635 he sent several expeditions to the Amur valley. Within nine years, he had succeeded in reducing the tribes in that area to tributary status. Just at this juncture (1643), he died.

Abahai's son who succeeded him (known as the Shun-chih emperor) was only five years of age; therefore, his uncle Dorgon (Abahai's brother) became the very competent regent to take over the interim reins of power. It was Dorgon who sent troops into China in response to a Ming plea. The Manchus then were not prepared to depart but rather had come to stay and established themselves in power as the Ch'ing dynasty. Indeed, the Manchu capital was quickly moved from Mukden to Peking. They felt at home and were remarkably well received by the Chinese government bureaucrats. The institutions venerated by the Chinese were essentially left unmolested: the examination system, the six boards, the Confucian ethic. The principal change was that the top positions in government were now encumbered by Manchus or Mongols—but many senior offices were filled by Chinese scholar-bureaucrats. One institution unique to the Manchus, the *Li-fan Yuan*, was brought to Peking, and although the Board of Rites would continue to handle matters concerning missions from the traditional tributary powers, the *Li-fan Yuan* would have cognizance over matters concerning the Mongols and other peoples to the north and northwest.

Abahai's grandson became the K'ang-hsi emperor at age seven when he ascended the throne in 1661. By the time he assumed personal rule in 1667, the feudatories in the south of China were growing increasingly independent. The young emperor made the decision that all China should be under the same rule. Thus, in 1673, eight difficult years of warfare began which would result in the total conquest of the south. The Manchus now would control all of China proper—and Manchuria. Two years later, in 1683, they captured the island of Taiwan and with it the last dynastic claimant of the Ming. The K'ang-hsi emperor now could concentrate his attention on achieving a lasting solution to the problem of the Russians, whose presence was becoming an ever greater irritant in the Amur River valley.

The dramatic spread of Muscovite authority across northern Asia, described in chapter 3, remained well north of Turkestan, Mongolia, and, certainly, China. The first meaningful resistance the Russian fur traders would encounter in their progression eastward was provided by the Tungusic-speaking tribes in the Amur River basin since they were, by the time of the arrival of the Muscovites, tributary to the Manchus. The Russians, of course, had no knowledge of Manchus, let alone awareness that they were in the process of seizing power in the Chinese Empire. Indeed, these Muscovite pioneers had only a vague notion of where such an empire might be.

At the same time, however, back in Moscow, there was a strong urge to pursue trade as deep into Central Asia as feasible with the ultimate hope of reaching fabled Cathay and its riches. Despite the fact that China and Russia had once been part of the same Mongol Empire, connections had been sundered now for hundreds of years. Whatever sense of unity had existed in the lands of Central Asia up to the late fourteenth century was shattered by the xenophobia of the Ming dynasty in China and the depredations of Tamerlane in Turkestan. By the fifteenth and sixteenth centuries, the steppes of Central Asia had become even more fragmented, confusing, and dangerous. Thus any Russian memories of China itself had become dim indeed.

What information the Muscovites did possess concerning the Chinese Empire was owed somewhat to Richard Chancellor, who had arrived in the White Sea in 1553, and those English and Dutch seafarers who followed him later in the century. The Muscovites began to absorb all of this knowledge just as their territorial horizons were being extended to the east. As the result of the early successes of Ivan the Terrible in his conquest of Kazan (1552) and Astrakhan (1556), a direct avenue of trade had opened up with the Persians via the Caspian Sea, and grand ideas arose concerning trade to the east.

Anthony Jenkinson was a representative of the English Royal Muscovy Company, the chartered entity established to handle trade with the Muscovites. As early as 1558 he received permission from Ivan the Terrible to travel through Muscovite lands in an attempt to reach the Central Asian caravan city of Bukhara with the aim of meeting traders from China. He successfully negotiated the manifold dangers of steppe and desert and reached Bukhara, only to learn that the caravans from the east had been disrupted, thanks to disturbances in eastern Turkestan occasioned by a struggle between the Oirats (western Mongols) and the Khalka Mongols for supremacy.

The next tentative effort to trade into the steppe region occurred a half-century later in 1608 and 1609 despite the disorder taking place at the time in Moscow (the Time of Troubles, discussed in chapter 3). At this juncture, the Khalka Mongols, led by the Altyn khan, had displaced the Oirats as the dominant force in western Mongolia and northeastern Turkestan. The Muscovite *voevoda* of Tomsk learned from Kirghiz leaders that it would be possible to make contact with China through the good offices of the Altyn khan. Accordingly, the *voevoda* sent a company of Cossacks in search of the Khalka leader. Because of the vagaries of nomadic movement and steppe warfare, the expedition failed in its mission.

The next attempt, undertaken after termination of the Time of Troubles and the advent of the Romanov dynasty, would be more successful. In 1616 an embassy under the leadership of Ivan Petrov and Vasili Tiumenets departed Tobolsk, proceeded southeast through Tomsk, and succeeded in reaching the mobile court of the Altyn khan. Although the expedition failed to approach any closer to China, the leaders came away with verbal pictures of a great and wealthy power farther to the southeast. This truly whetted the Muscovite appetite for more knowledge.

Such curiosity and dreams of riches quickly resulted in the Petlin mission, which would succeed in reaching China. Ivashko Petlin and his entourage departed Tobolsk in 1618. Proceeding via Tomsk, they struck southeast through western Mongolia and negotiated the Gobi Desert and Inner Mongolia in a relatively straight line toward Peking. Petlin was not an ambassador but rather an observer (or intelligence agent). The Ming court seemingly considered him to be the head of a tributary mission and housed his group in the courtyard set aside for just such missions under the purview of the Board of Rites. Petlin's report, submitted after his return to Moscow in 1619, provided the first eyewitness description of China and the Chinese by a Muscovite. He was deeply impressed by the Great Wall and even more so by the city of Peking. Interest was heightened in Moscow, but it would be three and a half decades before such curiosity could result in another mission since the Ming dynasty was entering its death throes.

One point should be made clear at this juncture. The Petlin expedition occurred at the very time that the fur traders to the north in the taiga were just beginning to build their forts on the Yenisei River. So there was no coordination between the activities of the fur trade to the north and the efforts to open a connection with China farther to the south.

In 1653, nine years after the Ch'ing dynasty asserted its control over Peking, the next Russian embassy was sent to China, this time under the leadership of Fedor Baikov. Baikov was given ambassadorial rank and detailed instructions as to how to comport himself; he was not to make obeisance to any person or symbol except the emperor himself. He was also instructed to maintain a meticulous record of observations about the land and people visited. His caravan was equipped with knowledgeable traders and well endowed with many fur pelts for presents and trade. After a long stop at Tobolsk, which was fast becoming the principal center of Muscovite Asia, his embassy departed in June 1654.

Prior to his departure, however, he had sent an advance party ahead under the leadership of Setkul Ablin, an experienced trader from Bukhara. Ablin was well supplied with presents and other goods, principally furs, for his role as herald preceding his superior, Baikov. He arrived in Peking in late 1655 but was not treated as a messenger. Rather, the Chinese understood him to be the expected Russian ambassador himself. He was housed at the expense of the Chinese government, and his presents were considered to be tribute in the sense of the traditional Chinese system of world order. There now was a difference in Chinese governmental responsibility, however. No longer was it the Board of Rites, but rather the *Li-fan Yuan*, the office designed by the Manchus for the handling of Mongol affairs, that had cognizance of Ablin's visit. Russians, arriving as they did from the northwest, logically were included in the same category as the Mongols. It is therefore almost certain that Ablin performed the kowtow (in Chinese *K'o-t'ou* or ''banging of the head''[1]) as required of tributary missions. Ablin was able to trade virtually his entire store of goods and then, loaded with presents from the emperor of China as befitted a tributary mission, departed Peking before the arrival of his boss, Baikov, in the spring of 1656. The two groups then passed in the steppe without encountering each other.

Fedor Baikov, with a much larger retinue, had followed the Irtysh River south into east Turkestan and thence proceeded across western Mongolia, the Gobi, and on into the border town of Kalgan (modern-day Changchiak'ou). At this point began the troubles that would doom the embassy to almost complete failure as a diplomatic mission. The Ch'ing officials in Peking were not prepared for the arrival of Baikov, thinking they had just dealt with the matter in the form of the tribute offered by Ablin. Thus no measures had been taken to welcome or accommodate Baikov's retinue. Finally granted permission to proceed from Kalgan to Peking, the ambassador refused to kowtow as requested at the gates of the capital. The embassy was properly housed by the *Li-fan Yuan*, but Baikov then insisted that his presents and credentials be delivered directly into the hands of the emperor rather than to subordinate officials. Clearly it was a conflict of Western diplomatic and commercial practices versus the Chinese system of tributary relationships. Fedor Baikov thus was forced to leave China without achieving his mission. He departed in 1657, arriving back in Moscow the following year. Although the embassy was not a diplomatic or commercial success, his reports provided a rich source of information on the great empire to the east. Also, like others who would make the trek, he provided data that added greatly to Muscovite knowledge of the geography of central and eastern Asia.

After his return from China, Setkul Ablin, the Bukharan, was very quickly sent back on another mission, this time solely as a messenger (which he really was on his first expedition). He was accompanied by a Russian named Ivan Perfilev. The undertaking, like its predecessor, was four years in duration (1658–1662). Again, it was treated in Peking like a tributary mission, but the Ch'ing court was most displeased that the letter from the tsar did not use the Chinese calendar and thus was not acceptable. However, the kowtow must have been performed since a fair amount of trade took place. The emperor himself directed that the embassy be treated considerately since the Russians did not have the benefit of Chinese "education and culture."[2] Although Perfilev and Ablin were relieved of much of their gain by Oirat Mongols on the way back to Moscow, they still realized a profit.

Ablin, by now an "old China hand," was sent on yet another mission to Peking, this one lasting from 1668 to 1672. It would be the first to arrive during the long reign of the K'ang-hsi emperor. That young, curious ruler even granted an informal audience to the Muscovites. Ablin performed the kowtow, and the visit progressed very smoothly. After a month in Peking, Ablin and his caravaneers departed, laden with a considerable quantity of Chinese goods and gems. When they returned to Russian lands, they calculated a return of more than 18,000 rubles on an initial investment of 4,500. Obviously, development of increased trade would be of great value to the Muscovites, particularly as a state monopoly.

Shortly before Ablin left Peking, a direct connection was made in Chinese minds between the missions from Moscow and the pushy Russian frontiersmen who, for the last twenty years, had been trying to establish a permanent presence in the Amur River valley to the north and to dominate the peoples living there. In particular, officials of the *Li-fan Yuan* complained to Ablin that certain tribute payers in the area had switched allegiance from the Manchus to the Russians. Of special concern was the case of one Gantimur, a tribal leader who had defected in the late 1660s with his immediate family and other followers in the number of about forty. He had been baptized into the Orthodox church, given the name Gantimurov, and awarded a princely title.

The nearest Muscovite authority involved was the *voevoda* at Nerchinsk, a town that had been built on the Shilka River, a major tributary of the Amur. In the late spring of 1670, about six months after Ablin's departure from Peking, the *voevoda* sent a strange letter to Peking suggesting the Ch'ing emperor recognize the suzerainty of the Muscovite tsar. Because of translation difficulties, the sense of the communication was misconstrued, and no offense was taken. However, the Chinese now realized more clearly the identity of the fur traders of the north. In the following chapter, we shall review events taking place in the Amur area.

The last great embassy to be sent to China by Muscovy prior to regularizing relations was one under the leadership of Nicholas Milescu in the years from 1675 to 1678. Milescu was born in Moldavia into a Greek family in 1636. He received an excellent education and grew into a haughty, talented aristocrat who was a master of several languages. He was appointed to the exalted office of *spathar*—or sword bearer—by the hospodar of Moldavia around the year 1658. Since he had been a bright intellectual light in the Orthodox Christian world, he was recommended for service to the tsar of Muscovy by the patriarch of Jerusalem in 1671—and was accepted. He rose rapidly in the tsar's service, making himself invaluable through his diplomatic and multilingual talents. He thus was a natural choice for the tough assignment of leading an embassy to the Celestial Kingdom.

Basically, the goal of Milescu's mission was to establish a sound basis for commerce between Moscow and China. He was equipped with many items for presents and trade and was instructed to invite Chinese merchants to make the trek to Moscow. He was given no instructions pertaining to the problem of the Amur valley, and the framers of the instructions obviously still had no appreciation of the Chinese system of world order which could countenance no equals—only the emperor and tributary kinglets.

Milescu departed Moscow in February 1675 and arrived in Tobolsk a month later. There, after filling out the personnel needs of the embassy, he proceeded eastward through the taiga, on the route of the fur traders, in order not to entrust the fate of this important enterprise to the vagaries of the steppe environment. He thus proceeded via Yeniseisk and Selenginsk (just south of Lake Baikal) to Nerchinsk. From there the group headed south through Manchuria until it reached Kalgan where it was held up by the Ch'ing authorities for two months before being allowed to proceed. Such delays incensed the proud Milescu and hardened his attitudes toward the country he was visiting. From Muscovite officials he visited while crossing Asia, Milescu had erroneously inferred that China was much weaker than he had previously been led to believe. Those who spoke to him about the mild Manchu responses to Muscovite actions in the Amur were unaware of the titanic struggle then taking place to complete the conquest of the southern part of China.

After months of fruitless argument with Ch'ing authorities, Milescu acquiesced and agreed, very reluctantly, to comply with Chinese practice. He was granted an audience with the emperor and performed the kowtow, albeit in such a hasty fashion as almost to make a mockery of the ceremony. Communication, although almost all confrontational during Milescu's visit, was greatly facilitated by a friendship of sorts that grew between the Orthodox Milescu and the Jesuit priest Ferdinand Verbiest. Verbiest's great value lay in his facility with Latin (which Milescu spoke), Manchu, and Chinese.

Milescu's pride on behalf of himself and his tsar was such that he could not bring himself to compromise with the Chinese. Accordingly, he finally submitted twelve articles to his hosts, which proposed a set of arrangements between Muscovy and Cathay, expressed in Western concepts of diplomatic relations and commercial intercourse. Even Milescu was forced to realize his mission had ended in failure when the Manchu response to his articles assumed the form of a blunt lecture on August 30, 1676, from senior Ch'ing officials, including the president of the *Li-fan Yuan*.

Milescu was informed that there was one—and only one—system of relations between Chinese and other peoples, namely the tributary system. He was told as well that the return of the traitor Gantimur was important and would be viewed favorably. To ensure that there was no misunderstanding, the words of the Manchu leaders were translated from Manchu into Latin, then into Russian, then Mongol, and finally back into Manchu. Milescu was then rather summarily dismissed and began the return trek in September, arriving back in Moscow in January 1678. Not for another decade would the Muscovites and Manchus be able to begin to achieve some sort of realistic accommodation.

NOTES

1. In performing the kowtow, the supplicant prostrated himself, touched his head to the floor three times, rose, and then repeated the routine twice more. In all, three prostrations and nine "bangings of the head" were required.

2. Lo-shu Fu, *A Documentary Chronicle of Sino-Western Relations (1644–1820)*, vol. 1 (Tucson: University of Arizona Press, 1966), 24.

5

Toward a Delineated
Sino-Muscovite Border

While Moscow had been approaching the Chinese Empire across the steppe, events had proceeded apace in the Amur region. As recounted in chapter 3, Vasili Poiarkov and a group of Cossacks had been the first Muscovites to trek into and out of the Amur valley (1643–1645). When they returned to Yakutsk with their report of the area, the local *voevoda* granted permission for an expedition into the Amur to an enterprising figure named Erofei Pavlovich Khabarov. In the early spring of 1649, he and 150 volunteers proceeded up the Olekma, a tributary of the Lena. In the dead of the following winter, they negotiated the Stanovoi Range and descended into the Amur basin. Based on the supplies of grain Khabarov noted in the possession of the native peoples known as the Daurs, he was convinced that the region held great promise as a possible source of food for the Russian fur trade. Leaving a garrison behind on the Amur, Khabarov made a rapid trip to Yakutsk in the spring of 1650. In his report, he strongly recommended that a positive effort be undertaken not only to conquer but also to colonize the area he had just seen. Then, before the end of the year, he returned to the Amur with reinforcements. His force wintered over in a town they fortified at the river's northernmost point, named Albazin.

The following summer, Khabarov's men ranged down the river, spreading terror along the way. They asserted their control over the Daurs and Duchers by destroying property, killing inhabitants, collecting tribute in the form of furs, and confiscating grain. In the process, they discovered the two points where the Sungari and the Ussuri rivers emptied into the Amur. Khabarov decided to fortify a site called Achansk between the mouths of the two tributaries since there was more grain available in this stretch of the river. It was at Achansk that the Muscovites' actions finally evoked a response from the nominal overlords of the native tribes. In March 1652 the Manchus decided to attack. In the ensuing fracas, they were in position to destroy the defenders when their commander issued the rather unrealistic order that the Russians were to be taken alive. The result was that the Manchus were easily driven off. This fact put the local tribes in the quandary of deciding to whom they should render tribute.

Khabarov nevertheless moved his Cossacks up river and spent the winter of 1652–1653 in an *ostrog* at a site named Kumarsk. He had been expecting a Muscovite invasion force of some magnitude based on his recommendations to the *voevoda* of Yakutsk. That official had indeed endorsed the need for positive action to Moscow, and the idea had initially been favorably received. However, in spite of original intentions to send out a substantial force under Prince Fedor Lobanov-Rostovsky, events in Europe had understandably taken precedence. Moscow and Poland were on the eve of the long struggle for the Ukraine. As a result, no army of any size was sent eastward. Instead, a nobleman named Dmitri Ivanovich Zinov'ev arrived on the Amur in the spring of 1653 with a small detachment to take charge. He arrested Khabarov and escorted him back to Moscow to answer charges of malfeasance. The Cossack Onufi Stepanov was left in command of the local forces, now numbering almost 400 souls. Stepanov would embody Muscovite authority on the Amur for the next five years.

The Russians, after wintering over near the mouth of the Zeia River, confiscated grain from the natives and began to ascend the Sungari River. Here they were met by a Manchu force which repelled them but did not follow up its advantage. Stepanov then moved back up the Amur to Kumarsk where his group spent the winter of 1654–1655. It was here they were briefly placed under siege and then attacked by Manchus in late March, but their firepower was sufficient to drive off the attackers. The Manchus now would resort to more subtle means to force the newcomers from the region. The various native tribes, principally the Daurs and Duchers, were ordered to destroy their settlements and withdraw up the tributaries south of the Amur, thereby depriving the Russians of their accustomed source of food.

Life now became more difficult for Stepanov and his followers. They even tried agriculture themselves, but not being farmers, their results were meager. They remained, however, since there was no permission to depart. At the same time, Moscow sought to provide a more authoritative government presence somewhat nearer the scene. In 1655 Afanasi Pashkov, *voevoda* of Yeniseisk, was ordered, with a force of 300, to establish a new *voevodstvo* at Nerchinsk, a site on the Shilka River 300 miles from its confluence with the Amur. The *voevodstvo* became a reality three years later. Stepanov managed to survive on his own during those three years—until the Manchus finally made a decisive move. While probing for food down the Amur, not far from the mouth of the Sungari, Stepanov and the more than 500 men with him were suddenly surrounded by a small river armada. Only 47 Muscovites escaped to make their way to Nerchinsk whereas almost 300 were either captured or killed. The rest deserted and became freebooters. The Amur now would become a no-man's-land for more than a decade. In 1660, Manchu forces destroyed a large band of

Russian outlaws and were in position to move up the Shilka and raze Nerchinsk. One reason they failed to follow up was the effectiveness of their policy of forced relocation of the Amur tribes: there was a lack of sufficient food supplies.

The period just discussed, concerning the activities of Khabarov and Stepanov, is frequently referred to as the "conquest" of the Amur region by Muscovy. As we have seen, such a description is an exaggeration. The Russians did manage to terrorize the native population and successfully fought off two Manchu attacks; however, they never established themselves in authority in any one location other than far-off Nerchinsk in 1658. They wintered over in a variety of places dependent, largely, on the availability of food. Once the Manchus took resolute action, the invaders were destroyed. The Manchus were unable to maintain a force of significant size because of the concurrent commitment of their relatively sparse population to the greater challenge of taking over the Chinese Empire.

The next interlopers into the Amur, a group of eighty-four desperate men under a Polish-born refugee named Nikifor Czernigowski, set themselves up in Albazin sometime around 1665. This haven for desperadoes would gradually acquire a population of some 300. Farmers must have been among their number since they began successfully to grow grain in the vicinity. It was around this period that the "Gantimur treason" took place. Gantimur came originally from the area not far from Nerchinsk. He had regularly paid tribute to the Manchus. Then, for a period of time, he paid tribute as well to the Russians. His priorities seemed apparent, however, from the fact that he fought with the Manchus in the 1655 attack on Kumarsk and in the 1658 Manchu victory on the Amur. However, when called upon to launch an attack against some of the renegade Russians in the Amur area in 1667, he defected. Since he was a chieftain of some influence, the Ch'ing dynasty in China was now considerably more worried about the security of the northern reaches of its original homeland.

This concern would be heightened by Russian actions taken in 1672. Moscow decided that the freebooters in the Amur valley should come under its control. Accordingly, two years later, the *voevoda* of Nerchinsk sent one of his officers to take charge in Albazin and to grant Czernigowski and his followers pardons for their past crimes. The timing of the action was remarkable in that it fairly closely coincided with the decision of the young K'ang-hsi emperor to deal forcefully with the conquest of southern China and with the Muscovite decision to send Milescu on his embassy to Peking. In 1682 a separate *voevodstvo* was created for the Amur with the *voevoda* resident in Albazin. Thus the period from 1672 until 1685 could be considered, if not the "conquest" of the Amur, at least the "occupation" of same by the Muscovites.

Eight years would be required for the completion of the conquest of mainland China by the Ch'ing authorities and another two to take over the island of Taiwan. The K'ang-hsi emperor now was free to pursue the problem to the north. He wasted very little time for, as he himself realized, control of the Amur meant ready access up the Sungari into the heartland of Manchuria.

Certain preparatory measures, defensive in character, had been initiated by the Manchus as early as 1676. A headquarters was established in Kirin on the Sungari River, and construction of a new river fleet commenced. Action was taken to ensure a supply of food, and reconnaissance missions were sent out to scout the topography, particularly the environs of Albazin. In the two years following the Ch'ing conquest of Taiwan, activity rapidly accelerated in the north. Despite the emperor's impatience, however, operations were not begun before the onset of winter in late 1684. The Russians began to observe Manchu patrols along the Amur, and a Manchu fort at Aigun opposite the Zeia River mouth gradually inhibited Russian riverine activity. Although the Ch'ing were operating at considerable distance (a thousand miles as the crow flies) from the center of power, the Russians were at an even greater disadvantage, their center being several thousand miles from the scene.

On June 23, 1685, the attack on Albazin commenced. The attacking force of 3,000 men surrounded the town and blockaded the river approaches. When the Manchus made preparations to burn the wooden perimeter of the stockade and the defenders' supply of lead and powder ran low, the Russian commander, Aleksei Tolbuzin, surrendered. Instructions from the K'ang-hsi emperor had been quite explicit that bloodshed should be avoided if possible and definitely minimized. Indeed, the Manchus had informed Tolbuzin before the attack that he and his followers (numbering between 350 and 600) could leave the area in peace. Now, following the surrender, the same liberal terms were offered. The majority of the Muscovites opted to proceed to Nerchinsk, but nearly forty-five, especially those with native wives (who could not be repatriated), decided to surrender to the Manchu authorities and became members of one of the Manchu Banners. The Manchus then withdrew to their base at Aigun.

The K'ang-hsi emperor now sent two letters, written in Latin by the Jesuit priests, addressed to the tsar of Muscovy. Therein he stated his desire to live in peace and harmony with the Muscovites but asserted that they in turn should permanently leave the Amur. When these letters and news of the loss of Albazin were received in Moscow, they elicited a favorable reaction. Matters in Europe were posing difficult choices for the Russians. Following the death of Tsar Alexis in 1676, his sickly son Fedor III assumed the throne for the next six years. Then, in 1682, the co-tsars Ivan V and Peter I reigned in name while their older sister Sophia acted as regent. Decisions of major magnitude were being made which brought Moscow into the crusade against the Ottoman Empire at the side of Catholic powers. Thus energies and resources were not available for problems in the Far East. Accordingly, the decision was made to send Fedor Alexeevich Golovin east with plenipotentiary powers and clear instructions for negotiation.

In the meantime, when Ivan Vlasov, the *voevoda* of Nerchinsk, learned that the Manchus had left Albazin, he sent a large detachment, numbering over 800 men, under the leadership of Tolbuzin, to harvest the Albazin grain. (It had been spared by the Manchu commander in disregard of the K'ang-hsi emperor's in-

structions). Feeling confident again, Vlasov directed Tolbuzin to reestablish Albazin and Russian authority along the Amur. The grain was harvested, and
Albazin was rebuilt. When word of these actions reached the K'ang-hsi emperor,
he ordered a siege that was put into effect by July 4, 1686. The siege remained
in force until raised by order of the emperor in December as the result of a
letter from Moscow that welcomed discussions and contained the news of Golovin's mission as ambassador. By the end of the siege, fewer than a hundred
defenders were still alive, and all of them were suffering from disease. Military
operations had thus ceased on the Amur by the end of 1686.

Fedor Golovin, who is best remembered as one of the closer confidants of
Peter the Great, departed Moscow on his important mission in January 1686.
He was thirty-five years of age. He was accompanied by 500 *strel'tsy*, the first
units of regular troops to be seen in Muscovite East Asia. By the time his party
had arrived at Selenginsk (October 1687), just to the south of Lake Baikal, his
military force had been augmented by some 1,400 Cossacks. Golovin was accompanied by a well-educated young Pole named Andrei Bielobocki to serve
as Latin interpreter. Golovin had received detailed instructions in Moscow, and
these would be augmented by courier during his trip east.

Selenginsk is located on the lower reaches of the Selenga River which flows
into Lake Baikal about twenty miles farther downstream. The Selenga is the
major river draining northern Mongolia, and Selenginsk is in an area populated
by Buriat Mongols. From this position, Golovin commenced correspondence
with Peking; therefore, the couriers transited eastern Mongolia which at the time
was dominated by the Khalkas, tribes tributary to the Manchus. Their leaders
were the Tushetu Khan, resident in Urga (modern-day Ulaanbaatar), and his
brother who was the Khutukhtu, or "Living Buddha," leader of the Mongolian
Lamaists. The various Mongol khans were unhappy that the Muscovites had
reduced their cousins, the Buriats, to tributary status, thereby depriving the Khalkas of political and economic advantage. Further, they believed the Russians
were granting asylum to fugitives sought by the Mongols. Indeed, the Khalkas
were sufficiently disturbed to send a small army to besiege the Russians at
Selenginsk, commencing in January 1688. The Muscovite defenses were adequate to withstand the threat, and two months later the Mongols suddenly lifted
the siege and left. The reason for their precipitate departure was an attack from
western Mongols under their charismatic leader Galdan. These Oirat Mongols,
now based in the Jungar Basin, are often referred to as the Jungar Mongols.
Their attack threw political matters in Outer Mongolia into considerable confusion, a condition we shall deal with in greater detail in the following chapter.

The immediate effect of Galdan's attack was to impress even more forcefully
on the K'ang-hsi emperor the need to put matters to right in the steppe. The
Khalkas fell back under his protection in Inner Mongolia. In the meantime, it
had been agreed between Golovin and the Chinese capital that talks should be
held in Selenginsk in the summer of 1688. Accordingly, the Manchu delegation
departed Peking in May. Before they had proceeded very far, the emperor

learned of Galdan's activities and ordered his ambassadors home. Thus the projected negotiations had to be delayed a year. Of interest is the fact that the delegation had included two Chinese scholars who were to provide a record of negotiations.

Golovin now proceeded eastward to Nerchinsk, and it was agreed that talks should take place at that Russian stronghold. The Manchu representatives departed from Peking on June 13, 1689, and arrived at Nerchinsk in late July. The head of the Manchu delegation was Songgotu, an uncle of the empress. His entourage included a military escort numbered variously between 3,000 and 15,000 men. Since the route to Nerchinsk was much more difficult than that to Selenginsk, no Chinese scholars were included to record the proceedings. Not only would it have been much more difficult for wagons to convey the bureaucrats, but time was a factor that demanded that all members ride horseback, an activity in which most Chinese scholars were not schooled. Two very important members of the Manchu negotiating group were Jesuit priests, the Frenchman Jean-François Gerbillon and the Portuguese Thomas Pereira, who provided not only their linguistic skills but also advice to the Manchus on Western norms of diplomacy. Each left a journal describing his experiences.

When the two groups met in August, each side had rather explicit instructions, the final positions of which were not that far apart. Golovin was to attempt to gain the Amur valley at least to the Sungari, but the final condition was to retain Nerchinsk on the Shilka at all costs. The Manchu position underwent considerable change from that which had been prepared a year before for the aborted Selenginsk meeting. The K'ang-hsi emperor now had greater worries about the Mongols and the possibility of cooperation between the Russians and the western Jungars. Therefore, although he wanted the Muscovites to withdraw beyond the Stanovoi Range, he no longer resisted totally the Russian desire to possess Nerchinsk. He was wise enough to realize that these new barbarians were different from the usual tribal alignments from the steppe, that there was a single driving authority that would not be easily fragmented. Therefore we see for the first time representatives of the Celestial Throne (albeit all Manchus) arriving to discuss and negotiate more or less as equals.

In view of the problem posed by the defection of Gantimur in the north and looking to possible future problems of a similar nature with the Mongols, the K'ang-hsi emperor came to the conclusion that a border must be delineated between the Russian territorial possessions and those of China. On the other hand, the Muscovites, in need of assets to pursue their struggles in Europe, had no desire to drain their resources further by a conflict with the powerful Chinese Empire. Quite the reverse, they viewed trade with China as an important means of increasing the wealth of their own state. Therefore two principal currents met at Nerchinsk: Russian desire for trade with China and the Ch'ing desire for a border that would exclude the Muscovites from the Amur valley. On the issue of Gantimur, the instructions were in direct opposition to each other. Golovin was ordered specifically not to surrender the defector whereas Songgotu was instructed to seek his return.

Negotiations at Nerchinsk commenced on August 22 and continued until signature of a treaty on September 6. The progress was painful indeed and in all probability would not have reached a treaty conclusion were it not for the patience and cleverness of the two Jesuit fathers. Constantly at stake was some aspect of national honor. For example, in order to surmount the problem of who should visit whom first, two tents were erected side by side with the openings facing each other so that the plenipotentiaries could negotiate without either having to pay a call on the other. For the occasion, the Russians had carted— all the way across northern Asia—musical instruments for a military marching display as well as costly Turkish and Persian carpets and a fancy desk and chairs.

Most of the negotiating was done by the Jesuits and the Polish interpreter Bielobocki, with only a total of three plenum sessions. The final product was the Treaty of Nerchinsk, a milestone in Chinese diplomatic history. It was a very brief document, containing only six articles. The first two met the requirements of the K'ang-hsi emperor for a delineated boundary. It was agreed that the border would commence, in the west, with the Argun River, that the left bank would be Russian and the right bank Chinese. Then, at the point where the Argun and Shilka rivers merge to form the Amur, the border would ascend the Shilka to the confluence of its left tributary, the Gorbitsa. This smaller stream would be the border to its very source in the Stanovoi Mountains. (This range comprises part of the watershed between the Lena and Amur riverine systems.) The border thence was to extend eastward along the watershed to the source of the Uda River and then down that stream to the Sea of Okhotsk. The wording of the treaty concerning the easternmost areas was understandably vague since neither side was at all well acquainted with the topography.

The third article simply called for the destruction of Albazin and the removal of all Russians and their equipment. The fourth article dealt with the matter of Gantimur. The Manchus were unable to secure his return and had to settle for wording that permitted any refugees at the time of the signing of the treaty to remain on either side of the border but provided that in the future all refugees were to be apprehended expeditiously and returned to the country whence they fled.

The fifth article met the Muscovite requirement for trade, albeit in rather vague terms: ''Whatever people who possess documents of passage from either side, for the sake of the presently inaugurated friendship, may freely come and go to both states for their affairs on either side and may buy and sell what is necessary to them and it shall be so ordered.''[1] The last article, the longest, was a general statement encouraging punishment of criminals and deploring any recourse to war in lieu of diplomacy. In this article, the Russians also agreed that the Chinese could place along the border stone markers with an outline of the treaty articles inscribed thereon. Interestingly, the town of Nerchinsk was not mentioned in the treaty at all, a victory on the part of the Russians.

As indicated above, the language of these negotiations in the wilds of north-eastern Asia was Latin. Therefore the authoritative versions of the treaty, the only ones bearing the seals of both countries, were in that language. The copy retained by the Chinese delegation listed the emperor first; that kept by the Russians listed the tsar first. The treaty was translated only into Russian and Manchu. Indeed, two centuries would elapse before an official translation would be made into Chinese. However, some border markers provided for in article 6 of the Treaty of Nerchinsk were placed along the Gorbitsa, and each contained a statement of the essential elements of the treaty in Latin, Russian, Manchu, and Chinese. Later, a Mongol translation would be added.

The Treaty of Nerchinsk was remarkable in that it represented such a radical exception on the part of the Chinese Empire in its relations with foreign powers. It was the first instance of an "equal" treaty. Although Western maritime powers had been prowling the western shores of the Pacific since the arrival of the Portuguese in the mid-sixteenth century, they were held at arm's length by the Chinese Empire and forced to adhere to the Chinese system of world order. It required the pragmatism of a ruler of the stature of the K'ang-hsi emperor to understand that the only means of realizing Chinese best interests on the continent was to negotiate with Moscow on the basis of equality.

For their part, the Muscovites had no desire to place a limit on the territory they would claim, but pragmatism was the order of the day. The two factors of the desire for what they considered a lucrative trade and the knowledge that they were in no position to offer a military challenge to the Chinese Empire at so great a distance made clear what was in the best interests of the state. Further, their stubborn insistence on the retention of Nerchinsk would in the future provide them with ready access to the Amur valley when the time was more auspicious.

NOTE

1. Mark Mancall, *Russia and China: Their Diplomatic Relations to 1728* (Cambridge: Harvard University Press, 1971), 282.

6

The Kiakhta System

One interesting fallout from military operations between the Manchus and Mus-covites in the Amur valley during the 1680s, including the capture of Albazin in 1685, was the growing number of Russians resident in Peking. The forty-five who chose to cast their lot with the Manchus rather than to accompany most of their fellows to Nerchinsk joined more than seventy others who had previously either been taken captive or had voluntarily chosen to defect. By decree of the emperor, all these Russians were organized into the seventeenth company of the fourth regiment of the Manchu Bordered Yellow Banner; they therefore retained their ethnic identity. This decision was in line with the Manchu practice that had included Chinese and Mongols in the Banner System much earlier in the century. The leader of the company was a Russian from Albazin named Urus-lanov who was made an official of the upper-fourth grade in the Chinese system. The company was given a special allocation of space in the northeast corner of the Tatar (Manchu) City in Peking reserved for the Bordered Yellow Banner.

The Russians constituted a household, rather than a line, company. They were therefore unlikely to be in danger of being employed in combat. Rather, their military usefulness was in support roles. Their daily task was that of making bows for the Manchu warriors, but a more unique role lay in the sphere of intelligence: their knowledge of geography in the north as well as their ability to speak Russian. Thus they came to be of limited use as low-level interpreters, particularly when Russian caravans began to arrive in Peking. However, virtually all were illiterate and thus not qualified as translators. Several were chosen from time to time to serve as couriers between Peking and Nerchinsk.

The seventeenth company of the Bordered Yellow Banner also included its own Russian Orthodox priest. In 1683 Maxim Leontev, a priest in Albazin, had been captured, along with a group of seventy or more other Muscovites, on a bank of the Amur River. The Manchu authorities looked favorably upon providing the means for Father Maxim to tend to his Orthodox flock and even provided him with an old Buddhist prayer house for the purpose. This was strictly in line with Ch'ing practices which similarly provided for Lamaist monks to serve the spiritual needs of the Mongol bannermen. Using the materials of the Buddhist structure, the Albazinians built a small church which they later named in honor of Saint Nicholas.

Moscow never had a clear idea of how many Russians were resident in China, for whatever purpose, but would regularly request the Ch'ing authorities to repatriate "Russian prisoners." The Manchus, particularly because of the Russian refusal to hand over Gantimur, would not consent even to discuss the matter. The Albazinians, despite their own parish priest, very soon lost their cultural identity as Russians. The succeeding generation included very few who could even speak the language.

The Muscovites quickly took advantage of the Treaty of Nerchinsk to begin sending caravans to the Celestial Kingdom for trade. At the outset, the caravans were conducted mostly by licensed traders. Because of troubles in the steppe between various Mongol elements, the safer but very laborious route was pursued from Nerchinsk to Peking (a round-trip between the two termini required from ten to twelve months). Thus Nerchinsk became the most important Russian trading center in the Far East.

Whereas the Russians were delighted that trade was now authorized, the officials in Peking were not. Although the treaty had ultimately been concluded in terms of national equality, the Ch'ing continued to view the relationship as that between the Chinese Empire and a tributary Muscovite state. Therefore the Russian caravans were treated like tributary missions in that they were housed and fed at the expense of the imperial court. The caravaneers were often excessively loud in their conduct and regularly engaged in drunken brawls, and the authorities in Peking became increasingly disenchanted with this new phenomenon in their midst—so much so that they commenced to apply various measures to discourage the caravans. A more subtle action was to flood the market with fur pelts, taken in Manchuria, when a Russian caravan was scheduled to arrive, thereby driving down the price. More direct means consisted of periodically restricting the numbers of caravans and the size of each.

Moscow, in turn, also entertained reservations about certain aspects of the trade. The traders were licensed, and the government of the tsar was concerned that an insufficient share of the profits found its way into the state coffers. Moscow became increasingly suspicious that too many of the traders were wily Bukharan caravaneers. But of greatest concern to the tsarist government was the amount of money siphoned off from the operations by governmental officials along the way.[1]

Not only was the system of commerce resulting from the Treaty of Nerchinsk far from satisfactory, but other, serious problems remained. The Manchus came to appreciate the fact that although they now had a border with Muscovy, it extended no farther west than the Argun River. As mentioned in the previous chapter, the Oirat Mongol leader Galdan presented a particular problem for the Ch'ing dynasty. Galdan first consolidated Oirat tribes under his leadership in the Jungar basin in the early 1670s and then managed to extend his control over all of east Turkestan by the end of the decade. In 1688 his Jungar forces invaded Outer Mongolia and delivered a crushing attack on the Khalkas (eastern Mongols) in the spring of 1688, forcing them to retreat into Inner Mongolia and causing cancellation of the embassy that had been sent to deal with the Russians at Selenginsk (see previous chapter).

Thanks to the security granted by the Treaty of Nerchinsk, the Ch'ing government in 1690 was now able decisively to repel an attack by Galdan's Jungars at Ulan-buting near the Great Wall and to send them packing back into the steppe. An immediate result was the complete formal subjugation of the Khalka Mongols to Manchu authority in a ceremony held the following year. Henceforth they were not merely tribute-paying neighbors but totally under the power of the Ch'ing. Thereafter, the titles of khan amongst the Khalkas would be conferred by Peking. The resolute K'ang-hsi emperor—in his typical way—decided now to meet this Jungar threat head-on. Gathering a great army of 80,000, he personally led it to an overwhelming victory over Galdan and his Jungar Mongols on June 12, 1696, at Jao Modo, not far from the Mongolian center of Urga. Galdan was forced to flee northwestward toward the Altai Mountains. The emperor then commenced preparations to move against him yet again, but the situation eased when the Jungar leader perished from illness or suicide the following spring.

Despite the removal of Galdan from the scene, the Mongol problem refused to go away. Even before Galdan's death, his nephew Tsewang Araptan had taken over as the khan of the Jungars in eastern Turkestan. This new leader by himself did not pose a serious threat to Manchu hegemony in Mongolia, but the fear persisted that he—or others like him—might make common cause with the Russians in the future. Thus the conviction grew in the mind of the K'ang-hsi emperor that the solution to the ''Mongol problem'' lay in a well-defined border with Muscovy extending across northern Mongolia.

In Moscow concern over profits from the caravan trade with China led to proposals for a state monopoly. As a result, a caravan sponsored by the government was sent out in March 1692 under the leadership of Eleazar Isbrant Ides. Originally from Denmark, Ides had been a successful merchant in the Russian north. He was not just in charge of a state-controlled venture but was instructed to examine carefully what the future role of the Muscovite state might be in the Chinese trade. He was, in essence, to make a market analysis of the city of Peking. Ides was designated an official ambassador and so was authorized to discuss diplomatic matters concerning implementation of provisions of the Treaty of Nerchinsk. He was specifically directed to request authority to build an Orthodox church in Peking for the use of Russian merchants.

The mission arrived in Peking in November 1693. Ides performed the kowtow as required, and despite Ch'ing displeasure that in the tsar's letter his titles had appeared above those of the emperor, the visit was rather amicable. Ides and his party were ensconced in the *Hui-t'ung Kuan*, the quarters in the southeast part of the Tatar City set aside for the guests of the *Li-fan Yuan* who hailed from the north and northwest. From this time onward, it would principally house visiting Russians; therefore, it acquired the name of *O-lo-ssu Kuan*, meaning "Russian Hostel." Ides was permitted to circulate freely throughout the city, a fact that greatly facilitated his careful market evaluation. During his wandering, he chanced across Saint Nicholas, the church of the Albazinians. Interestingly, he would mention this in his later book, but he did not include it in his report to the tsar.

As to diplomatic matters, in discussions concerning fugitives, the Manchus made the observation that it would be difficult to define Mongol fugitives until a border between Mongolia and Siberia had been delineated. The request for the construction of an Orthodox church for transient Russians was denied on the grounds that places of worship were authorized only for those permanently resident in Peking, a subtle way of explaining the presence of the Catholic church of the Jesuits. The Ch'ing officials also stated that all caravans should be limited to a total of 200 persons and restricted to visits every three years. The caravans would be housed at the *O-lo-ssu Kuan*, but the merchants would be required to pay for their own supplies and depart after a maximum stay of eighty days. Ides departed Peking in February 1694. Returning as he had come, via the Manchurian route through Nerchinsk, he arrived back in Moscow eleven months later. Based on his observations concerning the Peking market, Tsar Peter decided that henceforth the China trade would be a state monopoly.

Despite the restrictions on caravans outlined to Ides, Manchu control for some years was spotty at best. Similarly, although trade was a monopoly of the Muscovite state, many illegal entrepreneurs managed to insinuate themselves into the business, either by forged documentation or bribes to Ch'ing officials. The first state caravan, which departed Moscow in 1697, returned two years later. The fourth such caravan, under the leadership of Ivan Savateev, left Moscow in 1702 and took the usual route to Peking via Nerchinsk. Now that the Mongolian steppe had been pacified by the Manchu destruction of Galdan's forces, the Peking authorities permitted Savateev to return via Mongolia to Urga and thence to Selenginsk. The trip took only seventy days. The caravan bore with it a letter from the *Li-fan Yuan* suggesting this route in the future. One reason for the Manchus' action was their desire to establish a local control over caravan matters as far from Peking as possible. If the Russians were to use the route from Selenginsk, the Tushetu khan in Urga could act as a screen, checking documentation, proper form of any correspondence, and compliance with Peking directives such as the size of the caravans. In other words, Peking was employing the time-honored Chinese practice of "controlling barbarians with barbarians." The principal loser in this rerouting would be Nerchinsk, which to this time had been the chief entrepôt for trade from China.

At the very same time that the Sino-Muscovite treaty was being negotiated at Nerchinsk in August and September 1689, dramatic events had been taking place in Moscow. Peter, now a strapping youth of seventeen, seized power from his half sister Sophia, and began one of the more energetic reigns in Russian history. Peter certainly was aware of the situation in the Far East. Fedor Golovin, negotiator at Nerchinsk, was one of his closest advisors, who accompanied the tsar on his epoch trek to Western Europe from 1697 to 1699. But Peter's attentions were initially demanded in Europe. He was driven to modernize his country at a furious pace. The *strel'tsy*, created by Ivan the Terrible 150 years before, gave way to a more modern army. Peter's passion to send Russians to sea would create the first Russian navy. Although the patriarch of the Russian Orthodox Church had played a key role in Peter's seizure of power, the patriarchate would be replaced by a holy synod under a lay person. And Peter, the Great Prince of Moscow, would transform himself into the Emperor of Russia.

Peter's great plans for a new crusade of Christian powers against the Ottoman Empire were demoted in precedence since the Holy Roman Empire was more concerned about the ambitions of Louis XIV of France. As a result, he and the rulers of Poland and Denmark were emboldened to launch a war against the new king of Sweden, Charles XII, who was fifteen at the time of his accession to the throne in 1697. As it turned out, the youthful Charles proved to be one of the finer soldiers of his age, and the Great Northern War, begun in 1700, would not be concluded until twenty-one years later. After costly but educational losses to Charles XII, Peter's epic victory over the Swedes at Poltava in 1709 was the turning point, and from that moment he could begin to apply his prodigious energies in other directions.

The Russians for some time had attempted to lure Chinese merchants to their country, suggesting they bring with them gold, silver, and precious gems. The embassy of Ides from 1692 to 1695 had submitted a specific request to this effect, but it was rejected by the Ch'ing authorities. Nor had any Chinese diplomats made the long journey to Moscow. There was considerable surprise, therefore, when the Manchu official Tulishen actually made a trip westward. It was in connection with the Torgut Mongols. The Torguts, one of the four dominant tribes of the western Mongols or Oirats (called Kalmuks by the Turks) in the early seventeenth century, had decided to migrate westward from the troubled lands of western Mongolia. After successfully defending themselves from the Kazakhs and Kirgiz while passing north of the Aral Sea, they had arrived in the region of the lower Volga some time close to the year 1616. Here they settled, successfully defended themselves against the likes of the Nogai Tatars, and accepted the suzerainty of Moscow.

Almost a hundred years later, events brought this distant tribe to the attention of the emperor of China. The Torgut leader of the time, one Ayuka, had permitted his nephew, Arabjur, to make a religious pilgrimage to Tibet in 1698. After five years, Arabjur's return home was complicated by the presence of Tsewang Araptan and his Jungar Mongol horde. The Ch'ing dynasty was also deeply disturbed over Jungar intentions and wished to know the real situation of the Torguts in the west. Accordingly, Tulishen was sent on his mission, departing Peking in June 1712. After delays occasioned by late receipt of permission to enter Muscovite lands, the party arrived at Tobolsk in August 1713. Here Tulishen was advised that a visit to the tsar was not possible because of the war with Sweden. After a considerable rest, the group made its way to Saratov on the Volga and, following a long delay there, proceeded to the headquarters of Khan Ayuka, arriving in July of the following year.

If Tulishen had hopes of Torgut assistance against the Jungars, he was disappointed. The meeting was cordial, however, and would be a factor in the ultimate return of the Torguts to their original habitat, which will be discussed in a subsequent chapter. Tulishen's return trip was via the same rather awkward route through Tobolsk, bringing him back to Peking in April 1715. He was the first high-ranking Manchu to visit Muscovy, albeit only on the fringes, and his report was carefully perused by the K'ang-hsi emperor.

Tulishen's trek also was involved with matters concerning the Russian Orthodox church. Father Maxim, priest of the Albazinian flock, died sometime before Tulishen departed Peking, that is, in 1711 or 1712. In response to an Albazinian plea, the *Li-fan Yuan* sent a request to the governor-general in Tobolsk via Tulishen for a replacement priest. The Russian response was a bit overpowering since the church hierarchy viewed this as an opportunity for a real mission in Peking and even entertained dreams of establishing a bishopric. By the time Tulishen commenced his return from Tobolsk, he was accompanied by an archimandrite and nine lesser Orthodox clerics. As a result, the modest church of Saint Nicholas in northeast Peking would have a churchman for every five members of the congregation. The archimandrite, Ilarion Lezhaisky, although affable and well educated, was a very poor manager and an alcoholic. He only survived until April 1718, three years after his arrival. The mission was discouraged by lack of resources as well as the climate and cultural isolation of Peking. Slowly the numbers dwindled so that, by the time of the Izmailov embassy, described later in this chapter, only one priest and three junior clerics remained.

Peter's wars and his great expenditures, such as the building of his capital, Saint Petersburg, demanded an increasing income to the state. He was constantly seeking new sources of revenue and so responded very positively to reports that there was gold to be mined in Turkestan. Accordingly, in 1714, Lieutenant Colonel Ivan Bucholz was ordered to lead a contingent of 1,500 troops and Swedish mining experts, who were prisoners of war, to the upper reaches of the Irtysh to investigate in the region of Lake Zaisan. After reporting his findings, Bucholz ascended the river again the following year with 3,000 construction workers to build a fort near the lake. This evoked a response from the Jungar Mongols of Tsewang Araptan, who considered such activity an incursion into their lands. A force of some 8,000 was sent against the fort. The defenders were forced to withdraw and proceeded more than 700 miles down the Irtysh where they established themselves at a base they named Omsk.

In 1720 another expedition was sent up the river, this time under the command of Ivan Likharev. Like earlier attempts, it found no gold but did establish a permanent presence at Ust Kamenogorsk just downstream from Lake Zaisan. At this point, diplomacy and politics took over from the quest for gold. In the same year that Likharev ascended the Irtysh, the Jungars suffered a major defeat at the hands of the Manchus which drove them permanently out of Tibet and subjected the Tibetans to the Ch'ing dynasty for the next two centuries. The Jungars now were open to assistance from the Russians. In 1721 Peter the Great saw fit to send Captain Ivan Unkovsky to discuss an alliance with the Jungar khan, Tsewang Araptan. Although his round-trip required two years, Unkovsky was singularly unsuccessful in achieving a solid understanding.

Even had Unkovsky been successful, the fact would have been submerged by events taking place on a much higher diplomatic plane. The K'ang-hsi emperor, increasingly concerned by the threat to his empire by Mongol unrest, began to exert pressure on Saint Petersburg (Peter's new capital) to delineate a border north of the steppe. Convinced that China's chief leverage against the Russians was trade, the *Li-fan Yuan*, as early as 1717, sent signals to the Russians that they wished to restrict the flow of trade and suggested that such business should be conducted far from Peking. In line with this new attitude, a caravan headed by one Ifin was stopped at the Great Wall. By mid-1718 another caravan, under the leadership of Fedor Istopnikov, was detained. Part of the rationale given was that furs were available from Manchuria and that maritime traders from the West were bringing in adequate goods through their factors in Canton.

By late 1718, therefore, Peter the Great had decided that a positive approach to Peking would be the key to a brisker, more profitable commerce with the Chinese Empire. Accordingly, an embassy was ordered forth in 1719 under the direction of a captain of the Preobrazhensky Guards Regiment named Lev Izmailov. Officers of this regiment were particularly close to the tsar since he himself had formed it of his playmates while he was yet a child. Izmailov was accompanied by, among others, Lorents Lange, a competent engineer. Izmailov's mission is vaguely reminiscent of that of Milescu more than forty years before in that it was doomed to failure. Although Peter directed that his ambassador comply with Chinese ceremonial requirements and phrased his letter in the correct (Chinese) style, the assumption was that commercial relations between the two empires could be formalized along Western lines. Lange was to be left in Peking as a consul, to establish vice-consuls in various locations, and to ensure that Russian merchants would have free run of China.

Izmailov's embassy departed Saint Petersburg in July 1719. The leader was met at the Great Wall by Tulishen, now considered "an old Russian hand," and escorted into Peking in November 1720. Although the embassy was well treated and entertained and granted audiences with the emperor, the Ch'ing court made certain basic positions quite clear. Whereas Lange was very reluctantly accepted as a consular officer in Peking, he was to be housed at the expense of the court, a sign of tributary status. Istopnikov's caravan, still held up in Mongolia, was permitted to enter China but restricted as to size (200 persons) and length of stay (eighty days) in Peking. The most important talks, from the Manchu point of view, dealt with some 700 Mongols who had committed crimes and fled to Russian territory. This situation clearly indicated that peace in the steppe could be achieved only by delineating the border between Siberia and Mongolia. Indeed, there could be no discussion of commerce until the fugitive and border problems were settled. Izmailov departed Peking in March 1721 and arrived back in Moscow ten months later.

As provided for in the talks, Lorents Lange remained in Peking and assumed his consular duties. The next seventeen months would be extremely frustrating for him. He took up residency in the *O-lo-ssu Kuan*, which by now was somewhat dilapidated, and he found it extremely difficult to effect repairs through his contact, the *Li-fan Yuan*. His immediate problem was to look out for Istopnikov's caravan, which was in straits as the result of its long forced sojourn at Kalgan. The caravan did arrive in Peking, but many Chinese measures were taken to frustrate its success. Not only were thousands of pelts taken from imperial storehouses to drive down the prices, but trade itself was greatly inhibited by restrictions on the access of Chinese merchants to the *O-lo-ssu Kuan* and by the fees demanded by guards assigned to the compound. Lange experienced even more serious problems, and his credibility suffered when word was received in Peking of the Russian mission to the Jungars. It was this Manchu concern over Russian intentions in the steppe that finally resulted in Lange's expulsion on July 23, 1722.

The gravity attached to conditions in Jungaria by the Ch'ing government was finally appreciated by Tsar Peter after he studied the reports from Lange. An investigation was launched into the matter of fugitives, and Lange, who had withdrawn to Selenginsk, was instrumental in the extradition of almost a hundred Mongols considered, by the Chinese government, to be covered by the Treaty of Nerchinsk. It was these actions that doomed Unkovsky's mission to the Jungar Mongols.

A new factor in the scheme of things arose with the death of the K'ang-hsi emperor in December 1722 and the ascension to the throne of his fourth son, known as the Yung-cheng emperor. This new ruler would concentrate his energies on internal reform of the imperial bureaucracy, but he was aware of the importance of affairs in the steppe and, being much more xenophobic by nature, generally pursued his father's strategy of seeking a firm boundary line in the north. News of the new reign, when received in Saint Petersburg, was cause to believe that the time might be propitious for negotiations to restore the trade that had come to a full stop with the expulsion of Lorents Lange.

Peter the Great would survive the K'ang-hsi emperor by just over two years—that is, only about a year from the time of receipt of news of the emperor's death. Yet it was Peter who made the decision to negotiate with the Chinese.

He was convinced that he could not expend the resources required to pursue war with the Chinese Empire and that a fruitful trade would be more in the national interests of the Russian Empire. After Peter's death in January 1725, his widow ascended the imperial throne as Catherine I, the first woman to be sovereign of Russia. By this time, the nation was deeply involved in the grand politics of Europe, and there was a distinct wish on the part of the government to avoid adventures in Asia. Therefore one of the most important embassies in Sino-Russian history was set in motion, which was led by Sava Lukich Vladislavich.

Like so many servants of the Russian crown in the early eighteenth century, Vladislavich was not Russian by birth. Rather, he was from an aristocratic family in Illyria—or Bosnia. He was already sixty years of age by the time of his assignment. As an expatriate he had become a successful merchant following his arrival in Russia around the turn of the century. He had served as an advisor to the tsar and had carried out numerous delicate missions for Peter. Great care was taken in organizing the embassy, with stress on expertise. Lange, still in Selenginsk, was to be a chief advisor to Vladislavich, and Lieutenant Colonel Bucholz was in charge of the troop contingent accompanying the ambassador. There were also experienced topographers, geodesists, and priests. In all, the group comprised 120 staff members and 1,500 military personnel. Vladislavich not only was given painstakingly explicit instructions, like all such missions to Peking, but he steeped himself in the journals and reports of those who had gone before.

The embassy departed Saint Petersburg on October 23, 1725, and arrived in Peking just over a year later on November 1, 1726. Along the way, Vladislavich had picked up Lange and had familiarized himself as much as possible with the geography of Inner Asia. He had been displeased by the quality of maps prepared for him and had sent cartographers out to prepare more accurate and meaningful work. When he arrived at the Chinese capital, welcoming ceremonies proceeded without incident. Vladislavich was able to present his documents directly to the emperor and performed the kowtow. Three senior Manchu officials were assigned to negotiations, including the new president of the *Li-fan Yuan* and Tulishen, who now was vice president of the Board of War. The Manchu negotiators, however, were not given the careful guidance that the K'ang-hsi emperor would have provided.

For almost six months, the sessions continued in Peking. When Vladislavich appeared unreasonable to the Manchus, they resorted to harassment in the form of denying delivery of food and providing only brackish water, even to the point where members of the embassy took ill. Vladislavich, who patiently withstood the adverse conditions and environment, finally hammered out a general agreement on April 1, 1727. During this period, the services of the Jesuit priests, notably Father Dominique Parrenin, were invaluable, both as interpreters and as a source of intelligence on true Manchu attitudes. Understandably, therefore, the draft treaty was, like the Treaty of Nerchinsk, drawn up in three languages with Latin being the authoritative version.

It eventually became clear, however, that border delineation could not be concluded on the basis of available maps and that teams would have to survey proposed border areas. Vladislavich therefore departed Peking for Selenginsk on May 4. With him were the ubiquitous Tulishen, a senior Manchu official named Lungkodo, and Tsereng, a Mongol who was khan of one of the four major groups of the Khalkas. The Jesuits were not permitted to accompany the party north since the paranoid Yung-cheng emperor held them in deep distrust. It had been their bad judgment to support one of his brothers to succeed his father. As a consequence, communication now had to be via the Mongol language.

The maps he had directed be prepared were ready and waiting for Vladislavich. He therefore had a great advantage over the Manchus, and the Russians took the initiative in border delineation. Work commenced in June, but no progress was made initially because of the total lack of cooperation by Lungkodo. As a result, Vladislavich requested his recall. This was effected by mid-August when Tulishen was designated the senior Manchu negotiator, and on August 31 a general agreement outlining the border was signed, known as the Treaty of Bura. It was written in the Russian, Manchu, and Mongol languages. Once this step had been completed, teams composed of both nations commenced the actual siting of border markers. The anchor marker was located at Kiakhta, the site of a Russian guardhouse about a hundred miles south of Selenginsk, slightly to the east of the Orkhon River. The work proceeded rapidly so that two letters detailing the locations of the markers were drawn up in October. The first of these, known as the Abagaitu Letter, signed on October 23, detailed the locations of sixty-three markers positioned along the border from Kiakhta eastward to the Argun River. The second, the Selenginsk Letter, signed on November 7, listed the locations of twenty-four markers extending from Kiakhta westward to the Shabindobaga River on the northwest slopes of the Altai Mountains. These letters were written in Russian, Manchu, and Mongol.

The basic treaty that had been negotiated in Peking was not considered complete until it incorporated the Bura Treaty. The document was therefore forwarded to the Chinese capital where it was translated into Latin. When the final result was received by Vladislavich on the frontier, however, it was immediately noted that the Manchus had made substantive changes to the agreed text of the basic document. The Russians remonstrated energetically until finally the treaty in the agreed form was received at Kiakhta on June 25, 1728. Copies were signed and exchanged the same day.

The Treaty of Kiakhta contained eleven articles. The first required each side to exercise control over its own subjects. The second stated that henceforth all fugitives must be hunted down and expeditiously returned to the parent state. The third article gave a very general description of the border from the Argun River to the Altai Mountains. Whereas this met the basic aims of the Ch'ing, the fourth answered those of the Russians. It authorized caravan trade with a limitation of personnel to 200 and frequency to once every three years. All expenses henceforth were to be borne by the caravaneers. This article also provided for "lesser" trade at Nerchinsk and Kiakhta.

The fifth article was a rather radical departure from the past. It provided that the *O-lo-ssu Kuan*, which had housed Russians in the past, now could be permanently occupied by them. Further, a church could be built on the premises, and authorization was granted for the permanent presence of a priest and three assistant clerics. In addition, the presence of four young students and two older ones was authorized for the study of languages. Not only that, they were to be permitted to leave Peking after concluding their studies. The costs of supporting the students and priests were to be borne by the Ch'ing authorities.

The sixth article sought to clarify diplomatic avenues. Fundamentally, diplomatic correspondence would be between the *Li-fan Yuan* and the Russian Senate. This route could be abbreviated in certain instances by communications between the Tushetu khan at Urga and the governor-general in Tobolsk. The Kiakhta road was designated the official route. The seventh article confirmed the boundary from the Argun River to the Sea of Okhotsk, as defined in the Treaty of Nerchinsk, with exhortations that the Russians ensure the border not be violated. The eighth article insisted on quick and fair resolution of border problems. The ninth described how official envoys between the two states should be accommodated, and the tenth prescribed quick and drastic punishment for criminal activity along the boundary. The last article described the format of the treaty and how it was formally signed and sealed.

The Treaty of Kiakhta was a true landmark in the history of the Russian and Chinese empires. With very little change, it would govern relations of the two states for more than 130 years. The border defined in the treaty is, with some alteration (see chapter 20), that which divides Russia and Mongolia today. With such a finite border, the Ch'ien-lung emperor, who succeeded his father in 1735, would successfully destroy Mongol power in the steppe in 1755. The caravan trade, so desperately desired by the Russians, would die out in two decades since the trading center established on the border at Kiakhta would be much more convenient and efficient. Trade authorized to the north at "Nerchinsk" actually would be at the border town of Tsurukhaitu on the Argun River. Because of its relative inaccessibility, it would never rival the importance of the emporium at Kiakhta and the Chinese center facing it named Maimaich'eng (Chinese for "Business Town").

NOTE

1. Perhaps the most notorious case was the one involving Matvei Gagarin, for many years governor-general of Siberia in Tobolsk, who was executed in 1721 for accepting too many bribes from the traders.

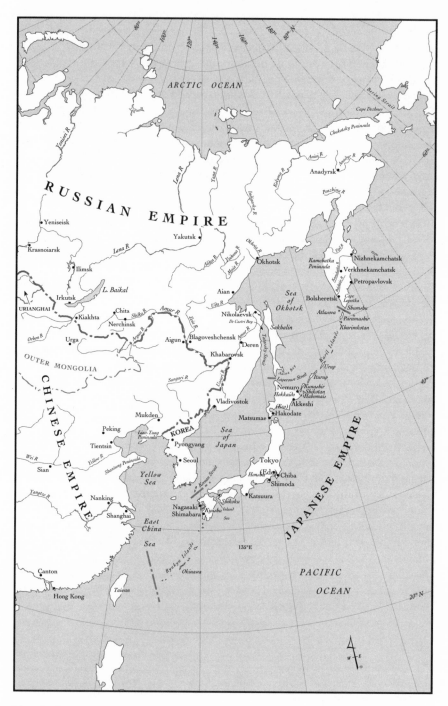

Map 5. East Asia, 1875.

7

Japan, Kamchatka, and the Kurils

The Japan of today comprises four main islands and thousands of smaller ones. The southernmost of the major islands, Kyushu, is separated from Korea on the Asian mainland by the Korean (sometimes known as the Tsushima) Strait. The northernmost island of Hokkaido is separated from the island of Sakhalin to the north by the La Perouse Strait and from the Kuril Islands to the northeast by the Nemuro Strait. Between Kyushu and Hokkaido stretches the largest island—Honshu. The fourth main island, Shikoku, lies just off the south shore of western Honshu and to the northeast of Kyushu. The water separating these three islands is known as the Inland Sea.

The greater part of the islands was inhabited by the aboriginal Ainu as late as the sixth century A.D. But after more than three centuries of warfare, helped by a thirty-year civil war amongst the Ainu, the Japanese managed to complete the conquest of Honshu. Interestingly, the end of the Ainu wars coincided very closely in time with the genesis of Kievan Russia. Yet, by the time the Japanese once again would focus seriously on the north, their closest neighbors would be Russians.

At the end of the sixteenth century, Japan came under the strong central authority of the shogunate established by Tokugawa Ieyasu. That worthy would exercise power from his stronghold at Edo while the emperor continued in residence in Kyoto. Ieyasu became concerned about the activities of Westerners in his realm, particularly the Christians. But it was his grandson, the third shogun, Iemitsu (1623–1651), who would become a thorough xenophobe and implement the exclusion—or seclusion—policy that is usually associated with the Tokugawa Shogunate. He commenced ejecting Europeans in 1623, finally expelling the Portuguese fifteen years later. In 1636 all Japanese were forbidden to depart the country, and any who did leave were not to return on pain of death. Two years later, the shogun decreed that no oceangoing ships were to be built. In 1637 occurred an uprising of Christian Japanese in Shimabara, in western Kyushu. It was put down with great ferocity the following year, thus effectively terminating Christianity as a force in Japan. Thirty thousand Christians died in the violence.

As a result, by the year 1640, just four years before the Manchus assumed imperial power in China, Japan had succeeded in isolating itself from the Western world. The lone exception was permission for the Dutch (who had provided naval support for the attack on Shimabara) to send a ship once a year to trade. This vessel was restricted to the port of Nagasaki where, on Deshima Island, the few Dutchmen allowed in the country were quarantined. The Japanese now were permitted to build only ungainly vessels used for moving rice and other supplies through coastal waters. Not only did the nation lose its ability to build high seas ships but also to navigate them. As a result, sailors on the coastal craft would be extremely vulnerable to high winds and storms. Many were blown far from Honshu and unable to navigate their way back. Either they perished at sea or were deposited on some inhospitable shore.

On Hokkaido by this time, a Japanese population had begun to grow very gradually in the southern part, on the Oshima Peninsula. These inhabitants were under the control of the Kakizaki family which was a subtenant of the Ando. In 1603 Tokugawa Ieyasu changed the family name to Matsumae and granted the head of the family the title of *daimyo* of Oshima. The Matsumae actually discouraged immigration into their island. They enjoyed a comfortable monopoly of Hokkaido's natural resources, and since all rice had to be imported, additional mouths were not welcome. They felt fortunate to be so far from the mind of the shogun. Although they would remain concentrated on the Oshima Peninsula, the Matsumae did establish a *basho*—or trading post—on the northeast corner of the island in the year 1620.

In the meantime, the Russians had reached the Sea of Okhotsk in 1639, just as the exclusion policy of Japan was being implemented. Just a few years later, the Russians had explored down the Amur and had viewed Sakhalin across from the mouth of that river. By mid-century, they had reached the end of the continent by an Arctic route and had established an *ostrog* at Anadyrsk far out on the Chukotsky Peninsula. No Russians, however, had yet come near Japan. When they did arrive, it would be by way of the Kamchatka Peninsula. After Poiarkov's exploration of the lower Amur River and southwestern shore of the Sea of Okhotsk (chapter 3), there was no probing by the Muscovites farther north and east along the shores of the Sea of Okhotsk toward Kamchatka; rather, remarkably, they would approach from the northeast. Mikhail Stadukhin had succeeded in making his way southwest from Anadyrsk in 1651 to the mouth of the Penzhina River, but since that stream empties into a long gulf, he was unaware that he stood at the neck of a huge peninsula.

Virtually no further exploration would take place in this region over the next half-century for two primary reasons: (1) the focus of attention on events in the

Amur River valley and (2) the warlike qualities of the native population to the south of Anadyrsk. The Koriaks were quite unlike most of the peoples encountered by the Russians as they pushed their way across northern Asia. These primitive folk fiercely resisted paying the tribute or *yasak* demanded by the newcomers. They were clever tacticians, and the warriors frequently would destroy themselves and their families rather than be captured by the Muscovites. As a result, when penetration of the region was pushed, it invariably resulted in considerable bloodshed. In 1669 a small fort was built on the upper Penzhina River with the intent of controlling the Koriaks, but any effective measures would have to wait until the end of the century.

There was a total ignorance of the geography of the farthest east on the part of both the Japanese and the countries of the West. Very few nautical explorers had bothered to probe the waters to the north of Japan, and those who did were unable to acquire a meaningful conception of the area because of the terrible weather conditions that rendered navigation and charting extremely hazardous and inaccurate. The Dutch explorer Maerten Vries entered the area in 1643 in search of "Islands of Gold and Silver"—or "Gama Land"—which had been reported in the previous century by Spanish sailors blown off course by storms. Because of the bad weather conditions encountered, particularly thick fog, Vries's reports led to more confusion since, for example, he missed the straits between Hokkaido and Sakhalin and between Hokkaido and Kunashir. Not only that, he believed the island of Urup was part of North America. To add to the distortion of the Russians' image of the Far East, Milescu, head of the Muscovite embassy to Peking in 1675–1678 (discussed in chapter 5), received very imprecise information on the location of Japan from the Jesuit Father Verbiest.

After conclusion of the Treaty of Nerchinsk in 1689, Russian energies, diverted from the Amur, now began to focus on the area south of Anadyrsk. In 1695 the *voevoda* of Yakutsk sent Vladimir Atlasov to take charge of affairs. Atlasov was extraordinarily observant and bright, but he possessed those qualities shared by so many in the brutal environment of northeast Asia: greed and cruelty. In 1696 he sent a deputy, Luka Morozko, to scout to the south. Morozko traveled almost halfway down the peninsula to the Tigil River and returned. Atlasov was so intrigued with his report of furs and fish that he himself led an expedition of sixty Russians and a like number of natives the following year to the southwest coast of Kamchatka. Although he did not proceed to the end of the peninsula, he was able to see a peak across the water, probably the Kuril island of Alaid (now called Atlasova). For the first time he encountered Ainu from the Kuril Islands and a prisoner of the Kamchadal people—a Japanese castaway named Denbei. Denbei was, of course, one of those luckless sailors of Tokugawa rice boats who had been blown off course by a storm and finally washed up on the shores of Kamchatka. Noting that Denbei was so different from his captors by virtue of courtesy, cleanliness, and education, Atlasov tentatively identified the castaway as a Greek.

Atlasov built an *ostrog* on the upper reaches of the Kamchatka River (which flows from the Sredinny Range northeastward into the Pacific Ocean) named Verkhnekamchatsk. In the summer of 1699 he returned to Anadyrsk, taking Denbei with him. He followed the standard tortuous course, returning to Yakutsk in July 1700. In almost record time, he arrived back in Moscow in February 1701. His vivid description of the riches and the peoples of Kamchatka made an appropriate impression on the government and the tsar. An even greater impression was made by Denbei since he was correctly identified as Japanese and spoke of the wealth of his homeland. Peter the Great instructed that the former castaway learn Russian and then teach the Japanese language to Russian students. Atlasov was designated *golova*, or boss, of Kamchatka, and an *ukaz* was issued directing the subjugation of Kamchatka and the collection of information about Japan.

In the meantime, back in Kamchatka, affairs were chaotic. The Koriaks in the northern part of the peninsula were constantly in rebellion against the Russians. To make matters worse, the Cossacks in the *ostrogi* regularly rose against and killed their leaders. Despite the general disorder, one of the few effective figures, Vasili Kolesov, directed a subordinate to explore the southern limits of Kamchatka. Therefore, in 1706, Mikhail Nasedkin and his fifty men became the first Russians to stand on Cape Lopatka and look southwestward toward Shumshu, the most northeasterly of the Kuril Islands. At this moment, they were less than 700 miles from the *basho* of the Matsumae on the northeast corner of Hokkaido.

The next six years would be especially violent in Kamchatka. Three leaders, including Atlasov, who had returned in 1707, were murdered by the Cossacks who then elected two of their members in traditional Cossack fashion to lead them. These were Danilo Antsyferov and Ivan Kozyrevsky. The former would soon die by burning at the hands of the Kamchadals in return for atrocities committed on their people. Kozyrevsky would survive to make a name for himself in other ways. Fearing tsarist retribution for the crimes committed on the peninsula, Kozyrevsky sought atonement in carrying out the desires of Peter the Great by exploring to the south. He made it across the seven miles of open sea to the island of Shumshu and brought back evidence of Japanese culture which, he was told, came from the south. Vasili Kolesov, who had departed the peninsula in 1706, was sent back to Kamchatka six years later to restore order. This he did by rather cruel but effective means. Kozyrevsky managed to survive the purge of mutineers and was sent out in 1713 on another expedition. In this instance, his party of somewhat more than fifty managed to sail their *baidarki* (boats made of seal skin stretched over a framework) to Shumshu and Paramushir, the next, larger island. Here many more Japanese artifacts were acquired, and the interrogation of Ainu from farther south in the islands revealed the rough extent of the islands and the clear indication that Japan lay at the end of the chain.

All this time the route from Yakutsk to Kamchatka had been the 2,800-mile-long trek using the path blazed by Stadukhin sixty-five years before. This involved the rivers Lena, Indigarka, and Kolyma, and the portages between them to reach Anadyrsk and thence overland into Kamchatka. Not only was it long and time consuming, but also dangerous. The Chukchi and Koriaks were very warlike, with the result that the loss of Russian life at the hands of these tribes was proportionally much higher than in other parts of Russian Asia.

Peter the Great relentlessly drove the landlubberly Russians to sea. They felt comfortable on land and rivers but not on the ocean. Peter's passion for the sea, which had built victorious fleets on the Sea of Azov and the Baltic, was to be felt in the Far East as well. In 1711 Petr Gutorov, commandant at Okhotsk, on the sea of the same name, was directed to attempt to sail eastward to reach Kamchatka. What would be a daunting nautical challenge at any time was far too great for the local talent at Okhotsk. Still, the clear logic of the directive was patent. The route of discovery pursued by Ivan Moskvitin almost three quarters of a century before—from Yakutsk up the Aldan tributary of the Lena, into the Maia affluent, across the Dzhugdzhur Mountains and thence down the Ulia to Okhotsk—would make available a much shorter path to Kamchatka provided navigation of the Sea of Okhotsk was possible. Therefore the job was done right in 1716.

In accordance with an *ukaz* of July 3, 1714, Kozma Sokolov, together with shipwrights and naval stores, which included rigging, anchors, tools, tar, and so on, was ordered to proceed via the Aldan-Maia-Ulia route to Okhotsk. Once they had arrived in the port, Sokolov and his crew constructed a seaworthy open boat which, in the summer of 1716, made a successful voyage across the northern reaches of the Sea of Okhotsk to Kamchatka and return. The following year, a sea voyage was made from Okhotsk to Bolsheretsk, near the mouth of the Bolshaia River which empties into the Sea of Okhotsk in the southwest corner of the peninsula of Kamchatka. From this time onward, the Okhotsk-Bolsheretsk route would become the normal path of communication. In little more than a decade, the peninsula would be removed from the jurisdiction of Yakutsk and subordinated to Okhotsk.

After receipt in Saint Petersburg of the information elicited by Kozyrevsky on the Kurils and their possible connection to Japan, Peter the Great sent two geodesists to Kamchatka. The two young men, Ivan Evreinov and Fedor Luzhin, received instructions in 1719 to carry out their assignment "not only north and south but also east and west."[1] They were expressly directed to determine whether Asia and America were joined. As a result, in June 1721, the two and their party set out from Bolsheretsk, headed south on an expedition conducted for the first time in a boat other than the native *baidarki*. Indeed, they were in an open boat sixty feet in length. They proceeded farther down the island chain than any Russians before them, but disaster struck when they were in the neighborhood of the sixth island, Kharimkotan. The force of the wind ripped their single sail, forcing them to lie at anchor. But the strength of the storm caused the anchor lines to part, and they were blown at the mercy of the elements, fortuitously being deposited back near Paramushir Island. Thence they were able to limp back to Bolsheretsk.

The expedition of the two geodesists was but the first effort made to glean scientific knowledge of the region. It would be followed by the two Kamchatka expeditions under the leadership of Vitus Bering. The impetus for the first Kamchatka expedition (1725–1730), like the Vladislavich mission to China, was provided by Peter the Great himself, although the event took place years after his death. Peter had the basic instruction drawn up and chose Bering for the task before he expired in January 1725. But it was his widow and successor, Catherine I, who issued the decree directing Bering to complete, in essence, the work of Evreinov and Luzhin, namely to determine whether Asia and America were divided.

Bering, although a Dane, had served in the Imperial Russian Navy since 1704. He chose as his top assistants two lieutenants: Martyn Spanberg, another Dane, and Aleksei Chirikov, a Russian. Loaded with the necessary supplies, Bering's group worked its way across Asia to Okhotsk and thence via the Sea of Okhotsk to Bolsheretsk. They then hauled their supplies overland to the *ostrog* of Verkhnekamchatsk where they wintered over. By the early spring of 1728, they had descended the river and commenced the construction of a decked vessel sixty feet long. Christened the *Sviatoi Gavriil*, the new ship departed on July 24, heading up the coast to the northeast. On the twenty-second of August, Bering and his party discovered Saint Lawrence Island and two days later arrived off the easternmost point of Asia (now called Cape Dezhnev). After the *Sviatoi Gavriil* moved about a hundred nautical miles farther to the north, Bering was satisfied that he had indeed rounded the eastern extremity of the continent and began his voyage home. On the twenty-eighth, Diomede Islands were discovered, but the visibility was so restricted that the party was unaware that the continent of America was less than forty miles distant.

Bering wintered over in Nizhnekamchatsk (at the mouth of the Kamchatka River) and in the spring sailed to Okhotsk. He then traveled back to Saint Petersburg as quickly as possible, arriving in March 1730. Many were disappointed by his seeming lack of achievement, but he contended that he had carried out his instructions. He also strongly recommended a newer and much more ambitious set of expeditions. The Empress Anna (ruled 1730–1740) decided in the Dane's favor, and the second Kamchatka expedition was approved and instructions issued in January 1733. It is obvious from the language of the directive that the moral authority of Peter the Great was still a major factor in the approval of the mission.

The second Kamchatka expedition essentially comprised three phases. The first was exploration of the Russian Arctic coast by teams descending the Ob and Lena rivers. The second was to locate the northwest coast of North America, a task to be undertaken personally by Commodore Bering and Lieutenant Commander Chirikov. Both of these will be discussed in subsequent chapters. The third phase of the expedition was to discover a route to Japan. The latter two phases were to be launched from Kamchatka. Thus the same long, difficult path was taken to haul the supplies, including anchors and cannon, needed for the voyages of discovery to America and Japan. Newly promoted Captain Spanberg was delegated the responsibility to search for Japan.

Spanberg arrived in Okhotsk in 1735 and spent the next three years preparing for his voyage. Three ships were outfitted for him and his two lieutenants: William Walton and Aleksei Shelting. He commanded the *Arkhangel' Mikhail*, Walton the *Nadezhda*, and Shelting the refurbished *Sviatoi Gavriil*, which had borne Bering to Cape Dezhnev. The three vessels set off from Okhotsk for the Kuril chain at the end of June 1738. Characteristically, in about a month, the ships became separated as the result of thick fog. Spanberg progressed as far as the island of Urup, fifth from the southern end, when he decided to return north. The three rendezvoused in Bolsheretsk in early September.

Early the following June, Spanberg's small fleet set out again. The course was set not along the Kurils but rather to the south, on the possibility of finding the "Islands of Gold and Silver." Failing to find land by the forty-fourth parallel of latitude, they then steered a southwesterly course until, on June 27, they made a landfall of northeastern Honshu at about 39°. The Russians were amazed at the lushness of the vegetation and the size of the towns dotting the shore. Spanberg anchored his vessels off one of these populated sites but decided not to land. However, scores of boats filled with curious Japanese came out to view the foreign ships, and certain bolder ones even came on board. The exchanges were very amicable, and Spanberg satisfied himself that this was indeed Japan. He then ordered anchors aweigh and headed back toward Kamchatka.

In the meantime, the Englishman William Walton, who now was skipper of the *Sviatoi Gavriil*, had detached his ship from the main group on June 25. He made a landfall at 37°42' and proceeded southward to a point just east of Chiba Prefecture, which forms a peninsula between the eastern waters of Tokyo Bay and the Pacific. Here, on June 30, he anchored and sent a party ashore for fresh water. They were the first Russians officially to set foot on Japanese soil. The reception was correct but friendly, and much swapping of trinkets took place between sailors and Japanese. In time so many Japanese boats crowded his vessel that Walton decided it safest to hoist anchor and depart. The *Sviatoi Gavriil* continued to move just south of west until anchoring off Katsuura on the east coast of Wakayama Prefecture at latitude 33°28' on July 4. The following day he weighed anchor and commenced the voyage home. The return trip provided an excellent opportunity to chart many of the Kuril Islands.

As luck would have it, Walton, who had ventured the farthest, was the first to return to Bolsheretsk—on August 5, 1739. He then made Okhotsk on September 2 where Spanberg joined him five days later. Remarkably, the journals of Spanberg and Walton were disbelieved by the Russian admiralty since they flew in the face of conventional knowledge, vague though it was. By this time, fifteen years after the death of Peter the Great, ethnic jealousies played a role between Russians and the Danish Spanberg and the English Walton. Further, technical errors were pointed out in the journals to buttress the government position. Not until later in the decade did the admiralty finally accept the authenticity of the explorations.

In Japan itself there was a flurry of activity resulting from the arrival of the Russians. A stream of reports was fed into the *Bakufu*, the shogun's government, describing the visits and asserting that the foreigners had been quickly sent on their way in accordance with Japan's exclusion policy. However, the Japanese would not know the identity of their visitors until some Russian coins and a playing card were sent to Nagasaki for positive identification by the Dutch merchants.

Spanberg was actually sent out on another expedition in 1742, but a combination of bad weather, indecision, and the deteriorating condition of the ships frustrated a return to Japan. Actually, further confusion resulted from this foreshortened voyage since one of his skippers, when charting Sakhalin, was unaware of the La Perouse Strait and thus showed Hokkaido extending much too far north. In the meantime, Bering had died while returning from his expedition to North America, and the momentum of Peter the Great's enterprises in the Far East finally ran out of steam. Back in Europe, Peter's immediate successors (Catherine I, Peter II, and Anna) had in a real sense been caretaker reigns. With the accession of Peter's daughter Elizabeth to the throne in 1741, a stronger hand was at the helm—one that would more deeply involve Russia in the affairs of Europe, particularly in the Seven Years War. Catherine II (the Great), who ruled from 1762 to 1796, would be most concerned, in foreign relations, with European politics.

The one serious attempt to settle and exploit the Kuril Islands was undertaken by the merchant Pavel Lebedev-Lastochkin who was granted a temporary monopoly of the Kuril fur trade in 1774. The following year he sent out a group in the *Sviatoi Nikolai* which landed at Urup. Their ship was wrecked, however, and they were forced to return to Kamchatka in *baidarki*. Two years following this disaster, Lebedev-Lastochkin caused another group, under Dmitri Shabalin, to move into the lower Kurils. They probed all the way to the *basho* at Akkeshi in northeastern Hokkaido in the summer of 1779. They were told trade was impossible, that they must leave, and that, in the future, any commerce was to be conducted via Ainu intermediaries. Shabalin returned to his base on Urup where he and his followers wintered over. On January 19, 1780, his ship, the *Natalia*, was thrown a quarter of a mile inland by a tsunami resulting from a series of earthquakes. Undaunted, Shabalin and his men managed a safe passage back to Kamchatka in *baidarki*. As the result of this half-decade of activity, Lebedev-Lastochkin chalked up some heavy losses, and commercial interest in developing the Kurils waned sharply. Also, Empress Catherine II decreed that Ainu henceforth were not required to pay *yasak*, a further discouraging action for any who would realize profits from the Kuril chain.

Meanwhile, in Japan, certain leaders were slowly gaining increased knowledge (called "Dutch learning" since it came through the annual Dutch ship admitted to Nagasaki) about the outside world. It was the eighth Tokugawa shogun, Yoshimune, whose interests in mathematics and science slightly liberalized the ban on Western publications. As a result, by 1763, there was already a Japanese translation of a Dutch atlas showing, however vague, Russia and Japan. Still, there was very little comprehension of the realities of the Russian presence in the Pacific.

This lack of knowledge would be dissipated by events that were put in motion by a bizarre incident that occurred in July 1771. It involved the person of Mauritius Augustus, count of Benyovszky, of Hungarian origin. It seems that, while fighting for Poland against the Russians, he was captured and exiled to Kamchatka in 1769. Despite a slightly favored situation by virtue of being tutor to the commandant's son in Bolsheretsk, Benyovszky led a mutiny in May 1771 which was facilitated by the inebriated state of the commandant and the guards. The mutineers escaped in a sixty-foot vessel named the *Sviatoi Petr i Sviatoi Pavel*. After one stop in the Kurils, they appeared on July 8 off the southeastern corner of the island of Shikoku where they took on foodstuffs from cooperative Japanese. They stopped again at Oshima Island off the southern coast of Kyushu. Here more water and food were provided, and Benyovszky prevailed on the local inhabitants to forward a letter to the Dutch in Nagasaki. The Dutch translated the missive and turned it over to the Japanese authorities. In this note, written on July 20, 1771, Benyovszky stated that it was his duty to sound an alert to a threat from the north. He warned that the Russians had reconnoitered the Japanese islands in preparation for an attack on Hokkaido to be carried out the following year. Further, he claimed that war materials had been stockpiled on one of the southern Kuril Islands for the attack. Benyovszky then sailed off for Macau and the rest of his short but colorful life.

The warning from Benyovszky was indeed incredible when one considers that the total Russian population along the entire eastern Asian seaboard at the time was about 2,000. On Hokkaido[2] itself, concentrated in the south, lived 30,000 Japanese, and the population of Japan was close to 30 million. Still and all, Benyovszky's letter would be a factor in awakening the Japanese to the Russian presence in the north and stimulating their first move in that direction since the defeat of the Ainu on Honshu nine centuries earlier.

NOTES

1. Basil Dmytryshin et al., ed. and trans., *Russian Penetration of the North Pacific Ocean: A Documentary Record 1700–1797* (Portland: Oregon Historical Society Press, 1988), 65.

2. Throughout the book, I have consistently referred to the northernmost of the four main islands of Japan as "Hokkaido." In actual fact, this name, with the proud meaning of "Region of the Northern Sea," was not assigned until 1869—after the Meiji Restoration. During the centuries before then it was generally called "Ezo," which carried the connotation of a somewhat alien frontier area whose people and territory vaguely extended beyond the island toward Sakhalin and the Kurils.

8

"Normalization" of Russo-Japanese Relations

As mentioned in the last chapter, interest in the Russian Far East waned during the reigns of Elizabeth and Catherine II, that is, for more than a half-century from 1741 to 1796. This was particularly true of the latter ruler. Catherine was indeed desirous of asserting Russian control over lands claimed by the empire, but she exhibited none of the passion of Peter the Great for exploration and discovery.

There was one notable exception during Catherine's reign, however, and it concerned the Laxman family. Eric Laxman, a Finn by birth, was a scientist who exercised considerable influence at the court of Saint Petersburg. In 1789, while on a visit to Irkutsk, a growing center located near the point where the Angara River disgorges from Lake Baikal, he met a Japanese castaway by the name of Kodayu. Kodayu and five of his fellow crewmen had been stranded in the Aleutians in 1783 and finally brought to Irkutsk six years later.

Eric Laxman was intrigued by Kodayu, who was a very bright young man, and came up with the idea of sending an expedition to Japan. The purpose was primarily to establish Russo-Japanese trade, hopefully based on Japanese good-will in return for repatriating their stranded seamen. Accordingly, Laxman took Kodayu and two of his fellows to Saint Petersburg in 1791 and submitted his plan to the court. On September 24 of that year, Empress Catherine II approved the plan and ordered the governor-general in Irkutsk to implement it. A year later, almost to the day, the ship *Ekaterina* was ready in Okhotsk. The nominal skipper was a barely qualified Grigori Lovtsov, but the de facto leader was Eric Laxman's son Adam whose assigned function was scientific research. The crew included a veteran, Dmitri Shabalin, whose expedition to the southern Kurils was discussed in the preceding chapter.

It was already mid-October by the time the *Ekaterina* arrived in northeastern

Hokkaido. Here, at Nemuro, the party was received by some local Japanese merchants who did not object to Laxman's desire to winter over; therefore, winter quarters were built, and the Russians remained. Adam Laxman then managed to send a letter to the authorities in Matsumae, the seat of the *daimyo* in southern Hokkaido, setting forth his instructions to deliver his Japanese castaways to the government at Edo. Matsumae immediately forwarded the package to Edo, and by the following spring officials from both Matsumae and Edo had arrived at Nemuro. They advised Laxman that travel to Edo was forbidden but that he could proceed to Matsumae.

The *Ekaterina* was sailed south and anchored in the harbor at Hakodate. From this point, a quaint procession of Japanese officials and Russian seamen wound its way past the fascinated local populace. After a trip of four days, the retinue arrived in Matsumae on July 27, 1793. The Japanese, although very hospitable, returned Laxman's letter to him, firmly denying authority to proceed to Edo with the castaways. Conversations continued through August 4, by which time the Russians were made eminently aware that trade was not authorized for any members of Laxman's party and that it could never be permitted other than in the city of Nagasaki. Laxman finally realized that his quest for entry into Edo was out of the question, and he turned Kodayu and his fellow castaways over to the officials on the spot. The principal concession on the part of the Japanese was the presentation of an official permit for entry into the port of Nagasaki.

Young Laxman took all this with good grace, believing it was all he could achieve under the circumstances. On Aug¨st 6 his party commenced the trip back to Hakodate. Eleven days later the *Ekaterina* weighed anchor for the trip back north. Laxman returned to Okhotsk on September 19, and he and Lovtsov were in Irkutsk the following January where they reported to Governor-General Ivan Pil. Pil, in turn, made a strong recommendation that there be a follow-up expedition to Japan, to be led by a much more senior personage. However, before further actions could be taken, two key actors left the stage. Eric Laxman died in January 1796, and his empress left this world the following November. As we shall see, the Nagasaki entry permit given Adam Laxman would not be used for more than a decade.

Finally, by the end of the eighteenth century, the Tokugawa Shogunate began to show real concern about its neighbors to the north and to take measures to deal with them. The Japanese had known virtually nothing about Russia or Russians until the arrival of Spanberg and Walton in 1739. They had very little idea of where Russia might be located until the translation of a Dutch map in 1763. Then, in 1771, the extraordinary Benyovszky wrote his letter warning that the Russians were planning an attack on Japan. Now, at long last, there was considerable concern. The Benyovszky letter was tightly held by the shogunal authorities, but rumors managed to leak out. A book written on the subject by a Sendai doctor, Kudo Heisuke, so concerned the *Bakufu* (government of the shogunate) that the *daimyo* of Matsumae was directed to report on the situation in the north. The resulting response was considered inadequate; therefore, an expedition to the area was planned for 1785. The most famous member of this undertaking was Mogami Tokunai. He explored Hokkaido, southern Sakhalin, and the Kurils as far as the fifth island—Urup. He had intended to proceed to Kamchatka but was frustrated by weather and the inadequacies of his vessel.

It was Mogami's practical knowledge of the geography to the north that gave strength to the arguments of various influential writers of the time, such as Honda Toshiaki and Hayashi Shihei, in favor of direct *Bakufu* rule in the north. Their position was then strengthened by the visit of Adam Laxman in the *Ekaterina* in 1792–1793. It was of course disconcerting to see a Russian ship in a Japanese port. But even greater concern grew out of the interrogation of Kodayu, the castaway who had been returned by Laxman. Kodayu had been living with Russians for nine years and had seen the Russian Empire from the Aleutians to Saint Petersburg. He had even had an audience with Catherine the Great. He was intelligent and a keen observer, and his answers did not calm the worries of the *Bakufu*. There was concern as well that the Matsumae, operating on their own as they had for centuries, had not very effectively carried out the exclusion policy during Laxman's visit.

The shogunate was finally moved to action in 1799. It launched an ambitious plan of development in the north which included the opening of lands in Hokkaido to agriculture and the building of roads. The plan provided for the detailed mapping of Hokkaido, Sakhalin, and the Kuril Islands and placed all the *basho* under officials of the central government. It also directed that the Kurils south of Urup be opened and that the Ainu on these islands and Hokkaido be assimilated into the Japanese way of life. Finally, it provided the resources necessary for implementation: military support and financial backing. In short, for the first time in over nine centuries, Japanese expansion to the north was to be resumed.

Symptomatic of this new approach were the voyages of discovery made by Mamiya Rinzo in the following decade. This intrepid figure explored much of Sakhalin in 1808, determining the fact that it was an island. The following year he again visited western Sakhalin and proceeded up the Amur River to the Manchu outpost at Deren. Thus Japan, at the time, was the only nation aware of Sakhalin's insularity and the location of the mouth of the Amur River.

The next chapter in Russo-Japanese relations would be related to the constant and pressing problem the Russians experienced in trying to feed their fur traders in East Asia and the North Pacific. By the end of the eighteenth century, the traders were spread across the northern Asian mainland, into the Kurils and across the Aleutian Islands to the mainland of Alaska. Wherever the Russians went, there was a surplus of game, but they could not subsist on a diet solely of meat and fish. They required vegetables and, especially, grain. As the fur traders initially pushed farther east across Asia, the principal source of grain was the Muscovite lands in Europe. By 1645 efforts at growing grain in the Yeniseisk area (the middle Yenisei River region) proved successful, thus bringing the source nearer to the traders. Then, forty years later, grain was successfully harvested in the Ilimsk area, that is, the portage between the Yenisei and

Lena river systems. This was a great help, but it was still a Herculean task to deliver food from Ilimsk to the north and east, to Okhotsk, Kamchatka, the Aleutians, and Alaska.

Not only were the distances staggering, but the environment was hostile and the means of delivery primitive and inadequate. From Ilimsk, the trip down the Lena to Yakutsk was 1,700 miles. The water route to Okhotsk required man-handling barges up hundreds of miles of the eastern tributaries of the Lena, a basic route at the time being up the Aldan, Maia, and Yudoma to a portage to connect with the Okhota River. Starting with the second Kamchatka expedition, however, a more direct land route came into use, known as the Yakutsk-Okhotsk Track. This path proceeded in a relatively straight line between the two centers. It required the crossing of numerous rivers and involved inhospitable elements such as bogs, steep mountains, and wild carnivores. There was no real track as such, no vehicles could be accommodated, and all goods had to be transported on pack horses. The maximum load for one of the Yakuti ponies was slightly over 200 pounds. Therefore all heavy items still had to be moved via the river route. Each caravan comprised between 100 and 150 horses, led by a Yakuti driver for every ten horses or so. An optimistic estimate of the time for the journey was two months.

Once the food had arrived in Okhotsk, much of it was transferred onto boats of questionable condition which proceeded through frequently vile weather to inadequate harbor facilities on Kamchatka. From this point, further transship-ment was required to support the Russians resident in the Aleutians and Alaska. In the North Pacific itself, improper packaging and stowage often resulted in spoilage, and the frequent loss of the ships themselves added a new dimension of frustration. Not only were the facilities greatly overtaxed to deliver a mini-mum of food support, but the cost was exorbitant. By the time the food arrived in Kamchatka, its cost had increased forty-fold.

Because of this very tenuous food support line, those in positions of respon-sibility were constantly seeking alternate sources to feed the Russian fur trade. Efforts to start agriculture around the Sea of Okhotsk were unsuccessful. In the mid-eighteenth century on Kamchatka, for example, the grain yield was often not even enough to provide seed grain for the next season. Following Adam Laxman's visit to Hokkaido in 1792–1793, Governor-General Ivan Pil in Irkutsk propounded the idea of establishing farming in the southern Kuril Islands. He recommended to Grigori Shelikhov, director of the Northern Company, that he undertake such a project. A towering figure in the fur trade and one whose company would ultimately be chartered as the Russian American Company, Shelikhov directed that forty men and women be settled on the island of Urup with seed and cattle. Although some of the settlers remained for ten years, the experiment was a disaster. The cattle could not survive, and the rigors of the island climate ensured that the grain harvest would be woefully inadequate.

Shelikhov had formed a fur trading company, together with Ivan Golikov and his nephew Mikhail, in 1781. They rapidly took over a lion's share of the trade in the North Pacific basin and in 1790, after the death of Ivan Golikov, reorganized the enterprise under the name of the Northeastern Company. Shelikhov had a very broad vision of Russia's future in the region; he strongly recommended to the Russian crown that North America be properly colonized and that the Amur River be used for Russian access to the Pacific. He dominated the company, renamed the American Company in 1794, from a headquarters in Irkutsk. It was here that a young visitor of noble birth by the name of Nikolai Petrovich Rezanov had met and fallen in love with Shelikhov's daughter Anna in 1790. Three years later they were married, with the thirty-six-year-old Rezanov receiving as dowry a large share of stock in his father-in-law's company.

Grigori Shelikhov died in 1795, and his strong-willed widow Natalia very competently attempted to continue the business against heavy odds. She might well not have succeeded had it not been for the astute services of her son-in-law Rezanov in Saint Petersburg. Largely through his effective lobbying, a merger was effected in 1798 of the Shelikhov and other commercial interests into the United America Company, which in turn was then transformed a year later into the chartered company called the Russian American Company. This new organization, in the tradition of the great chartered companies of the British and the Dutch, was given responsibility for the colonization of Russian territory in the North Pacific *and* for relations with Japan. The company's headquarters were first located in Irkutsk but moved to Saint Petersburg in 1800. The most influential director was Nikolai Rezanov.

The problems of supplying the Russian fur trade were not ameliorated by the creation of the Russian American Company, but there now was a more centralized direction of Russian activity in the Pacific. As a result, more creative ideas were forthcoming to find a solution. One thought, advanced shortly after the turn of the nineteenth century, was to send supplies from European Russia by ship and to pay for the voyage by delivering furs from the North Pacific to the Chinese port of Canton. This was in imitation of British and American skippers and stemmed from a suggestion advanced by Adam Krusenstern who, while seconded to the Royal Navy, had visited Canton on a British ship. Following a decision to implement the suggestion, two British vessels were purchased and named *Nadezhda* and *Neva*. Captain Krusenstern was placed in command of the former ship and of an expedition to test the new scheme. Lieutenant Commander Yuri Lisiansky was assigned as the skipper of the *Neva*.

Before the expedition got under way, it was decided to make another effort to open trade with Japan, with an eye toward using that island nation as a possible source of food supply for the Russian Pacific colonies. Another consideration was that the colonies should be inspected by someone in authority to examine their needs and attempt to provide for them. Rezanov, recently widowed, agreed to take on the mission and was duly empowered by the Russian American Company to conduct all necessary business in the Pacific. He also received the permit authorizing entry into Nagasaki harbor that had been presented to Adam Laxman in Matsumae in 1793. In addition, hopefully to insinuate themselves into the good graces of the Japanese, Rezanov had in tow a number of Japanese castaways who had washed ashore in the Aleutians in 1795.

The two ships departed Kronstadt in August 1803. They rounded Cape Horn and headed into the Pacific the following March. The voyage was almost a comic opera with the egos of Rezanov and Krusenstern in constant conflict despite the fact that Rezanov was clearly authorized to act as the senior personage. The two vessels separated at the Sandwich Islands, with Lisiansky in the *Neva* proceeding to the American colonies and Krusenstern in the *Nadezhda* to Kamchatka. After a two-month stay in Petropavlovsk (which had been established at Avacha Bay on the east coast of Kamchatka by Vitus Bering in 1740), where Rezanov succeeded in straightening out the chain of command, the *Nadezhda* headed for Nagasaki on September 27, arriving in that port on October 20, 1804.

The entourage, including the complement of the *Nadezhda*, would spend the next six months in Nagasaki harbor. Upon arrival, Rezanov presented a letter from his emperor requesting the opening of trade relations. The answer, after months of delay, was in the form of a resounding refusal, based on the traditional Japanese policy of seclusion. Rezanov was dumbfounded but was forced to accept the situation. Accordingly, the party departed Nagasaki on April 30, 1805, for the return trip to Kamchatka. Once back in Petropavlovsk, Rezanov and Krusenstern parted company. The latter, after exploring around the northern coast of Sakhalin and deciding that there was no passage between it and the mainland, sailed off with a load of furs to Canton, where he rendezvoused with Lisiansky in the *Neva*, and then proceeded back to Russia via the Indian Ocean and the Cape of Good Hope. He arrived in Kronstadt on August 25, 1806. By doing so, he became the leader of the first Russian group to circumnavigate the earth. Krusenstern was an astute observer, but his assessment that the Japanese could never become a naval power of consequence was far wide of the mark, as successor Russian naval officers would learn, to their sorrow, one hundred years later.

Rezanov quickly headed off to the American colonies. Here he carefully assessed the state of affairs and the needs of the colonists. The winter of 1805–1806 was particularly strenuous for the Russians in the North Pacific, owing to the loss of a ship bringing provisions from East Asia. Rezanov therefore resolved to find a solution in the Spanish port of San Francisco. He bought an American ship, the *Juno*, departed Alaskan waters in February 1806, and successfully returned laden with provisions the following May. This enterprise is discussed in more detail in chapter 10.

During his travels about the North Pacific in the winter of 1805–1806, Rezanov was accompanied by two young Russian naval officers, Lieutenant Nikolai Khvostov and Midshipman Gavriil Davydov. Khvostov was the skipper of *Juno*, and Davydov was given command of a small vessel, the *Avos*. Through this period of association, the two young men became intimately familiar with Rezanov's deep sense of indignation over his inability to open trade relations with the Japanese at Nagasaki in the winter of 1804–1805. Rezanov then authorized, on his own, naval activity by the two officers designed to force the Japanese to open trade. As it turned out, he gave conflicting instructions to the two, perhaps to relieve himself of responsibility if things went wrong (but since he died in Krasnoiarsk in March 1807, the matter was moot).

Khvostov, being eager and energetic, chose the activist interpretation of his instructions. He sailed the *Juno* to Aniwa Bay at the southern end of Sakhalin, arriving on October 18, 1806. The Japanese had only very cautiously ventured toward Sakhalin. Not until 1679 had they established seasonal fishing villages on Aniwa Bay. Finally, in 1790, the Matsumae clan had established a permanent trading facility with some guard posts. It was here that Khvostov vented his wrath. The Russians burned the warehouses after generously helping themselves to the contents. Four Japanese were captured, and all their boats and nets were burned. Khvostov left a copper plate with a message inscribed, in Russian, condemning the Japanese for not trading with Russia and threatening aggressive measures in northern Japan. He then sailed off to Petropavlovsk where he joined Davydov, still in command of the *Avos*, in early November.

Late the following spring (May 1807), the two enfants terribles sailed down the Kuril chain to Iturup where they captured, looted, and burned the principal Japanese settlement. One of the defenders happened to be Mamiya Rinzo who was slightly wounded while fleeing the fray. Fortunately, he survived to perform his exploratory feats around Sakhalin and the Amur River the following two years. The two Russian ships then moved north to the next island, Urup, where they discovered that the colonists sent there by Shelikhov in 1795 had all departed. They next cruised past Hakodate in southern Hokkaido where they sank a Japanese ship after availing themselves of its cargo. By June 23 they were in Aniwa Bay to assure themselves that no Japanese had returned. They next appeared off the northwest coast of Hokkaido where they looted more Japanese vessels and sent a message with released captives addressed to the Matsumae leader. In the note, Khvostov chided the Japanese for rebuffing Russian attempts to open trade and threatened further drastic measures if they did not cooperate.

The saga of Khvostov and Davydov in Pacific waters came to an end when the two arrived in Okhotsk on July 28, 1807. They were immediately arrested and thrown into confinement by the avaricious commandant, Navy Captain Bukharin, who confiscated their vessel and its contents. The Russian American Company successfully retrieved the ship and goods from Bukharin, and the two young naval officers escaped to Yakutsk after a harrowing trek. They later were court-martialed but survived to fight another day in the Baltic before their untimely deaths occurred in Saint Petersburg in October 1809.

The depredations of Khvostov and Davydov elicited positive actions from the shogun's government. The magistrate of Matsumae was dismissed from office. As we have noted, Mamiya Rinzo charted unknown shores of Sakhalin and the opposing Asian mainland. Additional garrisons were positioned on Hokkaido and Iturup, and all authority in the north was placed under the direct control of the *Bakufu*. However, there was no follow-up by the Russians as promised by Khvostov since he and his confederate Davydov had been removed from the scene. Inasmuch as the Japanese had only the capability to see to their coastal defense, there was no prospect of a retaliatory attack against Kamchatka or other Russian territory; therefore, a rather quiet four years ensued until Lieutenant Commander Vasili Golovnin sailed into the picture.

Golovnin was embarked in the war sloop *Diana* to conduct survey operations along the Kurils in the summer of 1811. Being aware of the Khvostov and Davydov escapades, he wished to avoid all contact with the Japanese. Despite his care, it would be his misfortune to fall victim to a trap. Golovnin was in need of water and provisions when he anchored off the southeastern end of Kunashir, that portion of the island facing Hokkaido across the Nemuro Strait. On the morning of July 23, he and seven others were enticed into the local fort to negotiate for the supplies and then suddenly were seized. They were ferried across to Hokkaido at night and, after a series of forced marches, arrived at Hakodate. After preliminary interrogation they were then marched to Matsumae. Here the Russian captives were thoroughly interrogated, with a particular view toward trying to associate them with Khvostov and Davydov. From mid-November 1811 on, they were well treated and for the most part lived in reasonable surroundings, despite a weeklong escape attempt in May 1812.

In the meantime, the senior officer remaining aboard the *Diana* was Lieutenant Commander Petr Rikord. When he became aware of what was happening ashore on Kunashir, he attempted to move in to bombard the fort but was unable to come within effective range because of shallow water. His complement was too small to support an amphibious attack; therefore, in frustration, he sailed back to Okhotsk for reinforcements. The request for a major military force was not approved since titanic events, which would threaten the very existence of the Russian Empire, were shaping up in Europe; therefore, Rikord was able only to augment the crew of *Diana* and to obtain the services of a brig named *Zotic*. Thus reinforced, he returned to southern Kunashir on September 9, 1812. Unaware of Golovnin's whereabouts, he was preparing to assault the Japanese fort when he fortuitously captured a ship with an unusual Japanese merchant aboard, Takadaya Kahei. Rikord sent a message ashore that he was taking Takadaya to Kamchatka but would return the following year.

After wintering over in Petropavlovsk, Rikord returned to Kunashir in June 1813 with Takadaya. The latter was an eminently wise man whose advice was critical in resolving this delicate Russo-Japanese crisis. Senior officials arrived from Matsumae with conditions for the release of Golovnin and the others. Rikord was obliged to proceed to Okhotsk to obtain an official statement affirming that Khvostov's actions were unauthorized and certification that the booty would be returned or was unrecoverable. He returned October 10, 1813. Golovnin and the others had in the meantime been brought to Hakodate. After twelve days of ceremonies, the prisoners were released and, reunited with their former crew members, headed back to Russia in the *Diana*. Thanks to the dogged persistence of Rikord, the proper and dignified demeanor of Golovnin, the wise counsel and participation by Takadaya, and the desire of the Japanese to put an end to the incident, the affair ended most amicably. However, despite the seeming warmth of relations between the Russians and Japanese in Hakodate, the Japanese made the clear statement that the law of the land forbade trade with Western nations.

After the Golovnin affair, there was a dramatic drawdown of Russo-Japanese relations. Russian imperial attention was glued to Europe as the result of the Napoleonic Age. Following this would be the new era of European revolutions, reflected in the Russian experience by the Decembrist movement in 1825 and the Polish insurrection in 1830. The Kuril otter population had been depleted, and Russian commercial fur trapping was drawn ever eastward. Also, the Russian American Company had begun to look farther east for sources to feed the fur trade—to Hawaii and the coast of California. On the Japanese side, after the departure of Golovnin and the *Diana*, interest in the north reverted to its centuries-old state of indifference. The *Bakufu* wished to withdraw its costly financial and military support, and the *daimyo* of Matsumae ardently desired the return of control over his fief. The shogunate auctioned off the *basho* on Iturup and Kunashir, and in 1814 garrison troops were withdrawn from the southern Kurils. Finally, in 1821, direct rule was officially abolished. The experiment had lasted but twenty-two years.

At the time that the two nations' contacts were in decline, great events were in progress which would force them together again just three decades later. The explorations of James Cook in the 1770s in the North Pacific and those of George Vancouver along the coast of North America two decades later presaged a British interest in the area. Jean La Pérouse of France and William Broughton of England had surveyed part of the coast of Sakhalin in 1787 and 1797, respectively. (Both entered the Tatarsky Strait from the south and concluded that Sakhalin was a peninsula.) In 1820 British and American whalers appeared in both the northern and southern Pacific Ocean in search of oil to grease the wheels of the Industrial Revolution. The Opium War (1839–1842) resulted in a victory by Britain over China. Thereafter we see a permanent British presence in the western Pacific centered on the island of Hong Kong, which was ceded by China in the Treaty of Nanking in 1842. In the same decade the United States burst upon the Pacific scene as the result of the Oregon Treaty of 1846 and the end of the Mexican War in 1848. Suddenly there was a three-thousand-mile American seaboard on the Pacific. Other Europeans, notably the French, were now active in the Pacific as well.

During the decade of the 1840s, a renewed Russian interest in the Amur Basin became evident (this will be discussed in more detail in chapter 13). Navy Captain Gennadi Nevelskoi, more determined than had been La Perouse or Broughton, ascertained in 1849 that Sakhalin was indeed an island. At the same time he also discovered the mouth of the Amur River. This occurred forty years after the feat of Mamiya Rinzo, but it achieved just as little notoriety—this time

because of Russia's desire to keep it a state secret. Nevelskoi was a true imperialist. He established a post on the lower Amur River in 1850, although it
was Chinese territory by treaty, and an encampment on the southern coast of
Sakhalin in 1853 right next to Japanese settlements.

As the world shrank, courtesy of the Industrial Revolution and its steamships
and need for markets and resources, Japan would be increasingly hard pressed
to maintain its isolation. The United States would be a leader in the pressures
to change the Japanese system. There were American whalers in the northwestern Pacific whose well-being in case of shipwreck was of concern. Further,
the increase of trans-Pacific trade with China meant that an ever larger number
of ships would pass along the shores of Japan while pursuing the shortest, great-
circle route. This invited the use of Japanese ports in case of emergency repairs
or resupply. The story of Commodore Matthew Perry and the "opening of
Japan" is quite well known. The decision to send a mission to Japan had been
made in 1851. Perry was chosen to head the effort the following year, and the
Treaty of Kanagawa was concluded on March 31, 1854.

Not so well known is the story of Vice Admiral Evfimi Putiatin. Russian
concern over the presence of so many Americans and British near the coast of
northeast Asia was heightened when word was received of the American plans
to send a naval squadron to Japan. The Russians therefore launched an expedition of their own. Putiatin had been involved in the formulation of Russian
Far East policy during the previous decade and so was a natural choice to serve
as plenipotentiary. His flagship *Pallada* departed from Kronstadt on October 21,
1852, and his small squadron of modest ships arrived in Nagasaki in August
1853, just a month and a half after Perry had delivered the American demands
in Tokyo Bay. The Russian presence therefore added to the pressure being felt
by the shogunate.

Russo-Japanese negotiations (which were conducted in Japanese, Chinese, and
Dutch) were carried on in an amicable manner and were adjourned in February
1854 for further Japanese research into the geography of the north. Putiatin
sailed to De Castri Bay on the Tatarsky Strait and, while there, learned of the
entry of Britain and France on the side of the Turks in the Crimean War, which
had broken out between Russia and Turkey in October 1853. Putiatin's mission
therefore became more complicated since he and his ships would be fair game
for British and French fleets on the high seas. At this time, at Putiatin's behest,
the Russian encampment on southern Sakhalin was removed as a gesture of
goodwill toward the Japanese. In the meantime, the Americans had concluded
the Treaty of Kanagawa, which provided for treatment of shipwrecked sailors,
revictualling, consular representation, and the opening of the ports of Shimoda
and Hakodate to trade. A similar treaty had been signed with the British; Putiatin
felt compelled to chance a voyage to Japan.

He arrived off Shimoda in a new frigate, the *Diana*, on December 4, 1854.
Eighteen days later, disaster struck. An earthquake caused a great part of the
city to slide into the sea. The *Diana* was violently swung about her anchor and

so badly damaged that she sank a few days later. This mutual disaster tended to bring the two sides together so that, on February 7, 1855, the Treaty of Shimoda was signed. The accord was quite similar to that concluded by Perry the previous year, but it included a third trading port (Nagasaki) and attempted to delineate a border. It was agreed that the Kuril Islands would be divided, with Japan receiving Iturup and the islands to the south thereof and the Russians receiving Urup and all islands to the north. No agreement could be reached on the island of Sakhalin; therefore, it was declared a condominium, granting access to both sides. A further clause called for reciprocal extraterritoriality. Copies of the treaty were exchanged in four languages: Japanese, Chinese, Dutch, and Russian.

An example of the mutual goodwill fostered by the disaster of the earthquake was the Japanese assistance in building a replacement ship for the Russians, thus initiating the Japanese once again into the art of constructing ocean-going ships. The vessel, built in the small port of Heda to the northeast of Shimoda, was christened *Heda*. It was ready in time for Putiatin to depart on May 8, 1855, and to make a speed run to the mouth of the Amur River (which was still Chinese territory). The *Heda* was too small to accommodate all of the *Diana*'s crew; they were mostly delivered to the north by Yankee skippers.

In 1859 the impatient and imperialistic governor-general of East Siberia, Nikolai Murav'ev-Amursky, in the belief that Putiatin had been too timorous in his dealings with the Japanese, took it upon himself to settle the problem of the Sakhalin frontier. To his surprise and frustration, he discovered that heavy-handed military threats were of no avail in winning Japanese acquiescence in ceding the entire island of Sakhalin to Russia. Nevertheless, from the end of the Crimean War in 1856, Murav'ev-Amursky continued to send an increasing number of Russians to Sakhalin. Japanese concern led to a mission to Saint Petersburg in 1862 under Takenouchi Shimotsuke and Matsudaira Iwami with a proposal that the island be divided at the fiftieth parallel of latitude. This was rejected by Nikolai Ignat'ev, hero of the Convention of Peking of 1860 (see chapter 13), who now was in charge of the Asiatic Department of the Foreign Ministry, but he did agree to a line that would follow natural topographical features slightly to the south. It was therefore announced that a joint commission should survey the area the following year. Unfortunately, domestic problems in Japan prevented the Japanese from taking part, and the project died.

The Japanese shogunate was shaken to its foundation by the events of the mid-1850s. The treaties with Western powers had been agreed to only because of military weakness. Since the Tokugawa Shogunate was the protector of the nation, its very raison d'être was now in question. Paradoxically, the shogunate was subject to harsh criticism for failing to enforce the seclusion policy which it had originally imposed. Led by western clans, notably the Satsuma and Choshu, dissidents rebelled against the Edo authority. This was climaxed, in 1868, by the so-called Meiji Restoration, whereby the authority of government nominally was restored to the emperor but was mostly exercised by young samurai, especially from the Satsuma and Choshu. They soon learned that they did not possess the technology to defend against the Western powers and so began massive importation of Western technology and institutions, particularly in the military realm. They wished to avoid the disasters they saw befalling China as the result of her weakness in the face of the Europeans.

In the meantime, the Russian pressure on Sakhalin increased, and attempts by the Japanese to reach a solution in 1870 and 1871 were fruitless. The energetic foreign minister Soejima Taneomi, on the advice of the U.S. Secretary of State William Seward, attempted to purchase the island for 2 million gold yen, but this too was turned down in 1872. With the fall of Soejima and the war party in late 1873, the sense of Japanese urgency cooled. A key personality now was Kuroda Kiyotaka, director of the *Hokkaido kaitakushi* (colonial office), who was dedicated to the effective colonization of Hokkaido and whose American advisers had such an impact on the ultimate development of that island. He personally believed that Japan should retain a claim on Sakhalin but had concluded that the island's climate was too austere for effective colonization and economic development. Other matters were absorbing Japanese external interests, such as difficulties with China over Taiwan and the Ryukyu Islands as well as the continuing problem of trying to establish diplomatic relations with Korea. Therefore the new foreign minister Terashima Muneori decided to solve the Sakhalin problem once and for all. Admiral Enomoto Buyo was sent to Saint Petersburg as minister plenipotentiary and envoy extraordinary with instructions to seek a division of the island or to cede Japanese claims in return for territory equal in area (the northern Kurils).

Although Russian interest in foreign affairs was being drawn toward Europe after the Franco-Prussian War and the rise of Germany, and events were taking place in Austria and Turkey that would lead to the Russo-Turkish War of 1877–1878, the Saint Petersburg government refused to divide Sakhalin. After many weeks of negotiation, the Treaty of Saint Petersburg was signed on May 7, 1875. This pact awarded the entire island of Sakhalin to Russia and all the Kuril Islands to Japan. The Japanese, however, were granted fishing rights in the waters washing Sakhalin. The border therefore was drawn between Hokkaido and Sakhalin and between the Kamchatka Peninsula and the northernmost Kuril Island of Shumshu. This is the only instance of a major border delineation between Japan and Russia based on normal diplomacy rather than the use of force or threat of war.

9

To the Farthest East:
The Rim of the North Pacific

It is generally accepted that the Cossack Semen Dezhnev was the first Muscovite to round the easternmost point of Asia as he moved in 1648 from the mouth of the Kolyma River, which flows into the Arctic Ocean, to the Anadyr, which empties into the Pacific. The second such achievement would have to wait eighty years, as we have seen, until the time of the first Kamchatka expedition when Vitus Bering sailed up the eastern coast of Asia into the Arctic Ocean in the year 1728.

The third voyage through the Bering Strait came as the result of an effort to conquer the eastern end of the Asian mainland. When the Muscovites were forced out of the Amur basin by the Treaty of Nerchinsk in 1689, their thrust was northeastward and thence south into the throat of the Kamchatka Peninsula. Their route was the laborious challenge via the upper Anadyr River. During this time, in the last years of the seventeenth century, so much energy was consumed pushing into Kamchatka that no attempt was made to press on to the end of the continent. And a considerable effort would be required to do so since the Chukchi natives turned out to be the most warlike of all the indigenous populations in East Asia. Following the first sea voyage between Okhotsk and Kamchatka in 1716, even less interest was given to the lands of Asia's ultimate east.

This attention void would be filled by the ideas of a Far East Cossack named Afanasi Shestakov, whose enthusiasm convinced the Russian Senate to approve, in April 1727, a plan for the conquest of the huge Chukotsky Peninsula. The enterprise, involving 1,500 men, was designed to split into two prongs, starting from Yakutsk. Shestakov himself was to advance to Okhotsk and thence to move northeastward. The remainder of the force, under an army captain named Dmitri Pavlutsky, was to pursue the old route via the Kolyma to the upper Anadyr River. Shestakov and his fellows successfully negotiated the trek to Okhotsk

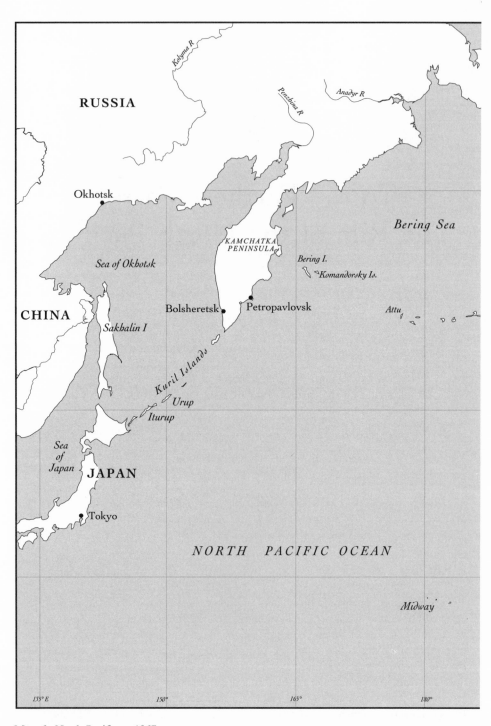

Map 6. North Pacific to 1867.

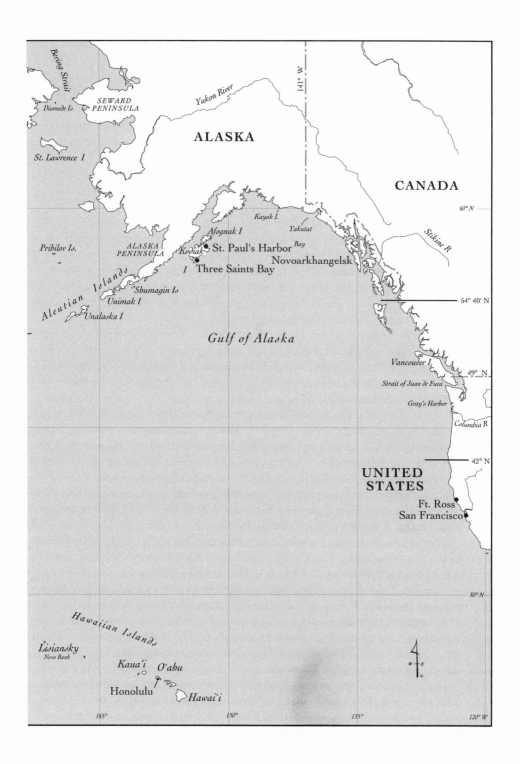

and beyond, but he was killed and his force defeated in their first encounter with the Chukchi, just north of the Kamchatka Peninsula, on March 25, 1730. When Pavlutsky learned of the disaster, he assumed overall command and sent word for the remaining personnel in the Kamchatka area to sail to the mouth of the Anadyr.

Thus, in the summer of 1732, a group embarked in the *Sviatoi Gavriil*, under the leadership of Ivan Fedorov and a geodesist named Mikhail Gvozdev, and proceeded along the coast, past the Anadyr, to the Bering Strait. There they found the islands of Big and Little Diomede and then moved eastward where they anchored three miles off the coast of Alaska's Seward Peninsula. There was no extraordinary excitement since they were quite unaware of their achievement. Also, Gvozdev's final report would be ten years late in arriving in Saint Petersburg. Gvozdev's group was of very little help to Pavlutsky since it immediately headed back to Kamchatka. Pavlutsky in the meantime had succeeded in pushing to the Bering Strait on land, but despite several victories over the Chukchi, he was unable to subdue them. He would return twice more, once in 1739 and again in 1743, in failed attempts to complete the job. On the last occasion, he lost his life in battle.

Peter the Great's passion for the sea provided the impetus that drove the Russians onto the Pacific Ocean in the early eighteenth century. Particularly impressive were the voyages launched by the second Kamchatka expedition of 1733–1742 which were resolved into three principal vectors. One of these, to the shores of Japan, we have discussed earlier. A second was to chart the northern limits of Russia's vast Asian empire—the Arctic shore from the White Sea to the eastern end of the Asian continent. Among Bering's many responsibilities as overall commander was to ensure adequate boats, supplies, and personnel at certain key river locations to support this undertaking. The effort was divided into five segments: from the mouth of the Northern Dvina River (Arkhangelsk) to the mouth of the Ob, from the Ob to the Yenisei, from the Yenisei to the Taimyr Peninsula, from Taimyr to the Lena, and finally from the Lena around Cape Dezhnev to the mouth of the Anadyr River.

The first segment was completed, after three failed attempts, in the summer of 1737 when a group under Lieutenant Stepan Malygin negotiated the northernmost point of the Yamal Peninsula. The second segment was attacked by a group from Tobolsk which headed down the Ob in the summer of 1734. After repeated frustrations, they succeeded in attaining the Yenisei in the summer of 1737 under the direction of Lieutenant Dmitri Ovtsyn. This same group then attempted, starting in 1738, to reach the northern tip of the Taimyr Peninsula. Despite their best efforts, ice prevented them from moving above 75°15' along the Taimyr coast. Meanwhile, another group commenced attacking the peninsula from the east, setting out from Yakutsk on the Lena River in the summer of 1735. By the following summer, they had managed to attain 77°29' but were forced to turn back. Renewed efforts in 1739 and 1740 under the leadership of Lieutenant Khariton Laptev similarly came close to reaching the northernmost point of the peninsula but failed. Indeed, the ship was lost in the summer of 1740. Laptev therefore decided to continue the mapping on shore, a task which was finally completed, all the way to the Yenisei, in 1741.

The final segment, from the Lena to the Anadyr, was even more daunting than the other challenges. The first effort was made by a group departing Yakutsk in the summer of 1735. After the usual frustrations and failure, a later attempt under Lieutenant Dmitri Laptev (Khariton's cousin) was launched from Yakutsk in 1739. This group arrived at the Indigarka River that year and the Kolyma the next. From this point, however, movement by ship was impossible because of ice, and survey by land was not feasible because of the threat of the warlike Chukchi. Therefore, in 1742, Laptev led his group up the Aniui (tributary of the Kolyma) to the short portage connecting with the Anadyr and on to Anadyrsk. This last segment of the Russian Arctic shore (from the Kolyma eastward) would not be successfully surveyed until eight decades later when Lieutenant Ferdinand Wrangel finally completed the job in 1823.

The remaining of the three vectors of the second Kamchatka expedition pointed eastward to North America, and this undertaking Vitus Bering reserved to his own immediate leadership. Some two years after Spanberg and Walton had piloted their ships to Japan, Bering and Aleksei Chirikov were finally ready for their challenging enterprise. Two ships, the *Sviatoi Petr* and *Sviatoi Pavel*, had been completed at Okhotsk in June 1740. By the following October, the two vessels dropped anchor in Avacha Bay on the eastern shore of Kamchatka where Bering had, the previous year, directed that facilities be built. A church was erected, dedicated to Saints Peter and Paul, and the new site was dubbed Petropavlovsk in their honor.

The following June 15 (1741), Bering, embarked in *Sviatoi Petr*, and Chirikov, in *Sviatoi Pavel*, weighed anchor and headed southeasterly into the Pacific. After a brief unsuccessful search for the fabled "Islands of Gold and Silver," the ships steered north of east. By sailing southeast from Kamchatka in search of the nonexistent isles and then to the northeast, the explorers totally missed the Aleutian chain and, incidentally, greatly increased the time consumed and the distance traveled in order to find the coast of North America. On the first of July, the ships drifted apart, and by the following day they had lost sight of each other, never to rejoin.

Chirikov and the crew of the *Sviatoi Pavel* were the first to sight land—on July 26 just north of latitude 55°. They were singularly unable to exploit their find as the result of two costly mishaps two days later. In an area near the northwest corner of Chichagov Island, Chirikov lost a boat which had been sent to reconnoiter and then his second boat which was ordered to investigate the fate of the first. Suddenly bereft of any means to effect a landing to take on fresh water, he was forced to return to Kamchatka. The crew of the *Sviatoi Pavel*, severely crippled by dehydration, barely managed to limp back to Avacha Bay, arriving October 21.

Meanwhile Bering, in *Sviatoi Petr*, made a landfall on July 27, a day after

Chirikov. This was farther north, above 58° north latitude. Personnel briefly landed on Kayak Island and, later, on the Shumagin Islands near the Alaska Peninsula. Bering was seriously ill and dispirited, and the elements combined to hinder progress homeward and to complicate accurate navigation. On the evening of November 17, the ship approached close to land and was suddenly lifted over the reef into a harbor. The crew was stranded on an island, now known by the name of Bering, just over one hundred miles east of Kamchatka. Bering died a month later, but the surviving crew members were able to cannibalize the *Sviatoi Petr* and build a smaller ship which they sailed back to Petropavlovsk the following summer, arriving September 7, 1742.

In the spring of 1742, Chirikov had headed eastward again toward America, hoping he might find Bering, and intending to start his exploration at the island of Attu in the Aleutians which he had charted on his return voyage the preceding autumn. He actually passed close to Bering Island and arrived at Attu, but the weather conditions and sickness amongst his crew forced him to return to Petropavlovsk. This would be the last gasp of the second Kamchatka expedition. Despite their achievements, neither Chirikov nor Bering had actually set foot on the mainland of North America.

Thus, seventeen years after the death of Peter the Great, the momentum finally went out of his great designs in the North Pacific. The results did not seem to justify the huge outlays of money which, from the central treasury alone, amounted to some 2 million rubles. With the death of the Empress Anna in 1740 and the accession to the throne a year later of Peter's daughter Elizabeth, strong supporters of the expedition, such as Andrei Ostermann, would be ousted from court circles. Further, there would be a deeper commitment to the affairs of Europe at the expense of eastward expansion. Therefore, although it was Russians who first approached the shores of Alaska in the early 1740s, the Russian Empire would not establish a permanent presence in North America until the lapse of almost half a century. It was one thing for adventurers, freebooters, and Cossacks to press across the mainland of Asia on foot and in sleds and river boats, but it was quite another to cross the northern waters of the Pacific Ocean. Much greater expenses were involved in ships and supplies, which could be met only by very large commercial companies or by the resources of a national government. The kind of people involved were practical seamen whose sole objective was to survive and amass as many fur pelts as possible. Scientific charting and survey were hardly their dominion.

As a result, the Russian presence in the North Pacific for the first decades after the voyages of Bering and Chirikov was primarily that of private traders, lured on as always by furs. The difference now was that not the sable but rather the sea otter was the target. Many entrepreneurs joined in this hunt, but there was no immediate pursuit into the environment by officials of the Russian government as there had been on the mainland. The furs had to be returned to mainland ports, of course, where the necessary duty could be collected. We therefore see neither Russian colonists nor Russian government representation being established on the islands or on the mainland of Alaska at this time.

As many as forty-two small companies sprouted up, in the two decades following the discoveries of Bering and Chirikov, which plied the waters washing the Aleutian, Pribilov, and Komandorsky islands in mad pursuit of the sea otters. These mammals were very different from the mainland fur sources in that their reproduction rate was dramatically lower. Whereas the exclusive sable might drop a litter of five, the social sea otter produced only one pup per year, and the pelt of the female of the species was more highly prized than that of the male. As a result, the waters of the northwestern Pacific became rapidly depleted of this rich source of fur, and the operations were perforce moved ever eastward. This, in turn, demanded longer voyages and larger ships so that gradually the smaller operators were forced out of business, and the number of competitive companies was radically reduced.

As the Russians pushed across Asia, a favorite means of acquiring fur pelts had been the taking of hostages from native tribes to ensure that the men of the tribe would provide the desired product in the desired number. In the North Pacific a somewhat similar system was employed. Aleut families were taken hostage to ensure that the men, who were superb hunters of the sea otter, wielding their spears with great dexterity from their kayaks, would serve with Russian mother ships. This meant long months at sea, ranging throughout the hunting areas which ultimately reached to the waters off the California coast.

In the previous chapter, we made brief mention of the merchant Grigori Shelikhov and the Russian American Company. When Shelikhov, together with Ivan and Mikhail Golikov, formed the initial partnership in August 1781, the arrangement was quite different from most in the fur trade in that it lasted for ten years rather than merely the duration of a voyage. The partners envisaged the establishment of a permanent company presence in the fur-trapping area to be supported by annual ships which would provide supplies and collect furs.

Although the Golikovs contributed the majority of the capital, Shelikhov was the man on the spot and the one in immediate charge. He and his wife Natalia proceeded to Okhotsk, supervised the building of ships, and on August 27, 1783, sailed eastward into the Aleutians. Because of storms, they were forced to winter over on Bering Island and then advance to Kodiak Island the following August. Here, on the southern part of the island, the first permanent Russian presence was established and named Three Saints Harbor. In the summer of 1786, having subdued the native population in the vicinity of Three Saints Harbor and having erected forts on the neighboring island of Afognak, as well as at Cape Saint Elias on Kayak Island, the Shelikhovs sailed back to Kamchatka. After a harrowing trek through the dead of winter, they made it to Irkutsk in April 1787.

Shelikhov immediately wrote a report on his activities which he submitted to the governor-general of Irkutsk, Ivan Yakobi. Now an expert for having been on the scene near North America, Shelikhov made a strong case for the assertion of Russian control over Alaska and its resources, for the establishment of per-

manent colonies, and for the propagation of the Orthodox faith amongst the
native population. He further recommended that this could best be done by one
company playing a monopolistic role supported by the imperial government of
Russia. Yakobi strongly endorsed the recommendations to Saint Petersburg. At
the same time, word was sent out from Irkutsk to Shelikhov's people in Kodiak
to place metallic insignia in certain strategic spots along the North American
mainland to proclaim that the land was integral to the territory of the Russian
Empire.

Catherine was opposed to monopolies and would not approve that key part
of Shelikhov's recommendations. Nevertheless, she authorized an expedition
under Joseph Billings, who had sailed as a midshipman with the English Captain
Cook, and Gavriil Sarychev to chart Russian possessions in the North Pacific
and the Arctic Ocean. The first phase of the expedition was an unsuccessful
attempt to map the Arctic coast east of the Kolyma river mouth in the summer
of 1787; as in the case of Dmitri Laptev four and a half decades earlier, the ice
rendered navigation impossible. Billings and Sarychev then proceeded to
Okhotsk, constructed ships, and spent two years (1789–1791) in the North Pacific doing survey work and ethnographic research amongst the native peoples
found therein.

At about the time of the Billings/Sarychev expedition, Catherine had even
been convinced of the desirability of sending a force of five naval ships from
European Russia to the North Pacific under the command of Commodore Grigori
Mulovsky to show the Russian flag. Catherine's priorities were quickly revealed,
however, when Mulovsky's small fleet was instead ordered to the Mediterranean
to take part in the crucial war with Turkey which erupted in 1787.

Aside from the Billings expedition, the greater effort was put forth by the
company of Shelikhov and the Golikovs. Although not granted a monopoly,
Shelikhov succeeded in gaining permission to set up a shipbuilding yard, to
settle peasants, and to establish an Orthodox mission in North America. Shelikhov passed away in 1795, before realizing all his dreams, but as noted in the
previous chapter, his company would be combined with those of two other major
merchants into the United American Company in 1798 and finally chartered as
the Russian American Company the following year. As such, it was designated
the agent for the Russian government in all matters on the North American
continent north of 55° north latitude, in the Aleutians, and even in the Kuril
Islands.

Whereas Catherine had an aversion to chartered companies, her son and successor Paul (ruled 1796–1801) so detested his mother that he reversed many of
her policies, and the conversion of Shelikhov's company into the Russian American Company proved to be no exception.

10

Baranov, California, and Hawaii

Between the time of the Bering/Chirikov voyages in 1741 and the chartering of the Russian American Company in 1799, other European nations began to appear in the North Pacific. Partially as the result of the Russian advance along the North American coast, the Spanish decided to move northward out of Mexico with cross and sword, starting with the founding of a mission and presidio at San Diego in 1769. By the middle of the following decade, they had established themselves at San Francisco, and Spanish captains had become active along the coast farther north. By 1779 Juan Francisco de Bodega y Quadra had probed as far north as 57° along the Alaskan coast.

The French also had shown their flag in the area. Louis Antoine de Bougainville was the first Frenchman to circumnavigate the globe in 1776–1779. In twenty years he would be followed into the Pacific by Jean François de Galaup, comte de La Pérouse, who visited many parts of North America and northeast Asia and whose name still graces many geographical features in the Pacific. He unfortunately would perish off the New Hebrides in 1788. The French Revolution and Napoleonic Wars would then combine to restrict any subsequent French presence of consequence until well into the nineteenth century.

Rather, it was the British and the Americans who came to challenge the Russians and the Spanish. The British claim could be traced to the appearance of Sir Francis Drake in the waters off western North America in 1579, but it would not be until 199 years later that Captain James Cook, while seeking a northwest passage, became the first English explorer to perform methodical charting of the northwestern coast of North America. His life was taken in February 1779 at Kealakekua Bay in Hawaii, but the account of his voyages, which was published in 1784, alerted many British and Americans to the wealth of sea otters in the North Pacific.

The British and Spanish interests clashed in Nootka Sound off Vancouver Island in 1789 when Spanish naval authorities seized the vessels of British fur trader John Meares. By the terms of the Nootka Convention of 1790, however, the Spanish made restitution and renounced claims to exclusive jurisdiction in the area. Within two years, Captain George Vancouver, who had been a midshipman with Cook, appeared in the North Pacific, charting the waters near the island bearing his name. At this same time, interests of the new American republic were represented by Captain Robert Gray who commenced a fur-trading operation to China in 1789. While in North American coastal waters not far from Captain Vancouver in 1792, Gray discovered the Columbia River after taking the dangerous chance of negotiating the treacherous bar at the river's mouth.

Late in the eighteenth century the British, in addition to maintaining a maritime presence off the west coast of North America, were also approaching the area overland. Alexander Mackenzie finally reached the Pacific just a bit north of Vancouver Island in July 1793, and Simon Fraser arrived fifteen years later, having descended the river named in his honor. David Thompson then made it to the ocean in 1811 via the Columbia river system.

In 1803 a vast tract of land, known as the Louisiana Purchase, became American territory. Within a year, Meriwether Lewis and William Clark set out on their trek to explore it, and they proceeded all the way to the mouth of the Columbia River. Building on their work, John Jacob Astor would form the Pacific Fur Company and attempt to dominate the fur industry in the entire area, based on his post (Astoria) at the mouth of the Columbia.

From the chartering of the Russian American Company in 1799, its dominant leader in North America for the next two decades would be the intriguing figure of Aleksandr Andreevich Baranov. Baranov was a short, sturdy man who had already spent nine years as the manager in charge of operations in the North Pacific for Grigori Shelikhov, and before that he had been involved in trade in the Chukotsky Peninsula. When he accepted Shelikhov's offer of employment in August 1790, he immediately set out for North America and barely survived a shipwreck which stranded him and his crew on Unalaska Island for the winter. Baranov showed his mettle and leadership by the high rate of survival among his men. They made the rest of the trip to Three Saints Bay in small native craft the following summer. The next year, he moved the headquarters to the eastern end of Kodiak Island at a site known as Saint Paul's Harbor. It was Baranov who got Shelikhov's shipbuilding program under way at the site of modern Seward, turning out the first vessel in 1794. A year later, he established the first settlement on the mainland, called Slavorossia, on Yakutat Bay.

As soon as the Russian American Company was chartered, Baranov was designated the chief manager for operations in the American colonies. He had earlier concluded that the sea otter population had been so depleted in the Aleutians that the center of gravity should be shifted farther to the southeast. Accordingly, one of his first moves was to establish a new center, named

Novoarkhangelsk (modern-day Sitka), on what is now called Baranov Island. The site was indeed closer to hunting operations, but it also was on land peopled by the Tlingit Indians (called Kolosh by the Russians).

Unlike the milder Aleuts, the Tlingits were very proud, tenacious warriors who would cause the Russians many woes. While Baranov was visiting Kodiak in 1802, in an attempt to get agriculture into operation, the Tlingits attacked the fort at Novoarkhangelsk, destroyed it, captured all the stores, and killed many of the Russians. Baranov was handicapped by a dearth of ships but, by 1804, had gathered four small vessels into an attacking force which was augmented by heavy weapons purchased from an American skipper. He was greatly helped by the arrival in June of the *Neva* under the command of Yuri Lisiansky, who had sailed with Rezanov and Krusenstern from Saint Petersburg until parting company with them at the Hawaiian Islands. Baranov led the attack against the Tlingits, who held out seven days before finally surrendering. He now set about rebuilding a greatly strengthened Novoarkhangelsk.

Lisiansky, after wintering over in the colonies, departed in the autumn of 1805 loaded with furs for Canton where he was to rendezvous with Krusenstern in the *Nadezhda*. En route he performed survey work, which is remembered by the names Lisiansky Island and Neva Bank in the Hawaiian Island chain. In Canton the two skippers were able to trade their furs, thanks to assistance from the British. When the Chinese authorities later became aware of the transaction, they were irate and firmly reminded the Russian government that Sino-Russian trade was permitted only at Kiakhta in Inner Asia.

This fact indicates even further the disadvantages under which Baranov and the Russian American Company had to labor. The best customers for their furs were the Chinese, yet the pelts had to be transported to Okhotsk, then by land track to Yakutsk on the Lena, up that river, and finally south to the trading center of Kiakhta. The British and Americans (whom the Russians dubbed "King George's Men" and "Bostonians," respectively), on the other hand, could sail directly from North America to Canton. Not only that, but they traded directly for furs with the North American natives in lands claimed by Saint Petersburg. To the even greater discomfiture of the Russians, among the items the Anglo-Saxons traded for the furs were weapons, ammunition, and, often, alcohol.

There was indeed stress in the Russian American colonies resulting from a chronic lack of basic needs—even the food necessary for survival. The winter of 1805–1806 was a particularly difficult period because of the loss of a ship bringing supplies from Okhotsk. Fortunately, at this time, Nikolai Rezanov was in Novoarkhangelsk, having just come from his frustrating failure to trade for food supplies in Japan. As we have seen, he was the most influential director of the Russian American Company, having played a major role in chartering the organization. He bought a ship, the *Juno*, from an American sea captain, John D'Wolf, and, with the energetic Lieutenant Nikolai Khvostov in command of her, headed south in search of food for his starving company employees.

Rezanov arrived in San Francisco in March 1806 and, despite considerable odds against him, succeeded admirably in his mission. Russia and Spain were on opposite sides in the War of the Third Coalition, and the highly restrictive Spanish trade practices would have seemed to militate against the likelihood of the Russian's success. However, Rezanov's aristocratic charm elicited a friendly response from the Spanish authorities, particularly from the family of the commandant, Don José de Argüello. Indeed, Argüello's daughter Concepción became deeply enamored of Rezanov, who had been widowed prior to his departure from Saint Petersburg in 1804. The attraction was mutual, and the Argüello family was startled when the forty-two-year-old widower and the sixteen-year-old señorita announced their desire to marry. Such a union would be complicated. Concepción required the approval of the pope; Rezanov the approval of his emperor.

Nikolai Rezanov was unable, because of political realities, to establish San Francisco as a regular source of supply, but he did manage to sail from the bay on May 20, 1806, with the food so desperately needed by the colonies in the north. He then hurried across the North Pacific to Okhotsk and commenced the arduous overland route to Saint Petersburg. His health had become undermined by the great exertions of the last three years, and the rigors of this journey proved too much. He died in Krasnoiarsk on March 13, 1807. Concepción, heart broken, took holy orders and became Upper California's first nun.

Rezanov shared the imperialistic fervor of his father-in-law Shelikhov and believed that the successors of Peter the Great had betrayed the tsar's vision of Russia's role in North America. Although the Spanish claimed their share of the condominium of "New Albion" (the coast north of San Francisco), established by the Nootka Convention of 1790 with the British, Rezanov had commented on the total lack of settlement and had discerned a future for Russian penetration into the area. In particular, he had carefully considered Discovery Bay inside the Strait of Juan de Fuca, Gray's Harbor, and the lower Columbia River as sites. As it turned out, the Russian settlement would be somewhat farther to the south.

Since Baranov did not possess the maritime strength to chase the foreigners from what he considered to be Russian waters, he attempted other stratagems. As early as 1803 he had struck a deal with an American skipper whereby the Russians would provide Aleut hunters under a Russian leader in return for transport and protection, the profits from both hunting and trading to be shared. This arrangement was repeated many times for the next decade. In the summer of 1808 Baranov sent two ships, the *Kadiak* and the *Nikolai*, southward with instructions to hunt, to attempt trade with natives, and to seek a place for a permanent settlement. The *Nikolai* ran aground near Gray's Harbor and was lost; its crew was either killed or captured by natives. The *Kadiak*, under Ivan Kuskov, was more successful, both in the hunt and in finding a site recommended for settlement. This was Bodega Bay, about fifty miles north of San Francisco.

Three years later Kuskov was sent out again, this time in the *Chirikov*, with explicit orders to found a permanent settlement in New Albion to serve as a headquarters for hunting off the California coast and as a source of agricultural products. By this time, the mouth of the Columbia was not an option since John Jacob Astor's Pacific Fur Company had established itself at what is now Astoria, Oregon, in March 1811. By June 9, 1812 (just as the armies of Napoleon were commencing the invasion of European Russia), Kuskov had supervised the construction and occupation of a site on a small inlet some twenty miles north of Bodega Bay.

The Spanish considered this new presence (named Fort Ross) to be an illegal incursion into their property but were hardly in a position to eject the Russians. They did, however, establish the San Raphael mission in 1816 as a defensive measure. Since the Spaniards refused to recognize the legal existence of Fort Ross, the Russians in 1817 negotiated a treaty with the Pomo Indians. This pact ceded territory reaching northward to the Columbia River, an area hardly under Pomo control. Matters, of course, were not changed by the Florida Treaty of 1819 whereby Spain and the United States recognized 42° north latitude as the border between their respective claims to Upper California and the Oregon Country (a boundary still existing between the states of Oregon and California). Unfortunately, for Russian plans, Fort Ross would never live up to expectations, particularly as a source of grain. As a result, there would still exist an urgent requirement to find an adequate supply of food. One possible solution to be considered was the Hawaiian Islands.

It was the visits to Hawaii by Captain James Cook (who named Hawaii the Sandwich Islands) in 1778 and 1779 that made the islands known to the peoples of Europe and North America. There are claims that the Spanish had visited earlier, but these are generally challenged despite the fact that, for more than two centuries before Cook's arrival, the annual Spanish galleon passed south of Hawaii on its western voyage from Acapulco to Manila and north of them on the return trip.

In 1790 an American vessel with its armament was captured by the Hawaiians as well as two British seamen who knew how to sail her and work the guns. These two, Isaac Davis and John Young, would become valuable advisors to Kamehameha, the rising powerful leader on the island of Hawaii. More help came from Captain George Vancouver. He arrived in 1795 in command of Cook's old ship *Discovery* and offered friendly advice to the Hawaiian chief. In that same year, Kamehameha, thanks to the technological edge of his ship, cannon, and advisors, launched his campaign for the conquest of the entire chain of islands. He succeeded in the rapid subjugation of all the major islands except Kauai. Kaumuali'i, leader of Kauai, finally recognized Kamehameha as the supreme sovereign of all the islands and was in return permitted to remain as the autonomous ruler of his own island.

In 1804, as mentioned in chapter 8, Adam Krusenstern in the *Nadezhda* and Yuri Lisiansky in the *Neva* arrived in the Hawaiian Islands. Krusenstern was singularly unimpressed by the place since he was unable to find adequate provisions during the three days he allowed himself to remain in the waters off the island of Hawaii. Lisiansky, who was not in such a hurry, spent three weeks in the islands and was able to take on ample supplies. While Kamehameha was on Oahu with his army, John Young was entrusted with matters on Hawaii. As soon as Young was made aware of the Russian presence, he arrived and facilitated provisioning. Lisiansky gave wide berth to Oahu, which was experiencing an epidemic, visited Kauai instead and so was the first Russian to meet the chief, Kaumuali'i. Baranov therefore received a first-hand account of the Hawaiian situation from Lisiansky when the latter arrived in July.

Lisiansky returned to Saint Petersburg in August 1806 in the *Neva*, and that sturdy ship was immediately prepared for a second voyage, departing in October under the command of Leonti Hagemeister and arriving in Novoarkhangelsk eleven months later. This trip was termed by the Russians the second ''round the world voyage'' (the first one being that of Krusenstern and Lisiansky). Just over a year later (November 1808), Baranov sent Hagemeister to Hawaii to assess the possibility of seeking supplies from that source. Hagemeister obviously was a very proud naval officer and did not get along at all well with Kamehameha. It seems that he preferred the company of Kaumuali'i on the island of Kauai. Accordingly, his report to Baranov upon his return to Novoarkhangelsk in late 1809 (by way of Kamchatka) was not an enthusiastic endorsement. He acknowledged that supplies were in abundance but suggested that the trade policies of Kamehameha were inimical to the interests of the Russian American Company. Since Baranov's attention by this time was diverted more toward California, no measures were taken at the time to develop Hawaii as a food source.

During the War of 1812 between the United States and Great Britain, several American skippers were happy to charter or sell their ships to the Russians. One such vessel was the *Atahualpa*, which was purchased and renamed the *Bering*. Baranov decided, in the light of the paucity of food being generated at Fort Ross, to open trade with the Sandwich Islands. Accordingly, the *Bering*, commanded by the American captain James Bennett, was sent to the island of Kauai. Here, in January 1815, the vessel ran aground in Waimea Bay. Much of the cargo was lost, and that which was saved was seized by Kaumuali'i. Bennett was finally able to gain passage back to Alaska with the unwelcome news for Baranov.

In Novoarkhangelsk at this time was the ship *Suvorov* which had been sailed from Saint Petersburg under the command of Navy Lieutenant Mikhail Lazarev, on the third of the ''round the world voyages.'' (During the trip, Lazarev discovered and named Suvorov, now Suwarrow, Atoll in the Cook Islands.) A passenger on the *Suvorov* was Georg Schaffer, a young German medical doctor who had spent some years as a surgeon in Moscow. When word arrived of the fate of the *Bering*, Baranov immediately made plans to recover the cargo of furs held by Kaumuali'i. Lazarev and Baranov managed to alienate each other to the point that the former would not comply with the latter's wishes to retrieve the furs and instead sailed back to Saint Petersburg.

Schaffer, who stayed behind, fully realized the importance of the food supply for the colonies and proposed that he see to the matter of the furs—and much more. As a result, he sailed for Hawaii on the American ship *Isabella* in mid-October of 1815. His instructions from Baranov were to establish friendly relations with Kamehameha and then to resolve the matter of the *Bering*'s cargo. Schaffer succeeded admirably in insinuating himself into the good graces of the Hawaiian king by virtue of his medical talents, which cured the monarch of a heart complaint and his favorite queen, Ka'ahumanu, of a fever. He was rewarded by being granted properties with a house on the island of Hawaii and permission to purchase lands for farming as well as a factory for Russian trade on Oahu. Schaffer's success was bound to worry the British and American merchants who had no desire to lose their favored trading position. They therefore advised the Hawaiian authorities that the Russians posed a threat to the realm. It seems that by the spring of 1816, John Young agreed with them, for he looked with disfavor upon the Russian position, especially the Russian fort on Oahu, which flew the flag of the Russian American Company.

Schaffer had been waiting patiently for ships to arrive to support him and facilitate the recovery of the *Bering*'s furs. The *Il'men'* and *Otkrytie* finally made an appearance in May 1816, but their very presence caused more local alarm and loss of favor with Kamehameha. Indeed, the king would not provide an order for Kaumuali'i to return the furs; Schaffer now proceeded to Kauai and met the local chief for the first time. The latter was quite apprehensive at first but, five days after Schaffer's arrival, consented to a remarkable series of agreements. On June 2, 1816, Kaumuali'i signed a pact that provided for the return of furs seized from the *Bering*, granted a monopoly of Kauai trade to the Russian American Company, gave permission to build Russian factories, and promised regular provision of food supplies. In return, the Russians were to provide Kaumuali'i with a fully armed ship to be paid for by sandalwood. On the same day, the ruler of Kauai signed an act of allegiance wherein he requested that the emperor of Russia receive Kauai under his protection.

Twenty-nine days later, a secret treaty was concluded between Kaumuali'i and Schaffer. This remarkable document had great ambitions indeed. Schaffer agreed that the Russians would provide arms and transportation and that he, Schaffer, would lead a force from Kauai to "reconquer" the other islands. Kaumuali'i was to provide soldiers and provisions and to pay for the Russian contribution with sandalwood. After the conquest, the Russian American Company was to receive half the island of Oahu, as well as all its sandalwood, and was to build forts and factories on the islands. All the islands were, of course, to be a protectorate of the Russian Empire.

The energetic Dr. Schaffer immediately set about building a Russian presence on the island of Kauai. A fort, named Elizabeth in honor of the wife of Alexander I, was established on the southwest shore at Waimea, flying the flag of the Russian American Company. Guards were mounted at the fort, and gardens were planted on land ceded by Kaumuali'i. Later in the year, further properties were made available to Schaffer, including those in Hanalei Valley in the northern part of the island where a second fort, named Alexandrovsk in honor of the emperor, was built. This stretch of land was even named Schaffertal ("Schaffer's valley" in German).

About two months after concluding the treaties, Schaffer signed documents committing the Russian American Company to the purchase of two American ships, the *Lydia* and the *Avon*, for use by Kaumuali'i in compliance with the treaty. The *Lydia* was an outright gift to the chief whereas the chief agreed to reimburse the cost of the *Avon* with sandalwood. The purchase agreement on the *Avon* stipulated payment in Novoarkhangelsk; therefore, the skipper, Captain Isaac Whittemore, sailed for Alaska on September 6, carrying with him the originals of the treaties signed by Schaffer and Kaumuali'i. Dr. Schaffer was now riding the crest of the wave. Unfortunately for him, matters would change drastically and soon.

Just sixteen days after the departure of the *Avon*, John Young shut down Schaffer's entire operation on Oahu, and the Russian personnel involved were sent to join Schaffer on Kauai. The American and British merchants continued to do all possible to frustrate Schaffer's designs, usually by trying to convince the Hawaiian leaders of the evil of the Russian enterprise. There was real concern about Schaffer's ultimate goals. John Young seized the fort that had been built by the Russians on Oahu and directed that it be strengthened to defend the port of Honolulu. Kamehameha felt compelled to have warriors in readiness in case of a Russian attack.

At this moment, in November 1816, Lieutenant Commander Otto von Kotsebue, who had been a midshipman with Krusenstern on his voyage of 1803–1806, sailed into Hawaiian waters in command of the *Rurik*, which flew the Russian naval ensign. Kotsebue, although only twenty-eight years of age, was in charge of a scientific effort sponsored personally by the wealthy and influential Count Nikolai Rumiantsev. Despite his youth, Kotsebue exhibited remarkable aplomb while assuming the role of a representative of the Russian throne. Earlier in the year, despite the objections of Kuskov at Fort Ross, he had negotiated with the Spanish in San Francisco, recognizing the North American coast south of the Strait of Juan de Fuca to be Spanish territory. Now, in the kingdom of Hawaii, he disavowed the actions of Schaffer as being totally without approval of the Russian government. Two weeks later, he made the same declaration to John Young on Oahu before sailing north to Alaska. This greatly undermined Schaffer's credibility, and he became increasingly isolated. By the end of the year, incidents began to occur on Kauai between Hawaiians on the one hand and Russians and their client Aleuts on the other. In January 1817, Schaffer received the unwelcome word from Baranov that purchase of the *Avon* had been repudiated and that further speculation was not warranted. Baranov directed that the two ships, the *Il'men'* and *Kadiak*, be returned to Alaska.

Kaumuali'i came to realize that Schaffer's authority was severely circum-scribed, and on June 13 he ejected the Russians from Kauai. Schaffer sent the *Il'men'* to Novoarkhangelsk and decided to sail the damaged *Kadiak* to Hono-lulu. Here indignity was heaped upon misfortune. The ship was barely able to make the harbor, and the only release for Schaffer was the generous offer of passage westward by an American skipper, Isaiah Lewis, of the *Panther*. Thus came to an end the adventures of Dr. Schaffer in Hawaii; however, because of the long time delays in communication, another few years would be required to sort the matter out fully.

Schaffer sent the original texts of the treaties signed by Kaumuali'i to Baranov in Novoarkhangelsk where they arrived on July 29, 1816. Copies forwarded directly to Saint Petersburg would not arrive until the middle of August 1817—two months after Schaffer had been ejected from Kauai. As we have seen, Baranov was disenchanted with the actions of his emissary to Hawaii; he therefore forwarded the original texts to Saint Petersburg without favorable en-dorsement. These documents arrived in Saint Petersburg just two months after the copies that were sent directly from Schaffer.

The directors of the Russian American Company in Saint Petersburg enthu-siastically approved of Schaffer's work. They sent a complimentary reply and gifts for Kaumuali'i via Captain Vasili Golovnin (whom we have met before) who departed the Baltic in the *Kamchatka* in September 1817 (i.e., before receipt of Baranov's endorsement and before knowledge of Schaffer's ouster). When the matter of the treaties was referred to the foreign ministry in January 1818, however, it met a cold response from the very conservative Count Karl Nes-selrode. By the following summer, Saint Petersburg had received letters written by Schaffer while en route back to the Russian capital, advising of the demise of his enterprise and submitting strong recommendations for decisive action to rescue the operation. His proposals had the support of the directors of the Rus-sian American Company but were opposed by Nesselrode.

The emperor himself made the final decision; he announced on June 24, 1819, that he disapproved of the act of submission signed by Kaumuali'i and asserted that relations with Hawaii should be on the same basis as those with any other sovereign country. He further directed that the gifts sent to the Pacific in the *Kamchatka* should be delivered to Kaumuali'i and an attempt be made to secure a special relationship through generous treatment. The decision and implement-ing instructions were then forwarded to Alaska with Lieutenant Zakhar Ponaf-idin, who conducted the fifth "round the world voyage" in the ship *Borodino*, arriving in Novoarkhangelsk in October 1820.

As indicated, Baranov had viewed Schaffer's actions in Hawaii with deep concern and had disavowed the purchase of the *Avon*. Baranov, constantly beset by troubles caused by the number of foreign ships in Alaskan waters, had no desire for Schaffer to enrage or offend those nations with mercantile interests in the Sandwich Islands. Also, he particularly wished to avoid any major prob-lems that might further delay his departure from the very demanding duties he bore in such a tempestuous environment. At the time of Schaffer's enterprise, Baranov was in his seventieth year and had been in the North Pacific area continuously for more than a quarter of a century. His desire was to retire in a comfortable climate. As it turned out, he did not have to wait long for his retirement.

Replacements for Baranov had twice been sent out, once in 1808 and again in 1812, but both men perished before arriving in the American colonies. Finally, Lieutenant Commander Leonti Hagemeister, who has already been featured in our story, departed Kronstadt in November 1816 in the *Kutuzov* on the fourth "round the world voyage." His instructions from the company directors included a provision that he replace Baranov if, in his judgment, it was the appropriate measure to take. It seems that there had been irregularities in the timeliness and accuracy of some of Baranov's reports (although the ultimate assessment of his stewardship was that it was remarkably free of corruption and self-aggrandizement).

Hagemeister succeeded Baranov as chief manager for the Pacific operations of the Russian American Company on January 11, 1818, and Kiril Khlebnikov became the senior administrative assistant in Novoarkhangelsk, a position he would fill for the next fourteen years. Because of health problems, Hagemeister decided in October to depart the American colonies himself and appointed Lieutenant Semen Yanovsky acting chief manager, a position he would hold until relieved by Matvei Murav'ev in September 1820. Baranov, freed of his duties now for several months, decided to depart the area in the *Kutuzov* with Hagemeister on November 27, 1818. His dreams of a quiet retirement were not to be realized, however. After so many years of rigorous existence in a demanding environment, his health had been undermined. The *Kutuzov*, after a brief stop in Guam, proceeded to Batavia in the East Indies, arriving on March 7, 1819. During a lengthy stay in that port, Baranov developed a fever to which he succumbed on April 16 when the ship was in the Sunda Strait. He was buried at sea the following day in the eastern reaches of the Indian Ocean.

11

Demise of the Russian American Company and Sale of Alaska

From the time of Baranov's departure from Novoarkhangelsk, the position of chief manager would be filled by officers of the Imperial Russian Navy, thirteen in all, from 1818 until the sale of Alaska to the United States in 1867. The rank authorized was originally lieutenant commander but was later revised upward to that of commodore. The stature of this officer corps was high in the first half of the nineteenth century. Founded by Peter the Great, the navy had enjoyed success primarily against the Swedes in the Great Northern War (1700–1721). After being neglected in the middle eighteenth century, the fleet was restored in the reign of Catherine the Great and won decisive victories over the Ottoman Empire. It was supported by Paul I (1796–1801) and his sons Alexander I (1801–1825) and Nicholas I (1825–1855). It performed well against the French and Turks in the Napoleonic period and played an important role in the historic victory of Russia and its Anglo-French allies over the Islamic navy in the battle of Navarino off the coast of Greece in 1827.

Although no Russian squadron was spared for duty in the Pacific during the period under discussion, Russian naval officers made sizable contributions in the area of maritime exploration. Already noted have been Krusenstern, Lisiansky, and Kotzebue. Other well-known exploits involved Faddei Bellingshausen who, with Mikhail Lazarev, was the discoverer of the first land inside the Antarctic Circle (1819–1821). Fedor Lutke did excellent survey work in the Bering Sea during his voyage from 1826 to 1829. As we have seen, Ferdinand Wrangel, who would be chief manager in Novoarkhangelsk from 1830 to 1835, succeeded in charting the last stretch of the Russian Arctic coast in 1823.

Other changes were in store for the Russian American Company since its twenty-year charter was due to expire in 1819. Indeed, the primary purpose of Vasili Golovnin's voyage in *Kamchatka* (1817–1819) was not just to deliver gifts for Kaumuali'i on Kauai but also to inspect the North Pacific sites and submit recommendations to the company directors. The new charter of the Russian American Company, promulgated in 1821, spelled out the duties of the chief manager in much greater detail and more precisely defined the organization for which he was responsible.

In September of the same year Emperor Alexander I, in response to the company's request, issued an *ukaz* that proclaimed a zone of denial to all except Russian subjects. This zone reached seaward 100 miles from Russian territory, which was defined as the Alaskan coast north of 51° north latitude, across the Aleutians, and down the coast of Asia through Kamchatka and the Kuril Islands, including the island of Urup. This declaration immediately met resistance from the British and Americans who, in the same year, entered into the Pacific in greatly augmented numbers in search of whales and their valuable oil. The *ukaz* also was a factor in the American decision to promulgate the Monroe Doctrine in January 1823. The lack of validity of the Russian *ukaz* lay in the fact that such an exclusion policy could not be enforced. A principal legal objection on the part of the British and Americans was that the original charter of the Russian American Company extended the company's authority only as far south as 55° rather than 51°. The matter was finally resolved through diplomacy.

By the terms of the Russo-American treaty signed on April 17, 1824, Russia recognized the United States' right to unrestricted navigation of open Alaskan waters in accordance with international law and granted permission to trade with the native population. The Americans recognized all land north of 54°40' north latitude (the southern coast of Prince of Wales Island) as being sovereign Russian territory and agreed that they would desist from trading arms and alcohol with the native Alaskans. A similar treaty was signed between Russia and Britain on February 28 the following year, which was, of necessity, more specific. After describing the east-to-west dimensions of what is now called the Alaskan "panhandle," the agreement defined the border of Alaska's hinterland with the rest of Canada as the meridian at 141° west longitude (a segment of the existing border between the United States and Canada).

As indicated previously, Fort Ross was intended not only to be the headquarters for hunting off the California coast but also to be a source of food supplies. Unfortunately, situated as it was between the coastal hills and the ocean, it was subject to heavy mists that drastically reduced the sunlight and, therefore, the agricultural productivity of the settlement. But the problems ran deeper. The early inhabitants of Fort Ross were Aleut otter hunters and Russian *promyshlenniki* (traders), not farmers. Indeed, for the first fifteen years, more effort was devoted to shipbuilding than to agriculture. Karl Schmidt, who replaced Kuskov in 1821 as commander of the installation, shifted emphasis; he devoted considerably more effort to growing food, including livestock, using the native population to augment the workforce. Within two years, Fort Ross was self-sufficient, but in spite of great efforts on the part of subsequent managers, especially Petr Kostromitinov (1830–1838), the site would be able to provide only part of the requirements of Novoarkhangelsk and none for Kamchatka or Okhotsk.

While the Spaniards were still in charge in Upper California, there was, from the time of Rezanov's visit in 1806, a modus vivendi whereby, despite strict Spanish restrictions on trade, barter flourished, particularly between Fort Ross and San Francisco. There would be an abrupt change, however, when Mexico achieved independence from Spain in 1821, for the Mexicans radically altered the economic basis of California, making San Francisco an open port. This meant that the Russians would be squeezed out of the market entirely by the higher quality, lower priced goods of the Americans and Western Europeans. Matters were not helped when the emperor of Russia, strongly influenced by the system of "legitimacy" stemming from the Congress of Vienna, refused to recognize the government of Mexico as legitimate.

During this period, the availability of sea otters was decreasing with the result that the expense of supporting Fort Ross greatly exceeded any advantages the site was intended to provide. By the late 1830s, American immigrants were beginning to purchase and settle on land that would restrict any further expansion of the Fort Ross settlement. In view of these mounting circumstances, the emperor decided in the spring of 1839 that Fort Ross should be abandoned. As a result, the land, cattle, and buildings all were sold to John Sutter, an American of Swiss birth whose name is forever linked to the gold rush of 1849 since it stemmed from gold discovered on his lands near Sacramento. The purchase price was approximately $30,000.

The Russian American Company, as we have seen, attempted to provision its sites by various means: the long trek across eastern Asia, from Fort Ross, from Hawaii, and through "round the world voyages." The company also regularly depended on supplies carried around Cape Horn by individual traders, particularly the Americans. Two major attempts were made to institutionalize such support from non-Russian sources. The first involved John Jacob Astor and his trading empire. Astor had grandiose plans to dominate the fur trade and wield virtual sovereignty over the Pacific Northwest at the expense of the British North West and Hudson's Bay companies. Toward this end, he commenced negotiations with the Russian minister to Washington, Andrei Dashkov, in 1809. His aim was to be designated the sole-source supplier of Russian needs in the North Pacific and to assume the role of close ally of the Russian American Company in cooperative fur-trapping operations. A year and a half later, an agreement was finally reached in Saint Petersburg which confirmed the arrangement since, in the Russian view, this would drive out the pesky individual American traders. But it was not to be. The War of 1812, which cost Astor most of his trading posts, including the one at the mouth of the Columbia River, drove his ships from competition.

In Astor's place now was the North West Company (a Canadian firm) which, in 1821, was merged into the Hudson's Bay Company. This powerful organization would flourish under the dynamic leadership of George Simpson for the next thirty-five years. It now dominated the entire area north of the Columbia River and so was face to face with the Russian American Company. In the middle 1830s, the British saw a need to bring furs out of the interior down the Stikine River, which enters the ocean in the Alaskan panhandle. The problem was solved by a meeting held in Hamburg, Germany, in 1837 between Ferdinand Wrangel, who had been the chief manager in Novoarkhangelsk from 1830 to 1835, and George Simpson. The matter of the Stikine River was settled to mutual satisfaction by a lease to the British of territory on either side of the river's mouth. At the same time, it was agreed that the Hudson's Bay Company would become a regular provisioner of the Russian American colonies. This was possible because of the highly successful farming efforts the company had launched in the Puget Sound area and the Willamette River valley. The arrangement, however, would be short-lived since the Oregon Treaty of 1846 ceded all of the mainland south of the 49th parallel of latitude to the United States, thereby depriving the Hudson's Bay Company of its agricultural base.

The charter of the Russian American Company was renewed for a period of twenty years in 1842. However, by this time, serious questions were being asked about the likely future of the company and, for that matter, of the Russian American colonies themselves. After the sale of Fort Ross in 1841, Russian claims were nowhere asserted south of 54°40'. The Oregon Treaty terminated any doubt about the status of the Oregon Country by dividing it between Britain and America. Then, two years later, the Mexican War was terminated by the Treaty of Guadalupe-Hidalgo, which ceded all of Upper California to the United States. Within a year after that, the discovery of gold at Sutter's Mill had ensured the growth of a sizable American population in the region and the development of San Francisco as an American port.

Next, the conduct of the Crimean War would bring into clear focus just how vulnerable the Russian American possessions could be to predations of major naval powers. Ironically, it was the overwhelming success of Russian naval technology (rifled, shell-firing guns) in the total destruction of the Turkish fleet at Sinop on the southern coast of the Black Sea ("Russian atrocity") that would be used as the casus belli for entry into the war by the British and French in March 1854. Although, as we shall see, the Russians made good account of themselves in the Pacific phase of the Crimean War, the successes of the Anglo-French allies in the Crimea drove home the vulnerability of far-flung areas to naval forces. Actually, the Russian American colonies were spared embarrassment primarily because of the wise agreement concluded between the Russian American Company and the Hudson's Bay Company in early 1854 which exempted their North American territories from hostilities. Nevertheless, shipping was fair game, and the Russians had to resort to chartering foreign vessels flying the flags of their parent countries.

The deeply conservative Nicholas I ("autocracy, orthodoxy, and nationalism") was indeed fortunate to pass from the scene in December 1855 and be spared the humiliation of the Treaty of Paris which concluded the Crimean War.

His son, Alexander II (ruled 1855–1881), known as the "Tsar Liberator," would usher in a new period known for its policy of *recuillement*, or looking inward, designed to cure Russia's internal ills. This would include such legislation as the emancipation of the serfs, judicial reforms, and revision of local governmental institutions. At this time, his brother and close confidant, the Grand Duke Konstantin, who was the naval minister as well, counseled against the retention of the Alaskan colonies since their proper defense would require too great an expense.

Another factor impacting on the future of the colonies included profitability. The value of the fur trade, the original raison d'être of the company, had long been drastically reduced. Efforts were made to fill the void by the extraction and shipment of other resources, such as timber, coal, and even ice. Still, the company was running a regularly rising deficit, requiring constant subsidy from the Russian government. The primary purpose of the company had thus become more strategic and political in nature rather than economic. It was as if the company were merely being reimbursed by the government for providing the administration of Russian sovereign territory.

Therefore, at the time when the third renewal of the charter of the Russian American Company was due in the early 1860s, forces were at work that were inimical to the continuation of the organization and even of the colonies themselves. Unfavorable reports on the operation of the company were submitted to a special governmental committee by two inspectors, State Counsellor Sergei Kostlivtsev and navy Captain Pavel Golovin, in 1861. Considerable wrangling ensued between the company and the governmental ministries concerned, resulting in a stalemate. The company continued to operate only by virtue of the authority of an imperial decree promulgated in 1861.

A strong advocate for detaching Russian America from the empire was the Russian minister to the United States, Edouard de Stoekl. He was directed, as early as 1857 and again in 1859, to sound out American attitudes on the future of the Russian possessions. Logically, it was the United States the Russians would approach since aggrandizement of British North America would be inconsistent with Russian goals in the "Great Game" being conducted by the Russians and British around the entire ring of Asia. Their two empires were at odds in Turkey, Persia, Afghanistan, Turkestan, and China. Thus, if sale there must be, the United States would be less threatening to the Russian Far East, and the deal might even usefully serve as a source of friction between America and Britain.

The initial feelers produced no results, and further contact was rendered infeasible by the American Civil War, which lasted from 1861 to 1865. During that conflict, significantly, the Russians gave strong moral support to the Union side. Finally, on December 28, 1866, Alexander II made the tough decision that to sell Alaska was in the best interests of the Russian state. Minister Stoekl, who attended the final session at the Winter Palace that elicited the decision, was instructed to approach American Secretary of State William Seward. Seward eagerly—too eagerly for tough bargaining—responded to the overture.

Seward's enthusiasm was widely shared on the Pacific Coast where Californians wanted a greater share of Alaskan trade and were well informed about the expiration of the charter of the Russian American Company. Indeed, a group was formed that wanted to bid for the charter. In the Washington territory there was a special desire for fishing rights in Alaskan waters. However, among most leading figures in Washington, D.C., including President Andrew Johnson, there was antipathy to expanding U.S. sovereignty over noncontiguous land. The rapid manner in which Stoekl and Seward were able to effect the purchase was therefore quite remarkable.

Conversations were begun in mid-March, and the purchase would become a reality three weeks later. Seward at first offered $5 million, a figure Stoekl was authorized to accept. However, aware of the secretary of state's eagerness, he held out successfully for the figure of $7 million. The United States then agreed to pay an additional $200,000 to cover exchange fees (an amount that neatly equated to the debt of the Russian American Company). This agreement was reached the evening of March 29, and the enthusiastic negotiators continued into the night, finally signing and sealing the treaty at four o'clock early the following morning.

There now remained the problem of securing ratification by two-thirds of the members of the U.S. Senate. The timing was optimum since Congress was nearing its spring recess. The matter was taken in hand by Senator Charles Sumner of Massachusetts. It seemed a hopeless task because of intense opposition in the Congress to the Johnson administration. To everyone's great surprise, the ratification vote, taken on April 9, was 37 to 2 in favor. It seems that much of the $200,000 of the final purchase price was liberally distributed as bribes by Stoekl to various senators.

One factor that seemed to sway some members of the Senate was the assumption, in the great surge of Manifest Destiny of the nineteenth century, that it was only a matter of time before Canada would become part of the United States, in which case Alaska would become contiguous to the rest of the country. In a sense, then, rationalization for the purchase might have been more difficult if the event had occurred three months later since, on July 1, 1867, the British North American Act granted self-governing dominion status to the Canadians.

There was considerable opposition within the Russian Empire to the sale of Alaska. This was especially true of the directors of the Russian American Company. One in particular was Admiral Vasili Zavoiko, hero of the Crimean War in the Pacific, who refused to sign the company release. Alexander II was very firm, however, and Zavoiko was banished from the capital to his estates. In such a manner did the Russian Empire, for the only time, voluntarily cede part of its territory to another nation.

12

Living with the Kiakhta System

The border established between Russia and China by the Treaty of Kiakhta in 1728 would remain static for well over a century. Such would not be the case on other borders of the Russian Empire. As we have seen, the Muscovites expanded into Kamchatka and down the Kuril Islands until they were close to the Japanese Empire. They extended their sway to the easternmost reaches of Asia, into the Pacific Ocean and onto the mainland of North America, proceeding until they encountered the power of the British and Americans.

Nor was such territorial acquisition limited to eastern regions. Peter the Great, in addition to his "window on the west" at Saint Petersburg, added a major part of the eastern shore of the northern Baltic to his empire. During the rest of the eighteenth century, Russian authority was gradually extended to the south and west, primarily at the expense of the Ottoman Empire and the kingdom of Poland. The most dramatic gains were made in the final decade of the century, during the reign of Catherine the Great, when the Zaporog Cossacks of the southern Ukraine were engulfed, and the Turks were pushed out of the northern littoral of the Black Sea. The third and final partition of Poland granted Russia a common border with Prussia and the Holy Roman Empire.

As the result of the Napoleonic Wars, Russian sovereignty was extended over Finland, and Russian arms earned great respect elsewhere in Europe. During the first half of the nineteenth century, Russian armies repeatedly launched campaigns against the Turkish sultan in the Balkans and Transcaucasus. So successful were the Russians that Great Britain became increasingly concerned for the viability of the Ottoman Empire and took measures to ensure that Russia would not expand into the Mediterranean. It was this anxiety that would bring the British into the Crimean War on the side of the Turks in 1854. In short, Russian expansionist energies in the west could be appeased only at the expense of the Great Powers of Europe by the middle of the nineteenth century. As we shall see, conditions in Asia were, at the same time, in the process of changes that would help provide political power vacuums to absorb those energies.

Although the Treaty of Kiakhta provided a modus vivendi between the Russian and Chinese empires for more than a hundred years, there were many border squabbles. In these remote regions, war was not a credible alternative, and misunderstandings usually were solved in favor of the Chinese because of their threats to suspend trade. An early problem concerned a Jungarian Mongol leader named Amursana. After the death of the Jungar khan Galdan Tseweng in 1745, order in Jungaria turned to turmoil. By 1752 the young Amursana, a son-in-law of Galdan Tseweng, rose to prominence and cast his lot with the Ch'ing dynasty of China. The Ch'ien-lung emperor, deciding to solve the Jungarian problem, sent an army of conquest in 1755 which pacified the area and left Amursana in charge. Almost immediately, however, Amursana turned on the Manchus and asserted his independence. Two years later, the government in Peking sent two new armies which defeated the Jungars and reasserted Manchu rule. Amursana, among others, escaped by flight into Russia.

Peking now commenced a systematic "final solution" to the Jungarian problem. This included the slaughter of thousands of the population as well as exile of others to the wilds of Manchuria. Peking also instituted direct Manchu rule to ensure tighter control. The Chinese government wanted the return of Amursana—and his followers—from Russia in accordance with the provisions of the Kiakhta Treaty. There was a reluctance on the Russian side to comply, but the matter was solved, in part, by the death of Amursana from smallpox. In partial appeasement of the Chinese side, Amursana's frozen body was transported from Tobolsk to Kiakhta for viewing in the spring of 1762. However, the Russians then buried the body, refusing the Chinese request that it be handed over for "posthumous punishment." The affair would fester for the next four years and be exacerbated by other misunderstandings to the point where the Chinese curtailed trade late in 1762 and suspended it three years later. Loss of revenues from duty on imports finally induced the Russians to accede to an agreement, signed at Kiakhta on October 18, 1768, that was a revision to Article X of the Treaty of Kiakhta. It prescribed explicit punishment for different crimes, such as public execution for murders, and even described the instrument for floggings: the lash for Chinese and the knout for Russians. The Chinese did concede that the new article would apply only to future criminals, including defectors. Copies of the treaty were signed in three languages: Russian, Manchu, and Mongol.

Another crisis arose just three years later when the Torgut Mongols (chapter 6) requested—and received—permission from the Ch'ien-lung emperor to return from the Volga to their old haunts. This meant that 90,000 Torguts now moved into Jungaria, which had been drastically depopulated by the Manchus in the late 1750s. The Russians objected on the grounds that the Torguts were defectors from the Russian Empire. The Ch'ien-lung emperor insisted, however, that they were merely nomadic peoples returning to ranges denied them for more than a century and a half. His decision prevailed.

A series of incidents, occurring in the early 1780s, resulted in the closure of the border by the Chinese in 1785. Not for seven years would it be reopened, and then only after the signature of an agreement couched in traditional Chinese terminology. An example from the first paragraph reads: "The mutual trade at Kiakhta really did not benefit China, but because the Great Emperor loves all human beings, he sympathizes with your little people who are poor and miserable; and because your senate has appealed to His Imperial Majesty, He has deigned to approve their petition."[1] This protocol, signed by both sides at Kiakhta on February 8, 1792, indicated both the desire of the Russians to reinstitute trade and the preoccupation of Catherine the Great with the Turkish War then in progress.

Early in the reign of Alexander I (ruled 1801–1825), it was decided in Saint Petersburg that the time had come to alter the relationship with China. Accordingly, a great embassy, reminiscent of those a century before, was proposed. The Ch'ien-lung emperor had abdicated the throne in favor of his fifteenth son in 1796 (to show his veneration for his grandfather, the K'ang-hsi emperor, by not exceeding that worthy's sixty-year reign). The new ruler, known as the Chia-ch'ing emperor (ruled 1796–1820), welcomed the idea of a tributary mission from the Russians. The embassy, under the leadership of Count Yuri Golovkin, comprised 200 luminaries, including scientists and linguists. Golovkin's instructions were ambitious, seeking to establish European-style relations with the Chinese Empire. Specifically sought were trade anywhere along the common Russo-Chinese border, entry for Russian caravans into any part of China, consent for Russian ships to trade at Canton, agreement for Russian navigation of the Amur River (in order to facilitate supply support for the Russian American Company), establishment of consulates at Canton and on the Amur, and assignment of a Russian diplomatic agent to be resident in Peking (or, failing this, recognition of the Russian ecclesiastical mission as a commercial agent).

The embassy arrived at Kiakhta on October 29, 1805. The prospects of success in its mission were dim indeed for the traditional reasons of differences of Chinese and Western concepts of world order. The Chinese made elaborate preparations to receive the visitors, but the entire enterprise crumbled in January 1806 at Urga where Golovkin was told he must perform the kowtow before a tablet representing the emperor. He flatly refused and returned to the border. Even if he had complied with the Chinese demand, it is highly unlikely that any progress would have been realized. At the very time Golovkin was approaching Urga, the skippers Krusenstern and Lisiansky, heroes of the first Russian "round the world voyage," were in Canton managing, with great difficulty, to trade their furs. Indeed, the day after they sailed, a directive arrived from Peking which would have prevented their departure. If he had gone on to Peking, Golovkin would certainly have encountered a hornet's nest.

Despite the seeming acceptance of the Kiakhta System by official Russian circles, there had been, from the time of the conclusion of the treaty itself, revisionist voices. Lorents Lange, as early as the 1730s, regularly proposed to the government that Russia should insist on the right to navigation of the Amur River. The historian Gerhard Muller was one of the scholars intimately involved in the second Kamchatka expedition and was the first real student of Russian eastward expansion. Based on the geographical knowledge thus acquired, he submitted a memorandum to the Russian government in 1741 suggesting a revision of the border which was so vaguely defined by the Treaty of Nerchinsk (the northern watershed of the Amur). Twenty-two years later, in a "secret" memorandum to the Senate, he detailed the advantages of a successful war against China, including the occupation of the Amur valley. By the mid-1750s Fedor Soimonov, later governor-general of Siberia, had planned an expedition down the Shilka River, hoping to chart the Amur, but was turned back by the Manchus. He envisioned a system of colonization based on the town of Nerchinsk.

Nevertheless, such voices became muted after conclusion of the supplement to the Treaty of Kiakhta in 1768. Indeed, the matter then would lie dormant for eight full decades. During that time, however, fatal events would be taking place in China. The glory of the High Ch'ing, exemplified by the reign of the Ch'ien-lung emperor who addressed Catherine II of Russia and George III of Britain as one would naughty children, steadily dimmed commencing with the advent of the nineteenth century. It was not just the Chinese dynastic cycle in operation, but rather a new, insidious factor which came into play—opium.

As the Ch'ien-lung emperor stated in his lectures to the Western monarchs, China lacked nothing in resources or wares and therefore had no need for trade. Thus precious metals streamed into the Middle Kingdom to pay for the Chinese products that were so sought after by the West. By the end of the eighteenth century, however, the British East India Company had discovered a substitute for gold and silver in the debilitating derivative of the Indian poppy. The net result was a reversal of the flow of metals and an opium drug problem of epic proportions in southern China, centered on the port city of Canton (to which site all trade with the Western maritime powers was restricted).

A forthright Chinese attempt under the energetic direction of Commissioner Lin Tse-hsu to stamp out the trade resulted in the First Opium War of 1839–1842 between Britain and China. The technological backwardness of the Ch'ing army and navy was mercilessly exposed to the world. Almost a century of peace had taken its toll as well as the ascendancy of the scholar-bureaucrat over the military man. As a result, China was humbled by the Treaty of Nanking of 1842. The Chinese were forced to abolish their monopolistic trade system and to accept a fixed tariff. They agreed to open five ports to trade, permitting resident consuls and merchants in those ports. The island of Hong Kong was ceded to the British "in perpetuity," and the Chinese government was obliged to pay an indemnity of $21 million.

To certain observers in Saint Petersburg, the results of the Opium War had meaningful prospects. On the one hand, they were concerned that China might become another India, with the British gradually taking over the entire country. On the other hand, there was the clear recognition of Chinese weakness as an invitation for Russia to seek territorial and commercial advantages. One indirect result of the Opium War was the advent of the Taiping Rebellion (1850–1864). This cataclysmic event, which would result in millions of deaths, rocked the Ch'ing dynasty to its very roots. Troops were withdrawn from border areas to defend against the insurgents. In the end, the dynasty was saved not by the Manchu Banners or by the Green Standard Army but rather by the provincial militias organized by Chinese governors, such as Li Hung-chang and Tso Tsung-t'ang.

A further factor that would draw increased Russian attention to Chinese lands was the attitude of the Ch'ing emperors toward Manchuria. Interestingly, the Ch'ien-lung emperor, who was concerned about repeopling the Jungar basin, initiated a policy that prevented migration of Han Chinese into Manchuria. This was designed to preserve what he considered the true patrimony of the Manchus as a land whither they could repair to renew their warlike qualities in the hunt. As a result, the northernmost part, Heilungchiang Province (which included most of the lands along the Amur River), remained a very sparsely populated space that was only occasionally patrolled by Manchu border units.

Another consideration was the Russian ecclesiastical mission and the language students who had been provided for in the Treaty of Kiakhta. From the very beginning, the ecclesiastical mission had virtually no flock to attend to, and even that lot spoke little or no Russian. The clergymen sent to Peking distinguished themselves more by drunkenness and outrageous behavior than by their missionary zeal. Much more successful had been the efforts of a few of the language students, one of whom, Aleksei Leontev, was of great value in negotiating the Convention of 1768. However, by the eighth decade of the eighteenth century, the realization that the mission had great potential value other than propagation of the faith resulted in the assignment of persons of greater quality and intelligence. The archimandrite Ioakim Shishkovsky, who arrived in Peking in 1781, received instructions to conduct surreptitious intelligence gathering.

The mission was extraordinary in that it occupied the premises of the *O-lo-ssu Kuan*, which had served as the Russian hostel for the caravans. Thus the site, in the southern part of the Manchu City of Peking, continued to maintain a Russian identity, the only location in the city associated with a European country. It even boasted a satellite location since one of the responsibilities of the mission was the Albazinian church, in the northeast sector of the Manchu City. Here dwelt the bulk, usually less than a dozen, of the Orthodox faithful. In the 1800s, even greater care was taken in choosing the members of the mission so that by the middle part of the century a veritable Russian embassy was functioning in the heart of the Ch'ing capital.

Meanwhile, voices in Russia encouraging a reexamination of the Kiakhta system were rising. Yet, as long as Karl Nesselrode continued to encumber the position of foreign minister (he did so from 1816 to 1856), there would be strong resistance to any deviation from correct observation of the terms of the Kiakhta Treaty. From the very signing of the treaty, Russian fur trappers had regularly ranged into the Amur side of the watershed in search of pelts, but official violations were very rare. Therefore not until the fifth decade of the nineteenth century, in the wake of the Opium War and the Treaty of Nanking, would Russian official activity in the region become manifest.

In the two years 1843 to 1845, a noted scholar and energetic explorer named Aleksandr von Middendorf led an expedition that traversed the Taimyr Peninsula, Yakutia, eastward to the Sea of Okhotsk, and then proceeded westward along the Amur side of the river's northern watershed. He discovered that the Chinese indeed had put markers along the border but that they were located on the Amur tributaries at the upstream limit of navigability. They were, therefore, somewhat to the south of the real watershed. His report, together with his maps, stimulated a new interest in the area.

It might do well at this point to review both the gradual Russian advance southward along the eastern coast of Asia and the prevailing view of geographers as to the relationship of Sakhalin to the Asian mainland. The port of Okhotsk, the first Russian toehold on the Sea of Okhotsk, had been recognized for its shortcomings as a port by the time of Vitus Bering's activities in the North Pacific. Primarily, its handicap was its lack of elevation. It flooded readily, the harbor regularly silted up, and fresh water was a major supply problem. Also, as described in chapter 8, the overland route between Okhotsk and Yakutsk was a huge headache. After seemingly endless indecision, measures were finally initiated to build a new harbor at Aian, 275 miles farther down the coast. The survey of the harbor in 1840 and commencement of port construction three years later were under the direction of Lieutenant Vasili Zavoiko of the Imperial Russian Navy. By 1845 the transportation arrangements from Yakutsk were completed; Aian now provided a much more accessible and greatly improved port facility. However, events we shall discuss shortly would rapidly relegate it to obscurity.

By the 1840s, 200 years had elapsed since Poiarkov's expedition down the Amur and 150 years since the Russians had been pushed out of the Amur basin. Hence, knowledge of the geography had become dim indeed. The whereabouts and configuration of the estuary of the Amur were unknown. The true nature of Sakhalin was generally a riddle—was it a peninsula or an island? The voyages of discovery by La Pérouse in 1787 and William Broughton exactly a decade later, both of which approached the Tartarsky Strait from the south, led general European opinion to the conclusion that Sakhalin was a peninsula. This tended to be confirmed by Krusenstern, who approached the strait from the north in 1805. As we have seen, those few Japanese who were interested were aware of the insular properties of Sakhalin by virtue of the explorations of Mamiya Rinzo in 1808 and 1809. By the 1840s, however, no Europeans were cognizant of this or of the location of the mouth of the Amur River.

Now, with Aleksandr von Middendorf's report in hand, it was decided in Saint Petersburg to launch an expedition, albeit very quietly. The Russian American Company was given the task and admonished to maintain a low profile. Virginia tobacco was even issued to the crew so that in the event of challenge by the Manchus, they could claim their identity as Americans. Ensign Aleksandr Gavrilov, embarked in the *Konstantin*, was sent out in 1846 from Novoarkhangelsk to Aian and thence south toward Sakhalin. Gavrilov was beset by bad weather, but he located the Amur and ascended it some miles in a small boat. However, he failed to find a fairway and concluded that the river could be entered only by vessels of very shallow draft. Because of weather conditions and time constraints, he was unable to determine the insularity of Sakhalin.

Based on Gavrilov's report and the adverse attitude of Foreign Minister Nesselrode, the government for the moment seemed to lose its enthusiasm for taking a more aggressive line toward the Amur. However, just a year later, one of Russia's greatest imperialists, Nikolai Nikolaevich Murav'ev, would be appointed governor-general of Eastern Siberia. The ensuing thirteen years would ensure the demise of the Kiakhta System.

NOTE

1. Lo-shu Fu, *A Documentary Chronicle of Sino-Western Relations (1644–1820)*, vol. 1 (Tucson: University of Arizona Press, 1966), 322.

13

A New
Russo-Chinese Border
in the Far East

Nikolai Murav'ev was born into an aristocratic family of modest means in 1809. He sought his fortune in the army, serving first with distinction in the Caucasus. Rising rapidly, he was designated governor of the province of Tula by his thirtieth year. It was here that he made a very favorable impression on Nicholas I during an interview on the imperial train as it was passing through the province. As a result, he was chosen to become the governor-general of East Siberia in 1847. He was thirty-eight years old and a major general.

From the time of Boris Godunov in the sixteenth century, the Muscovite capital of Siberia had been Tobolsk on the Irtysh River. Despite its great distance from the power centers of East Asia, Tobolsk would be the seat of Russian authority in Asiatic Russia for almost two and a half centuries. Finally, the Russian reformer Mikhail Speransky, while in disfavor with the court of Alexander I and serving as governor-general of Siberia at Tobolsk, recommended certain administrative reforms. One that was approved in 1821 was the division of the Russian Empire east of the Urals into West Siberia and East Siberia, separated at the Yenisei River, each to be governed by a separate governor-general. The new capital for East Siberia was Irkutsk. Also established in 1821, at the suggestion of the farsighted Speransky, was a Siberian Committee to provide a coordinated policy for the vast realm of Russian Asia, but preoccupation with wars and radical movements in Europe rendered this committee moribund, and it was disbanded in 1838.

Irkutsk, whither Murav'ev was bound to assume his new duties, was situated next to Lake Baikal, and so was very close to the Chinese Empire. It was a dynamic environment spiced by the presence of numerous intellectuals exiled from Europe. Included were many Poles and even Decembrists (those who staged a brief attempt at revolution at the time of the death of Emperor Alexander I in December 1825) who by now had endured more than two decades of punishment.

While in Saint Petersburg in the winter of 1847–1848, preparing for his new duties, Murav'ev soon discovered that he would have many masters in the imperial bureaucracy. One of his first recommendations therefore, readily adopted by the emperor, was the establishment of a successor to Speransky's former Siberian Committee, renamed the Amur Committee, to coordinate policy in the Amur basin. Of particular importance was the designation in 1850 of Crown Prince Alexander, who would reign later as Alexander II from 1855 to 1881, to chair the committee. Before leaving the Russian capital, Murav'ev arranged to have Lieutenant Commander Gennadi Nevelskoi dispatched to the Far East in a newly constructed vessel, the *Baikal*. The first directive of the Amur Committee authorized a "small naval expedition"[1] to scour the shores of the Sea of Okhotsk to learn if there were any European ships in the area. If any were discovered, their presence was to be reported to the Chinese. Nevelskoi was directed by Murav'ev to explore the southeastern shores of the Sea of Okhotsk, although it was understood between the two of them that the goal was to find the fairway at the mouth of the Amur.

The first move toward the great river was actually taken by the Russian American Company in the summer of 1849. A small group, under an exile named D. I. Orlov, was sent in *baidarki* from the port of Aian south along the Okhotsk coast toward the Amur to scout trade with the Giliak peoples who lived in the region. The following summer, Orlov and a larger group now came by land from Aian to establish a trading center at Petrovskoe about twenty-five miles north of the mouth of the Amur.

In contrast to these tentative moves, Commander Nevelskoi, who never permitted bureaucratic timidity in his superiors to inhibit his passion for extending the sway of the Russian Empire, sailed from the north into the waters separating the mainland of Asia from Sakhalin in the summer of 1849. Through sheer dogged persistence, he braved daunting elements, including sandbars and rocks, to find the fairway of the Amur. He then pressed southward and traversed the narrowest part of the Tatarsky Strait, formed by Cape Lazarev on the mainland side. In one bold move, he had discovered the navigable entrance to the Amur and had established the fact of Sakhalin's insularity. This knowledge was not published in the standard manner of warnings to mariners but rather was tightly held as a Russian state secret.

Nevelskoi returned the next year with supplies and, in direct contravention of explicit orders, entered the Amur and established a post, raised the Russian flag, and called the site Nikolaevsk in honor of his tsar. When news of this event reached Saint Petersburg, Foreign Minister Nesselrode was apoplectic, and there was call for a court-martial. Nicholas I, however, made his famous comment that "Where once the Russian flag is raised, it must not be lowered."[2] Nevertheless, amplifying instructions cautioned that if other European powers were to learn of the fact and were to object, the prescribed answer was that Nikolaevsk was merely a trading post of the Russian American Company. In the course of the next three years, the energetic Nevelskoi established sites on Sakhalin, elsewhere on the lower Amur, and on the seacoast south of the Amur.

After Murav'ev assumed his gubernatorial duties, he set about familiarizing himself personally with the geography of his vast domains. He became the first governor-general to take the overland track to the Sea of Okhotsk and thence to Petropavlovsk on Kamchatka, a trek he made in 1849. One result was to designate Petropavlovsk in place of Okhotsk as the center for Russian naval strength in the Pacific. His time for the rest of 1849 and 1850 was largely taken up defending the bold actions of Nevelskoi before the Amur Committee. Murav'ev was extremely fearful that, if Russia did not act, the British and Americans would shortly be on the banks of the Amur. He was very fortunate that in 1850 the thirteenth ecclesiastical mission arrived in Peking. The new archimandrite was Palladi, a true student of the Chinese. He had already served in the twelfth mission and was fluent in the language. During his tenure, a steady flow of intelligence would be forthcoming from Peking to Irkutsk.

There was virtually no military force at Murav'ev's disposal until he convinced the Amur Committee to convert 20,000 mining serfs to Cossacks. Thus reinforced, and with Russians now resident in the lower Amur, Murav'ev sought authority to send Cossack reinforcements down the river to Nikolaevsk and points beyond. Approval was forthcoming, but the imperial proviso cautioned that there was to be "no smell of gun powder."[3] Murav'ev was ready to move by the time the Amur was ice free in early May 1854. His written advance notice to the Tushetu khan in Urga was purposely not sent until April (relayed to and received in Peking in July); in it, he stated that the British had occupied Russian island possessions in the Pacific and that he was on his way to expel them. The stunned Manchu governor at Aigun could do nothing other than to let the flotilla of barges, led by a steamer (built in Nerchinsk) and carrying supplies and 1,000 armed men, pass. By being pleasant but firm, Murav'ev successfully arrived at Nikolaevsk at the end of June. He immediately sent 300 troops to reinforce Petropavlovsk on Kamchatka.

Murav'ev had made a shrewd—or lucky—guess, for word was received in July about the entry of Britain and France into the Crimean War. During this time an allied squadron had been in pursuit of the Russian frigate *Aurora* across the Pacific, from Chile toward Kamchatka. This would lead to the main phase of operations in the Pacific theater of the Crimean War. Rear Admiral Vasili Zavoiko, the commander at Petropavlovsk, positioned the *Aurora*, which had arrived ahead of her pursuers, and one other ship so that their broadsides were facing seaward. The remaining guns were transferred to augment the shore batteries. The allies arrived in late August. The Russians not only were able to withstand the allied bombardment but also routed the landing force with a bayonet charge that inflicted more than 300 casualties. Allied gloom was intensified by the suicide of Rear Admiral David Price the night before the abortive attack.

Murav'ev realized how vulnerable Petropavlovsk was to a concerted naval attack; therefore, he ordered Zavoiko to withdraw with all personnel and equipment. The allied fleet missed intercepting the evacuees in mid-April 1855, but a month later Commodore Charles Elliot's force spotted the Russian ships in De Kastri Bay on the mainland side of the Tatarsky Strait. Fortune entered to spare Zavoiko and his tiny force. Mists shrouded the area, and the ice between Sakhalin and the mainland broke up, permitting the Russians to negotiate the northern end of the strait and reach the safety of the Amur. The British, still unaware of Nevelskoi's discoveries, relied on their own charts which indicated a bay to the north of them; only later in the year would they learn the truth about the insular nature of Sakhalin. The Russian secret had been well kept from the rest of the maritime world for six years.

Also in 1855, Murav'ev sent an even larger flotilla down the river, numbering 3,000 people, including settlers. The Russians apprised the Manchus of their success against the despised British the previous year as rationalization for continued navigation of the Amur. The Chinese, however, were not impressed. They issued an edict stating firmly that there was no valid Russian claim to such use of the river and that it must cease when the need to defend against the British was ended.

Murav'ev could find no legal basis for Russian penetration of the Amur basin. Although the Treaty of Nerchinsk was somewhat vague, and there had never been a joint survey to show exactly the location of the watershed on maps, no feat of legerdemain could produce a credible Russian case. This was particularly true so long as Karl Nesselrode was the foreign minister. However, that worthy was a casualty of the Crimean War and in 1856 was replaced by Alexander Gorchakov (who would serve as foreign minister for the next twenty-six years). Still, a catalyst was required to effect a change in the Far East. It would be provided by the British and French.

The Arrow War, sometimes called the Second Opium War, grew out of differences concerning implementation of the provisions of the Treaty of Nanking which had concluded the First Opium War in 1842. The *Arrow* was a vessel manned by a Chinese crew, but of Hong Kong registry, which was seized by the Chinese authorities in Canton in 1856. Although difficult to envision as a casus belli, the incident took place at a time when the British were growing increasingly impatient over the continued refusal of the Ch'ing government to permit entry of their ships into Canton as provided by the terms of the 1842 treaty. Further, London had higher ambitions, such as opening more trading ports and establishing a diplomatic presence in Peking. Therefore, since the Chinese were unyielding in their refusal to apologize for the detention of the *Arrow*, the incident was seized upon by both the British and French as a basis for taking military action.

In order to exact satisfaction, an Anglo-French fleet set sail for the Far East in 1857 under the leadership of the British Lord Elgin and French Baron Gros. The Sepoy Mutiny in India caused Elgin to divert his troops temporarily to

Calcutta, but by the spring of 1858 the force had managed to capture Canton and to take position at Shanghai while contemplating future movement.

When news of these developments in the *Arrow* affair reached Saint Petersburg, Russian Foreign Minister Gorchakov observed that it was now the time to "activate Russian Far Eastern Policy."[4] Murav'ev was accorded plenipotentiary powers, and Vice Admiral Putiatin, who had negotiated the Shimoda Treaty with Japan, was sent to Peking to seek a more favored Russian position vis-à-vis the Chinese Empire. In the meantime, Governor-General Murav'ev had been increasingly active in the Amur River valley. In 1856 and 1857 he sent even more men down the Amur to settle in what was still legally Chinese territory. Then, in 1858, Murav'ev himself made a triumphal descent in an armed steamboat down the Shilka into the Amur. His instructions permitted this action but also cautioned that there was to be no employment of military force unless required to free any Russians who might be taken prisoner. When he reached Aigun, he was unable to persuade the Manchu governor, I-shan, to agree to sign a treaty placed before him. Murav'ev therefore resorted to threats and an ultimatum, followed by a series of unnerving cannonades. As previously noted, the Manchu garrisons were greatly under strength, and an intimidated I-shan, more frightened of the Russians than of his own imperial masters, finally signed the treaty on May 28, 1858. Murav'ev then continued on down the river with his large contingent of troops and colonists, establishing the settlement of Khabarovsk at the confluence of the Amur and the Ussuri rivers. By the following September, a grateful Alexander II promoted Murav'ev to the rank of full general and awarded him the title of count and the honorary suffix to his surname of "Amursky."

The Treaty of Aigun was very brief, consisting of only three short articles. The first provided that the left bank of the Amur River would henceforth be under Russian sovereignty and the right bank under Chinese sovereignty as far downstream as the confluence with the Ussuri. The land between the Ussuri and the sea was to be treated as a condominium until such later time as a more precise border might be determined. This article also stated that navigation of the Amur, Ussuri, and Sungari rivers would be forbidden to all nations other than Russia and China. The second article permitted reciprocal trade to the subjects of both nations who lived along the three rivers. The final article provided that the Chinese side would remit copies of the treaty in Manchu and Mongol to the Russians and the Russians in turn would remit copies to the Chinese in Manchu and Russian.

In the meantime, it will be remembered, Admiral Putiatin had been dispatched to Peking. When he arrived at Kiakhta in the spring of 1857, he was refused entry into the lands of the Chinese Empire by the local officials. Undismayed, he moved eastward, descended the Amur, boarded the ship *Amerika*, and sailed to Tientsin on the north China coast. Here his efforts to get to Peking were again frustrated by the Ch'ing authorities. Putiatin became convinced that he could not get to Peking without a military force—something that was not available to him. However, the British and French had powerful troop strength in the area, concentrated at Shanghai, and were preparing to force their will on the Chinese Empire. He quickly made his way to Shanghai.

Although Putiatin possessed no forces, his presence was welcome by virtue of his charm, his interpreters, and his knowledge of the waters off northeastern Asia. He was persuasive in confirming the allies' belief that a show of real military force would be required in the region of Tientsin, the port city for Peking. Accordingly, Anglo-French forces moved northward and stormed the Taku forts which protected the water approaches to Tientsin. With the forts in allied hands, Putiatin offered himself as a mediator, and the Chinese agreed to negotiations which resulted in the Treaties of Tientsin. In the case of the British, French, and American pacts, the Chinese granted all but one of the concessions demanded (permanent diplomatic representation in Peking). Granted were an expanded number of treaty ports, access to the interior, diplomatic representation, payment of an indemnity, and exchange of ratifications at Peking within one year.

Unknown to the allies, the treaty negotiated at Tientsin by Putiatin and signed on June 13, 1858, was somewhat different. While the others kept squeezing more concessions from the Chinese, Putiatin had sweetened his approach with the offer of cannon, military instructors, and 20,000 rifles. His treaty provided for joint demarcation of Sino-Russian frontiers "not as yet determined." Thus Putiatin, unaware of the agreement concluded sixteen days earlier by Murav'ev in Aigun, had made the same territorial claims but was forced to settle for vague wording which possibly could be construed as not incompatible with his demands. The treaty also agreed that correspondence in the future would be conducted between the Russian Foreign Ministry and the senior member of the Chinese Council of State. Provision was made as well for the designation of ad hoc emissaries to each other's capitals to be received by the appropriate senior ministers. Russia was to enjoy most-favored-nation status; six ports were opened; consuls were authorized in all land and sea ports; and Orthodox missionaries, with proper passports, were permitted to propagate the faith. About the only advantage gained by the Chinese was that, in the future, the cost of the ecclesiastical mission and language school would be borne by Russia. This Russo-Chinese treaty set a new pattern in that the copies were written in Russian, Manchu, and Chinese.

The allies departed Tientsin in the belief that their mission was accomplished. However, the Chinese were extremely reluctant to play host to Westerners in Peking and attempted to have ratifications exchanged in Shanghai instead. The British and French were adamant, and in June 1859 they attempted to force a passage by the Taku forts to proceed up the Pei-ho River toward Peking. This evolution was very casually undertaken, and the allies were surprised and embarrassed when they were repulsed by the determined defenders. The following year, Lord Elgin and Baron Gros would again bring military force to bear.

The success of the Chinese in repulsing the allied attack on the Taku forts emboldened them to refuse ratification of the two treaties signed with Murav'ev and Putiatin. This action—or inaction—would bring onto the stage an aristocratic, twenty-seven-year-old major general named Nikolai Pavlovich Ignat'ev. He had already been an aide to the tsar, a military agent in London, and a plenipotentiary in Paris at the conclusion of the Crimean War, and he had been sent on a delicate diplomatic mission to the khanates of Central Asia.

In March 1859 Ignat'ev was ordered to accompany the Russian weapons and instructors to China in accordance with the understanding reached between the Chinese and Putiatin. At the Russo-Chinese border, he learned of the new attitude of the Hsien-feng emperor (ruled 1850–1861) toward the recent treaties, including a refusal to receive the rifles and instructors. Undaunted, and with remarkable aplomb, the young general proceeded to Peking, lived in the Russian ecclesiastical mission, and tried, with notable lack of success, to persuade the Manchu government to ratify the Aigun and Tientsin treaties.

Just as the future looked darkest to Ignat'ev, he caught wind of the planned movement of Lord Elgin's allied fleet. He managed rapid overland travel to Tientsin and thence proceeded by a Russian ship to rendezvous with the allied leaders who were then in Shanghai. Like Admiral Putiatin two years before, the young Russian general proceeded to charm Elgin and Gros. Like Putiatin, Ignat'ev had no soldiers or naval forces; rather, his value to the British and French was his knowledge of northern China. Not only did he have a map of Peking but he was accompanied by interpreters who spoke the Peking dialect and Manchu.

Ignat'ev therefore became a welcome addition to the expedition to Peking, although neither Elgin nor Gros had the slightest idea that Ignat'ev was after much bigger game than having diplomats resident in Peking. As had Putiatin before, Ignat'ev now encouraged the allied military advance into northern China. By October 1860, the allied forces had landed, retaken the Taku forts, and fought their way overland to the walls of Peking. The emperor fled northward to Jehol, leaving his brother, Prince Kung, to handle matters of state. At this juncture, Ignat'ev maneuvered himself into the position of mediator between the allies and the Chinese.

It was the French and Chinese especially who sought the young Russian to serve as arbiter. The Ch'ing authorities were fearful of the British and deeply resentful of their conduct; therefore, Ignat'ev preyed on this fear and hate to drive a hard bargain for his services: general approval of Russia's territorial demands. At the same time, allied solidarity was being sorely tried by policy differences in Europe, and the French were not nearly as insistent on treaty matters as were the British. Thus Baron Gros saw in the Russian diplomat the best key to a speedy termination of the matter. Ignat'ev obliged the allies by persuading the Chinese to accept all their demands. On the other hand, he proved his good intentions toward the Ch'ing negotiators by convincing the allies not to place ambassadors at Peking until a somewhat later date.

The Anglo-Chinese Convention of Peking, signed on October 24, 1860, not only ratified the Treaty of Tientsin between those two nations but also ceded to Great Britain the Kowloon Peninsula (about 3.5 square miles on the mainland directly opposite Hong Kong Island) in perpetuity. The Franco-Chinese Convention was signed the following day, and Ignat'ev now intensified his negotiations with the Chinese. In addition to ratification of the Sino-Russian Treaty of Tientsin, he pressed for the cession of both "Amuria" (the territory on the left bank of the Amur) and "Ussuria" (the territory on the right bank of the Ussuri and lower Amur, now known as the Maritime District) to Russia. He convinced the Chinese that the allies would support his position and warned that their troops would depart only at his request. Then, wishing the French and British presence no longer than necessary to his plans, he persuaded Elgin that because the winter weather of Peking was singularly hostile to the health of Westerners, the troops must be withdrawn to the south.

Finally, on November 14, Ignat'ev achieved all his objectives. The Russo-Chinese Convention of Peking, signed on that date, ratified the Treaty of Tientsin; it also "confirmed and clarified"[5] the terms of the Treaty of Aigun by agreeing that "henceforth" all territory north of the Amur and east of the Ussuri rivers was to be part of the Russian Empire. Ignat'ev had managed this coup totally without British or French knowledge.

The young diplomat had succeeded in the transfer of 350,000 square miles of territory from Chinese to Russian sovereignty in East Asia. The reasons for such dramatic Russian successes in the sixth decade of the nineteenth century are not hard to find. The Russians possessed a superior intelligence source in the ecclesiastical mission and Manchu and Chinese interpreters from the language school associated with it. They also practiced much tighter state security of information, such as Nevelskoi's discoveries. Thanks to centuries of association with members of the Mongoloid race, the Russians did not exhibit the same sense of racial superiority that was so evident among the other Western powers. There was as well the advantage of continuity. Gorchakov served as Russian foreign minister for twenty-six years. In Great Britain, continuity could be assured only until the next election. There was, on the part of the Russian diplomats and officers—Murav'ev-Amursky, Nevelskoi, Putiatin, and Ignat'ev—a total dedication to state and emperor. And, finally, the Russians were extraordinarily lucky, particularly in timing. The allied application of military force came at the most opportune of times. After the Conventions of Peking in 1860, the British would assert a dominating presence in China. A year later, the Russians would have been prevented from taking such actions. Ignat'ev fully realized this; it was the reason why he was so determined to have the allies ease their requirement for immediate positioning of diplomats in Peking. As he stated, "It was quite obvious that the English Minister who would take up residence in Peking after the recent disasters for the Manchus would be the sole Master of China."[6]

NOTES

1. P. V. Shumakher, "K istorii priobreteniia Amura; snoshenii s kitaem s 1848 po 1860 god," *Russkii Arkhiv* (1878), 265.

2. P. I. Kobanov, *Amurskii Vopros* (Blagoveshchensk: Amurskoe knizhnoe izdatel'stvo, 1959), 131.

3. Shumakher, "K istorii," 277.

4. I. P. Barsukhov, *Graf Nikolai Nikolaevich Murav'ev-Amurskii po ego pis'mam, offitsial'nym dokumentam, razskazam sovremennikov i pechatnym istochnikam*, vol. 1 (Moscow: Synodal'naia tipografia, 1891), 287.

5. William Frederick Mayers, ed., *Treaties between the Empire of China and Foreign Powers, etc.* (Shanghai: *North China Herald* Office, 1902), 100.

6. John Evans, *The Russo-Chinese Crisis: N. P. Ignatiev's Mission to Peking, 1859–1860* [Translation of Ignat'ev's report on his mission to Peking] (Newtonville, Mass.: Oriental Research Partners, 1987), 132–33.

2. Jenghis Khan (1162–1227). Creator of the Mongol Empire. His grandsons ruled the greatest land power in history.

3. Ivan IV ("The Terrible") (ruled 1533–1584) receiving Siberian sable pelts sent by Yermak, "Conqueror of Sibir."

4. K'ang-hsi Emperor (ruled 1661–1722). Second ruler of the Ch'ing dynasty. Largely responsible for delineation of the Russo-Chinese borders.

5. Peter I ("The Great") (ruled 1682–1725). His energy pushed Russian exploration to the end of Asia and into the North Pacific.

6. Vitus Bering (1681–1741). Russian naval officer of Danish birth who was placed in overall charge of expeditions of exploration to the Arctic, Japan, and Alaska.

7. Grigori Shelikhov (1747–1795). Energetic merchant and strong proponent of Russian colonization of North America.

8. Nikolai Rezanov (1764–1807). Son-in-law of Shelikhov who successfully chartered the Russian American Company.

9. Aleksandr Baranov (1746–1819). Chief manager for the Russian American Company in North America.

10. Evfimi Putiatin (1804–1883). Russian admiral who negotiated key treaties with Japan and China.

11. Nikolai Murav'ev-Amursky (1809–1881). Energetic governor-general of East Siberia who pushed Russian claims into the Amur basin.

12. Nikolai Ignat'ev (1832–1908). Able Russian diplomat who concluded the Convention of Peking with the Chinese Empire.

13. Mikhail Cherniaev (1828–1898). General whose impatience was a major factor in the Russian conquest of Central Asia.

14. Konstantin von Kaufman (1818–1882). Aggressive governor-general of Russian Turkestan.

15. Sergei Witte (1849–1915). As finance minister was largely responsible for the construction of the Transsiberian Railway.

16. Aleksei Kuropatkin (1848–1925). Russian general who was a major player in the Russo-Japanese War and in Central Asia.

17. Vasili Blucher (1890–1938). Important Russian military figure in events involving China, the Soviet Union, and the Far Eastern Republic.

Map 7. Central Asia, late nineteenth century.

14

New Borders
for Russia in Central Asia

Whereas the Convention of Peking in 1860 demolished the Kiakhta System, the first chink in the Chinese armor had really appeared almost a decade earlier—in Central Asia—in the form of the Treaty of Kuldja (also known as Ili) in 1851. This agreement was an anomaly, contrary to Chinese policy. It resulted from Russian pressures at a time just after the death of the Tao-kuang emperor (ruled 1820–1850) and the accession of the eighteen-year-old Hsien-feng (ruled 1850–1861). Further, that nemesis of Chinese fortunes—I-shan—was present[1] in Kuldja. Indeed, he was the military governor of the region. The Russians had repeatedly tried to gain permission to trade at Tarbagatai and Kuldja in the Jungar Basin and at Kashgar in the Tarim basin. The treaty, as signed in 1851, permitted trade only at Tarbagatai and Kuldja, but a major Chinese concession permitted Russian consuls to reside in those two towns.

The conclusion of the Treaty of Kuldja was only one small aspect of a much larger Russian expansionist movement which would involve Russia, China, and British India as well as many Turkic-speaking and Indo-Iranian-speaking peoples of Central Asia. The Treaty of Kiakhta of 1728 had extended the Russo-Chinese border westward from the Argun River to the Altai Mountains in northwestern Mongolia. To the west and south of this point lies the vast area in Central Asia which historically has most frequently been termed Turkestan. That portion to the east of the T'ien Shan and Pamir mountain ranges, southwest of Mongolia and northwest of Tibet is East Turkestan. It consists essentially of two basins: the northern one, the Jungar basin, is defined by the Altai Mountains in the north and T'ien Shan in the south; the other, the Tarim basin, is situated south of the T'ien Shan and north of the Tibetan Plateau.

As recounted earlier (chapter 12), Ch'ing armies destroyed Mongol power in the Jungar basin in 1757. Within two years, other Manchu forces rapidly completed the conquest of the Tarim basin and its Turkic population. Just to the west lay lands subject to the khan of Kokand, and fear of Manchu power at this time caused that ruler to recognize the Ch'ien-lung emperor as his lord. Ch'ing authority therefore nominally reached part way into western Turkestan, the vast area stretching from the T'ien Shan range to the northern Caspian Sea. However, Chinese authority west of the T'ien Shan would be tenuous at best.

The Muscovite eastern expansion had remained in the taiga, north of the Turkic peoples of the Asian steppe. In the time of Peter the Great, in the early eighteenth century, modest probes were made up the Irtysh in the east and toward the Aral Sea in the west, but they were discontinued after the decision was taken to cooperate with the Chinese in concluding the Kiakhta Treaty. The Russian advance thus stopped at Semipalatinsk and Ust-Kamenogorsk on the Irtysh. Still, there was a constant threat to Russian security from the south, starting in Bashkiria. The Bashkirs inhabited the area on both sides of the southern Ural Mountains. It was the conquest of the Kazan and Astrakhan Tatars in the mid-sixteenth century that had brought Muscovy face to face with the Bashkirs. Although these Turkic-speaking, Islamic peoples soon nominally recognized the suzerainty of Moscow, they would exercise independence of action for almost two more centuries. Therefore the fortress town of Ufa, founded by Boris Godunov in 1586, would long be an exposed outpost.

It was the policies originated by Peter the Great that would finally result in the conquest of Bashkiria although, as in the case of the Kamchatka expeditions, implementation of such policy would take place during the reign of the Empress Anna (ruled 1830–1840). The momentum of Peter's ideas was initially carried by one of his pupils, Ivan Kirillov. Although he would not live to see his plans to fruition, Kirillov commenced the relentless program of domination known as the Orenburg Project. By 1741, as the result of campaigns implementing the Orenburg Project (which were extraordinary for their brutality), Bashkiria became an integral part of the Russian Empire. The beheadings, hangings, enserfment, and exile of 30,000 Bashkirs not only ensured the obedience of the population but also sent a warning message to the steppe people to the south and east: the Kazakhs. The Russians, incidentally, were assisted in their campaigns against the Bashkirs by the Torgut Mongols who had migrated from East Turkestan to the southern Volga in the early seventeenth century and, as mentioned previously, would return to their former haunts in 1771.

The principal strategic cornerstone for Russian operations against the Bashkirs was the newly established fort of Orenburg, which was erected on the Ural River. This site would also become a key location in the conquest of all of Central Asia. Orenburg was, by the middle of the eighteenth century, the western strong point of a line of forts that extended from the southern Urals in a wide arc to the northeast, through Omsk, until anchored in the east by the forts of Semipalatinsk and Ust Kamenogorsk. The line thus described extended more than 1,500 miles and was designed to protect against the nomadic Kazakhs in the steppe to the south.

By the end of the sixteenth century, the Kazakhs were organized into three hordes. That one nearest the Urals was known as the Lesser Horde, the one closer to the Irtysh River as the Middle Horde, and the third—south of the other two, roughly between the Aral Sea and Lake Balkhash—as the Greater Horde. Although Khan Abulkhair of the Lesser Horde nominally recognized Russian suzerainty as early as 1730, all Kazakhs considered themselves free, and their mobility made them an ephemeral object of Russian control. Their frequent raids into Russian lands were a constant irritant and resulted in the enslavement of many of the tsar's subjects who were then sold to the emirates to the south of the Kazakh steppe.

That area south of a line stretching eastward from the Aral Sea to Lake Issyk Kul (now Ysyk-Kol) in the T'ien Shan and east of the Amu Darya River was known as West Turkestan proper. It was dominated, commencing with the late eighteenth century, by two khanates (Kokand and Khiva) and the emirate of Bukhara. Kokand lay east of the Syr Darya River and included the Fergana Valley and the Kirgiz people; Bukhara occupied most of the area between the Syr Darya and Amu Darya; and Khiva held sway over the land on both sides of the lower Amu Darya. These relatively well-organized polities comprised mostly sedentary populations and were economically prosperous. To the west of Khiva, stretching to the Caspian Sea, were the Turkmens who, like the Kazakhs to the north, were essentially nomadic peoples moving across what is for the most part a sparsely vegetated sand desert. The Turkmens, like the Kazakhs, lived closer to the Russians and, whenever the opportunity was presented, enslaved their Slavic neighbors, most frequently near the shores of the Caspian. These slaves also were sold to the emirates of Turkestan.

The Turkmens were separated from another Islamic, Turkic-speaking people, the Azerbaijanis, by the southern Caspian Sea. In the first three decades of the nineteenth century, Russian authority had been extended beyond the Caucasus Mountains into Asia at the expense, mostly, of the Persian shahs. The kingdom of Georgia was annexed in 1801, and the heart of Azerbaijan was ceded by Persia by the Treaty of Gulistan in 1813. Fifteen years later, most of modern-day Armenia was ceded by the Treaty of Turkmanchai. Saint Petersburg, however, would never succeed in converting the Caspian into a Russian lake.

The Russians particularly relished the idea of regular trade with the Central Asian states, but the caravans that carried out the trade were frequent victims of nomadic raids. The government wished to be in a more dominant position to curb the Kazakh forays into Russian territory and looked with avid eyes on the lush land of the northern steppe. The plan was therefore formulated to draw a noose tightly about the Kazakh territory. From Orenburg in the west, the Russians began gingerly to push southeast toward the Aral Sea in the mid-1840s. In 1847 a Russian fort, named Raimsk, was established near the point where the Syr Darya enters the Aral Sea. Six years later, General V. A. Perovsky moved eastward up the Syr Darya some 200 miles and captured the town of

Ak-Masdjid. It was renamed, for obvious reasons, Perovsk (and is now known as Kzyl Orda or Qyzylorda).

At the same time, farther east, there had been a gradual Russian movement southward from the Irtysh River through areas that the emperors of the Ch'ing dynasty had for almost a century considered as theirs. This penetration continued, east of Lake Balkhash, across the Ili River. In 1854 a Russian fort called Verny (modern-day Alma Ata or Almaty, the capital of Kazakhstan) was established about halfway between the Ili River and Lake Issyk Kul. At this stage, Verny and Perovsk were separated by only 600 miles—the last "gap" in the noose to enclose the Kazakh steppe.

Matters then came to a standstill because of the Crimean War and the ensuing period of the internal reforms of Emperor Alexander II. A further factor was the unclear question of territorial sovereignty in the region just to the west of the northern T'ien Shan. This latter matter was resolved as a by-product of the Russo-Chinese Convention concluded by General Ignat'ev in Peking in 1860, which forced cession of Amuria and Ussuria from China to Russia (chapter 13). The second article of the convention provided that the border in Central Asia follow "the direction of the mountains" from the westernmost border marker provided for in the Treaty of Kiakhta of 1728. The Chinese thus were committed to withdraw any claim to West Turkestan. This agreement was implemented by the Treaty of Tarbagatai of 1864, which delineated the border in detail.

In the same year, 1864, Russian expansion in West Turkestan recommenced after the hiatus of a decade. Interestingly, there were forces militating against such expansion. The policy of *recuillement*, or "looking inward," of Alexander II tended to divert emphasis from territorial aggrandizement. Further, there was concern about British reaction to any Russian encroachment into Central Asia which might be viewed as threatening the security of India's northwest frontier—the traditional invasion route into the subcontinent. Reluctance in Saint Petersburg, particularly on the part of Foreign Minister Alexander Gorchakov, was overcome by two factors: (1) the assignment of General Nikolai Ignat'ev as chief of the Asiatic Section of the Foreign Ministry and (2) the precipitate actions on the part of impatient military officers on duty in Central Asia. Ignat'ev and the minister of war—General Dmitri Miliutin—both were strong advocates of conquest in the region. Thus, when Colonel Mikhail Cherniaev—in direct disobedience to orders—captured the fortress of Suzak in the "gap" area in 1863, his actions were strongly supported by Ignat'ev and Miliutin. Since there was no great international outcry, authority was given to complete the closure of the gap in the following year.

Accordingly, a column under Colonel A. N. Verevkin moved eastward from Perovsk while Cherniaev led a force westward from Verny. They easily swept all opposition before them and joined together to capture the Kokandian center of Chimkent on September 22, 1864. Gorchakov, the foreign minister, then promulgated a circular letter to the Great Powers, stressing the fact that the operation had been necessary to control a turbulent steppe and that further expansion was not necessary since the sovereign entities to the south were more regularly constituted states. However, even before Gorchakov's message was written, Cherniaev had already made an unsuccessful attempt to storm the great city of Tashkent. This failure, in turn, encouraged the Kokandians to attack a Russian fort. Although this effort failed, Russian concern over "face" compelled Cherniaev to conduct an authorized, and this time successful, storming of Tashkent in June 1865. This fortress would become the most important administrative Russian center in West Turkestan.

The following year, Cherniaev (who had been promoted to the rank of major general after the 1864 campaign) was recalled because of his unpredictable actions. This in no way put the brakes on the Russian advance, however. Cherniaev's successor, General D. I. Romanovsky, led a drive up the Syr Darya with such force and success that the khan of Kokand agreed to become a vassal of the emperor of Russia. The following year, a new figure was appointed to the recently established post of governor-general of Turkestan in Tashkent: General Konstantin von Kaufman. Russian attention now was directed at the emirate of Bukhara.

In May 1868 Kaufman launched a sharp offensive, capturing the caravan city of Samarkand, and then, on June 2, won a decisive battle over the main body of Bukharan troops. In the ensuing settlement, Samarkand and most of the of the Zeravshan River (a tributary of the Amu Darya) valley were annexed to the Russian Empire, and the remaining territory of the Bukharan emirate became in effect a Russian protectorate. Indeed, Russian arms came to the rescue of the emir when his authority was challenged militarily by his eldest son later in 1868. However, the fiction of Bukharan sovereignty was maintained so as not to anger the British since the southern border of Bukhara was the upper Amu Darya River, across which lay the emirate of Afghanistan.

At this point, only Khiva remained as an organized challenge south of the steppe. It was not easily accessible since it was an isle in a sea of deserts. Saint Petersburg had several scores to settle, not the least of which was the number of Russians held in slavery. There were also past indignities. In 1717 Prince Aleksandr Bekovich-Cherkassky had led an expedition to Khiva, and all the members of the expedition were massacred. More than a hundred years later, in 1839, V. A. Perovsky failed miserably; his columns did not even reach Khiva because of the harsh winter weather. Finally, in the spring of 1873, Khiva again became a prime target. In view of past difficulties, very little was now left to chance. Troops were launched toward Khiva from Tashkent in the east, from Orenburg in the northwest, and from two locations on the Caspian Sea in the west. Such overwhelming force made Kaufman's entry into Khiva on May 29 essentially a ceremonial occasion. Khiva had become a protectorate of the Russian Empire.

After this action, the Turkmens now were surrounded by Russian authority on the southern Caspian and in the lands to the north and east. To their south lay the frontier with Persia, the northern portion of which was coming increasingly under Russian influence. (This trend gained momentum when the Cossack Brigade was established under Russian officers in Persia in 1878). Russian attitudes toward the Turkmens were strongly influenced by the large numbers of the tsar's subjects who had for centuries been enslaved along the eastern coast of the Caspian Sea. To add to the urge, the ''New Imperialism'' of the last quarter of the nineteenth century was at flood tide and abhorred a political vacuum.

Military successes in the Russo-Turkish War of 1877–1878 brought Russian troops to the very gates of Constantinople. The British were so concerned that they sent their war fleet to the Turkish capital. The situation was finally defused by the Congress of Berlin which was convened by German Chancellor Otto von Bismarck in the early summer of 1878. However, wary of the outcome of such a gathering and wishing to put pressure on London, Saint Petersburg had ordered General Kaufman to have 20,000 troops in readiness to march on Afghanistan.

After agreements in Berlin eased tensions, the troops stood down, but a column under General N. P. Lomakin was directed to move from Chikishliar on the Caspian into the land of the Turkmens. The venture failed. The following year, 1879, Lomakin's forces suffered more loss of face when a siege operation at Dengil-Tepe went awry, resulting in a Russian retreat. Such embarrassment had to be avenged; therefore, the following year, a force of 11,000 fully supported troops were put at the disposal of General Mikhail Skobelev. The campaign began in November 1880 and reached its climax two months later when the fortress of Geok-Tepe, some thirty miles from modern-day Ashkhabad, was stormed. The ensuing butchery, which dispatched thousands of inhabitants, including a high percentage of women and children, broke the Turkmens' will to resist. With most of its principal centers now occupied by the invaders, the land of the Turkmens became an oblast of the Russian Empire named Transcaspia. To complete the picture, the oasis of Merv (modern Mary), some 200 miles farther east, voluntarily submitted in 1884. The southern border of Russia in Asia now stretched along the countries of Turkey, Persia, and Afghanistan, to the Pamirs. Here, among the highest peaks in the world, the territories and interests of Russia, China, and the British all met together.

The Russian operations in Central Asia were to have repercussions in Chinese Turkestan as well. As described in the last chapter, the Ch'ing Empire was buffeted by the Taiping Rebellion during the decade and a half that started in 1850. Even before that insurrection was finally quelled, China was rocked by other uprisings. One of these was the Muslim revolt, which started in Shensi Province in 1862, largely as a result of acts of discrimination on the part of Manchus and Chinese toward Islamic inhabitants. Since Ch'ing officials were so involved in fighting the Taiping forces, the rebellion flourished and spread westward into Chinese Turkestan. The rebels captured the important town of Urumchi in July 1864 and commenced to besiege the capital, Ili (Kuldja), the following November. Ili fell on March 6, 1866.

The Muslims in Chinese Turkestan had a problem of unity of leadership and asked for a leader of preferred lineage who was living in exile in the khanate of Kokand. The choice, the Khoja Buzurg, arrived in early 1865 accompanied by a general named Yakub Beg who, within five years, would usurp the mantle of authority from his nominal superior. Yakub had a history closely associated with West Turkestan and indeed had been born in the khanate of Kokand. While still in his twenties, he became governor of Ak-Masdjid until that fortress was captured by Perovsky in 1853 as outlined above. He rose to the position of commander of the Kokandian army and was in command at the time of Cherniaev's unsuccessful attempt to capture Tashkent in 1864. By being posted to Chinese Turkestan in 1865, he avoided the humiliating defeats suffered by Kokand in ensuing campaigns.

As Yakub consolidated his power in the Tarim and Jungar basins, he affected sovereign authority. He established his capital in Kashgar, and his state was usually referred to as "Kashgaria." His domains enjoyed a common border with the Russian Empire and British India, a fact that he attempted to exploit to the utmost. The Chinese requested the two Great Powers not to recognize the usurper Yakub Beg, but the British looked favorably on him as a valuable Islamic buffer against the spread of Russia and, in 1874, concluded a treaty with him. The Russians, in contrast, were much more circumspect. They feared the spread of British influence and were not happy to see Islamic insurgents successfully defying Chinese authority in East Turkestan. There was the constant fear that the Kokandian Yakub Beg would cause trouble in his former home to the west. Further, renegades from Kashgaria commenced cattle raiding into Kokand. Still other problems for the Russians included the loss of warehouses in the towns of Tarbagatai and Kuldja which had been important to the trade authorized by the Treaty of Kuldja of 1851.

Governor-General Kaufman, whose powers were virtually those of a viceroy in Central Asia, became increasingly disturbed by events in East Turkestan. In August 1870, he directed that operations be conducted up the valley of the Ili River aimed at the capture of the strategic Talki and Muzart passes in the T'ien Shan. In compliance with these orders, Major General G. A. Kolpakovsky moved swiftly up the valley the following spring. He occupied Ili (Kuldja or modern-day Yining) itself and extended a Russian enclave two-thirds the distance from the border to Urumchi. The area occupied amounted to a total of 1,224 square miles. When word of these developments finally filtered out, the Chinese requested explanations but were met with rather vague responses. The Russian position finally settled on the theme that since the Ch'ing government was not in a position to control events in Kashgaria, the Russians were merely helping out. Saint Petersburg professed that Russia would be happy to restore the territory to the Chinese as soon as the Chinese were in a position to take charge themselves. Of course, the existing chaos in the Celestial Empire seemed to bode poorly for such a prospect. To the surprise of many, however, China did manage to respond to this challenge.

In 1874 Tso Tsung-t'ang, one of the heroes to emerge from the Taiping

Rebellion, was given the job of recovering Chinese Turkestan. Realizing the long lines of supply and communication involved, he levied requirements of 10 million taels on the imperial government. The gravity of the situation evoked a critical debate in Peking. In essence, it centered on whether such a huge sum should be expended for protection of a land frontier so far away, or for maritime defense in the eastern part of the empire where the threat of the Western powers was so real and evident. Tso, citing the historic threat to China from the north-west and the steppe, ultimately carried the day, and he was provided with the necessary tools to approach his task. Accordingly, in early 1876, his forces penetrated into the northern part of the Jungar basin, then wheeled to the south and commenced to sweep everything in its path. On August 18, Urumchi was captured and its garrison massacred. The following year, the Chinese rejected British offers of mediation and captured Turfan. Yakub Beg was now in full flight. An apparent suicide on May 29, 1877, spared him the agony of a Chinese execution. The following year, Tso Tsung-t'ang completed the conquest of all of what we now may properly call Sinkiang—or "New Territories"—with the exception of the Russian enclave in the Ili River valley.

The Russians were caught quite unawares by the successes of Tso's troops and provided only vague responses to Chinese queries concerning the Ili valley. The Ch'ing government, in a sharp break with tradition, was at this time in the process of sending out permanent diplomatic missions to the capitals of the Great Powers; therefore, the emissary Ch'ung-hou, who was assigned to Saint Peters-burg in 1878, was given the mission of securing the return of Ili to China. Ch'ung-hou was a Manchu of no unusual accomplishments; he was not a gifted negotiator. Indeed, he had very little appreciation of the authority with which he was entrusted, nor of the details of the situation in the Ili valley. The time was not propitious for Chinese gain since Russia was still smarting from the diplomatic defeat of the Congress of Berlin which had been concluded just a few months prior to Ch'ung-hou's arrival. The not surprising outcome of his visit to the seat of the Russian Empire, during which he was neatly finessed by the Russian diplomatic team, was the Treaty of Livadia (so named for the tsarist palace at Yalta in the Crimea), which was signed on October 2, 1879.

The treaty provided that (1) Russia would still retain a large portion of the valley, including the strategic passes; (2) Russia would be granted seven new consulates in the Chinese northwest, one as far east as Chiayukuan, at the west end of the Great Wall; (3) Russia was given the right of navigation of the Sungari (principal river of Manchuria); and (4) China was to pay an indemnity of 5 million rubles to reimburse Russia for the expense of protecting the Ili valley for eight years. The response in Peking was one of disbelief. Tso Tsung-t'ang was outraged. Ch'ung-hou was stripped of his offices by the court and sentenced to death by beheading.

Ch'ung-hou's hide (and head) were saved by an international outcry from the Great Powers, including a special plea from Queen Victoria of Britain. However, it was obvious that the Chinese court could not ratify the Treaty of Livadia, and

Tso Tsung-t'ang counseled a strong position, even though it might mean war. In 1880 the Chinese Tseng Chi-tse, son of the military hero Tseng Kuo-fan, was given the delicate mission of revising the treaty. Thanks to his diplomatic presence and Russian concern over their diplomatic isolation, revision was possible. Saint Petersburg, and especially deputy foreign minister Nikolai Giers, wanted to resolve expeditiously what had become a sort of minor but annoying irritation. Also, considering the military strength Tso Tsung-t'ang had mustered in Sinkiang, and with no rail east of the Ural Mountains to support Russian forces, there was no desire for a major war in the east. Finally, on February 24, 1881, the Treaty of Saint Petersburg settled the Ili problem. All the Ili enclave was to be returned to China, including the strategic passes, except for a small strip at the west end which was supposedly for refugees from Sinkiang. However, in order for the Russians to save face, the amount of the indemnity was increased to 9 million rubles. Navigation of the Sungari was not mentioned, and the number of new consulates was reduced from seven to two. Timing was fortuitous in that the signing took place just five days before Alexander II was killed by an assassin's bomb.

The Sino-Russian border in Central Asia now was largely agreed upon and was worked out in detail by a protocol of 1884. However, this extended the border only to the Uzbel pass in the Pamirs. That is, it in essence defined the eastern extent of the lands of the Kirgiz but not those of the warlike Tajiks just to the south. Finally, in 1895, a border commission's proposals were accepted which divided the Pamirs among Russia, Britain, China, and Afghanistan. The most salient feature was the awarding of the Wakan valley to Afghanistan so that that country would have a common border with China, thereby separating the lands of the Russian Empire from those of the British Empire.

Despite the cataclysmic events of the last century, the Central Asian borders of Imperial Russia and the Soviet Union, which were defined in the nineteenth century, have remained remarkably unchanged. This is so despite the existence of new states that emerged after the partition of British India in 1947 and the breakup of the Union of Soviet Socialist Republics in 1991.

NOTE

1. I-shan had played a less than noble role in the Chinese withdrawal from Canton in the Opium War in 1841. Then, as noted in the previous chapter, he signed the Treaty of Aigun in 1858 which deprived China of the left bank of the Amur River. In the Kuldja situation of 1851 treated above, he permitted the first Russian economic penetration into Sinkiang.

15

Russian Railroads in Asia: Arteries of Empire

By the ninth decade of the nineteenth century, thanks to the growing weakness of China and the political fragmentation of Central Asia, the Russian Empire had expanded dramatically deeper into the Asian continent. By that time, however, such expansion had begun to encounter ever stronger resistance—principally in the form of the economic and military power of Great Britain. This was true from southeastern Europe, where the British supported the decaying Ottoman Empire, eastward through Central Asia, where the British presence in Persia and Afghanistan was at its height, and on to East Asia, where the Royal Navy's mobile strength militated against the further spread of Russian influence.

Russia's possessions in Asia were indeed vast, so much so that the defense of so great a territory was difficult and would become even more so if the existing means of communication were not drastically improved. This could be done in the late nineteenth century only by the construction of railroads together with telegraph lines. The completion of the Union Pacific (1869) and the Canadian Pacific (1885) railroads across the North American continent had demonstrated the effectiveness of rail in unifying other large nation-states. But such a modern, capital-intensive undertaking would be a major challenge to the relatively primitive economy of the Russian Empire. After the debacle of the Crimean War, Tsar Alexander II had instituted many social and political reforms, but the Industrial Revolution, aside from arms manufacture, had barely made its appearance in Russia. Still, the nation would be forced to respond to the urge of empire.

The first penetration of railroads into Asiatic Russia would occur in Central Asia. As early as 1864 a post-road system had been established between Tashkent and Orenburg which grew to include fifty-five post houses and 239 teams of horses. A normal caravan required approximately two months to traverse the

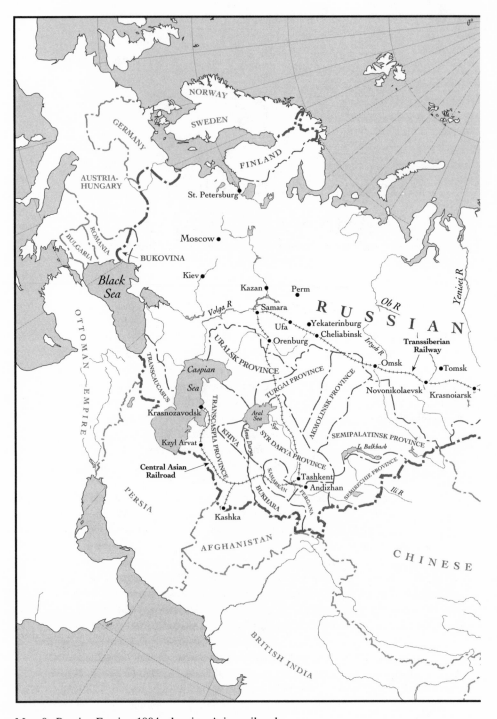

Map 8. Russian Empire, 1904, showing Asian railroads.

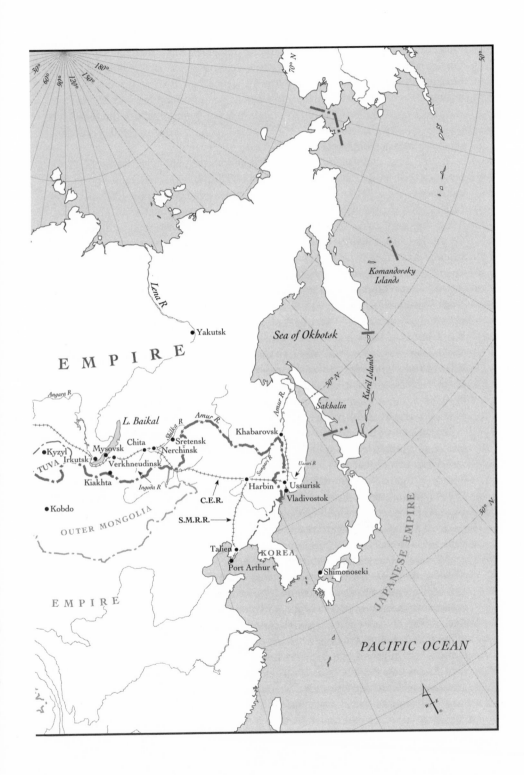

EMPIRE

70° N

50°

30°
180°
60°
90°
120°
150°

Lena R

● Yakutsk

Sea of Okhotsk

Komandorsky
Islands

50° N

Kuril Islands

Sakhalin

E M P I R E

Angara R.

L. Baikal

Shilka R

Amur R.

Amur R.

● Khabarovsk

● Kyzyl   ● Mysovsk   Chita
Irkutsk   ● Sretensk
TUVA   Verkhneudinsk Nerchinsk

● Kiakhta

Ingoda R.

Singari R.

Ussuri R.

● Harbin   ● Ussurisk

C.E.R.

● Vladivostok

● Kobdo

OUTER MONGOLIA

S.M.R.R.

30° N

JAPANESE EMPIRE

● Talien   KOREA

Port Arthur

● Shimonoseki

EMPIRE

PACIFIC OCEAN

N
W   E
S

route, and couriers about half that time. A telegraph link, implemented in 1867, greatly accelerated the speed of written communications, but movement of supplies and troops still caused great logistic headaches. Despite the fact that such an imposing figure as Ferdinand de Lesseps proposed a grandiose scheme of a railroad from Calais to Calcutta, including a leg from Orenburg through Tashkent to Peshawar, forty years would elapse before the dust of the post road would be replaced by steel rails.

The first railroad was built in connection with the campaign against the Turkmens described in the preceding chapter. This rail section, built by military engineers, reached 145 miles east from the Caspian Sea to the Turkmen town of Kzyl-Arvat (now Gyzylarbat). Since it was not completed until 1881, it was not a major factor in General Skobelev's victory in 1880, but it turned out to be the base to which would be added most of the rest of the rail system in Central Asia. It was largely concern over the British power projection into Afghanistan and particularly the Penjdeh clash between Russian and Afghan troops in 1885 that prompted Saint Petersburg to extend the Transcaspian railroad eastward through shifting sands 500 miles to the Amu Darya by 1886. The river was bridged and the railroad pushed another 260 miles to Samarkand via Bukhara just two years later. Finally, in 1898, the line was extended to Tashkent, and a spur was built from Merv (present-day Mary) in Turkmenistan south to Kashka (now Gushgy) to provide ready access to Afghanistan. Then, in 1899, a spur was constructed through the Sanzar Pass ("Tamerlane's Gate") into the Fergana valley to the town of Andizhan. The system now was renamed the Central Asian Railway.

By the end of the century, therefore, more than 1,000 miles of rails had been laid in Central Asia, but access to the region was still restricted in that people and cargo had to be transported by water from European Russia to the Caspian port of Krasnozavodsk before they had access to the railroad. Further, the Volga River and northern Caspian were closed to navigation for a few months each year. This situation would finally be resolved through the efforts of General Aleksei Kuropatkin,[1] who became minister of war in 1898. He succeeded in gaining approval for starting the direct line from Orenburg to Tashkent. This 1,150-mile railway was completed in 1906.

The difficulties of building railroads in Central Asia would be dwarfed by the much greater challenge of extending rails eastward from the Ural Mountains to the Pacific Ocean. This daunting effort would involve the construction of more than 4,000 miles of track through forests, over mountains, along steep river valleys, and atop swamplands and permafrost. It would be performed in a wilderness area requiring the arduous transport of supplies, equipment, and workmen to the construction sites. It would be the greatest test of rail engineering of the nineteenth century. Yet it would be completed in a remarkably short period of time. In many ways, it was the result of the strong wills of two sturdy Russians: Emperor Alexander III and Sergei Yulevich Witte. After the assassination of Alexander II in 1881 by an anarchist's bomb, the throne was assumed by his son Alexander III. The new ruler was much like his grandfather, Nicholas I, in his conservative view of political and social matters. His physical strength was extraordinary, and his trust in and support of the ministers he appointed was steady. Thus it was that, despite his hard line against change, belief in one of his ministers—Finance Minister Witte—resulted in a dramatic change of the nation's outlook on railroads.

Witte was born in 1849 in the Georgian capital of Tiflis (now Tbilisi) where his father and grandfather had served as colonial administrators. Witte was a bear of a man who was impatient with others he considered not his intellectual equal. He took a degree in mathematics at Novorossiisk University and early on was attracted to a life in the railroad business. He made a name for himself by his handling of military supplies in support of the Russian armies during their successful operations against the Turks in the War of 1877–1878. The following year, he was called to Saint Petersburg and from that point saw a rapid rise in the imperial bureaucracy. Alexander, who met him first in the 1880s, was impressed by his no-nonsense manner. He was appointed director of railroad affairs in the Ministry of Finance in 1889 and became minister of finance just three years later. Witte was interested not only in railroads but in the larger matter of economics and industrial development. He saw Russian Asia as a vast treasure house that could be tapped only by means of a railway system. Although a dedicated Russian imperialist to the core, he believed not only that penetration should be achieved by economic means but also that railroads were the only way to ensure exploitation of Russian lands and to guarantee their retention in the empire.

At the time Witte rose to the top circles of government, transport east of the Urals had made some progress—however limited—since the initial Russian expansion to the Pacific in the sixteenth and early seventeenth centuries. The tricentennial of Yermak's conquest of Sibir had been celebrated just a decade before Witte was advanced to the position of finance minister. As we have seen, from the beginning of the expansion across Asia, the Russians for the most part used the riverine system for transportation—sledge in winter and boat in summer—with very few portages. Such a means, however, added many miles to a straight-line route. Therefore longer portages, avoiding the meandering of long tributaries, were adopted. With time, these portages became ever longer, especially for the use of couriers on official errands. Rude carts came to use these routes, and gradually a track was worn in the earth, really a set of ruts, as distinct as some of the trails across the western United States in the nineteenth century.

Finally, after the completion of a highway from Moscow to Yekaterinburg (named Sverdlovsk for most of the Soviet period) on the east slope of the Urals in 1763, efforts were made to extend it gradually farther into Asia. Known as the Siberian Highway, it had been completed as far as Irkutsk by 1838. It was a dirt road, supposedly twenty-one-feet wide. It was usually iced up, filled with mud holes, or covered with dust up to a foot deep. From Irkutsk it branched south to Kiakhta for the China trade or to the northeast toward Yakutsk. Later

on, Governor-General Murav'ev-Amursky would extend post roads from Lake
Baikal to Khabarovsk and thence south to Vladivostok (after that port was
founded in 1860). These roads were so precarious, however, that rivers were
generally preferred: the Shilka and Amur from Chita to Khabarovsk, and the
Ussuri for the greater part of the journey on to Vladivostok. The rivers still
came into play as well in West and East Siberia—particularly from Tiumen to
Tomsk—for the shipment of supplies, and a canal connecting the Ob and Yenisei rivers was actually begun in 1882. A great weakness of heavy river transportation, of course, was that it was restricted to an annual operation of only a
few months because of ice.

One of the earliest and most energetic proponents of a transsiberian railroad
was an American entrepreneur named Perry McDonough Collins. His interest
was primarily in selling steamboat navigation of the Amur, and he managed to
be designated U.S. commercial agent to the "Amoor River" by Secretary of
State William Marcy in March 1856. Collins proceeded directly to Saint Petersburg where he met Governor-General Nikolai Murav'ev, who was visiting
from East Siberia. Armed with introductions from that worthy, he traveled to
Moscow and thence via the Siberian Highway to Irkutsk. Negotiating the icy
road in January and February, he covered the 3,545 miles in thirty-five days,
changing horses 210 times in the process. After enjoying Murav'ev's hospitality
in Irkutsk and a short round-trip to Kiakhta, he set out the following month for
Chita. Here, as the guest of Governor Mikhail Korsakov, he awaited the spring
thaw and then sailed down the Ingoda, into the Shilka, and thence into the Amur,
finally arriving at Nikolaevsk near the mouth of the river on July 10, 1857.
Collins made strong recommendations to Korsakov for construction of a railroad, including a leg from Irkutsk to Chita via Kiakhta. Korsakov was an enthusiastic supporter of the project, as was his superior Murav'ev, and their voices
were heard in Saint Petersburg. However, the sheer size of the undertaking and
the costs involved ensured a strongly negative voice from the Finance Ministry,
so that action would be deferred for more than a generation.

Collins was by no means the only proponent of the railway. Many Russians
believed there was a vital need for it. One of the most dedicated proponents
was Admiral Konstantin Pos'et who, as minister of transport communications
(1874–1888), made a detailed proposal in 1875 to build a railroad from the
Volga River to the Amur. This was successfully defeated by the minister of
finance, and the Russo-Turkish War of 1877–1878 deflected consideration until
the 1880s. Pos'et, who continued to be the major figure in favor of the railroad,
gained the support of the War Ministry. The minister of war, also a senior
military officer, shared the concern over the defense of the Russian Far East. In
particular, the Amur valley had not proven to be the bountiful source of grain
anticipated, with the result that food for the Russians in the Far East was being
imported from China and Korea. Thus, in the event of war, the forces there
would be in jeopardy. Nevertheless, the competent and crusty old minister of

finance, Ivan Vyshnegradsky, successfully defended the imperial treasury from such expenditures with tough fiscal arguments.

Alexander III (ruled 1881–1894) instinctively favored the construction of a transsiberian railroad, and the capital received regular pleas from Governor Andrei Korf in Khabarovsk and Governor-General Aleksei Ignat'ev (brother of Nikolai) in Irkutsk. The fact was, however, that there were conflicting currents of thought prevalent at the time. As mentioned, military leaders believed it essential to the defense of the empire, but conservatives entertained a basically negative attitude out of fear that it might impact unfavorably on the existing order of things. They were quite sensitive to the effect of cheap Siberian land and grain on the profitability of agriculture in European Russia. There was concern over the growth of regionalism among the Russian population in Asia which could be compared to that of the English colonists in North America a century before. Others feared that if communication to the Pacific coast were too convenient, it could lead to the rapid influx of outside ideas which would enhance the feeling of regionalism. Visionaries, on the other hand, looked to the development and economic growth of Asiatic Russia as a great benefit to the nation at large. In the final analysis, conservative thinkers became persuaded that the threat to the integrity of the empire outweighed that to the political order. As a result, Finance Minister Vyshnegradsky's obstructionist tactics were facing an increasingly strong force favoring the transsiberian venture.

The first break in the stalemate occurred in February 1891 when the Committee of Ministers outvoted Vyshnegradsky to approve a railroad from Vladivostok to Khabarovsk and to endorse a vague program of railroad construction from the Urals to Khabarovsk. As a result, Alexander III issued a decree on May 31 implementing the work of the ministers. On the same day, his son Nicholas presided at a ceremony in Vladivostok inaugurating the construction of the Vladivostok-Khabarovsk Line.

The following year, Vyshnegradsky was forced to retire because of illness, and Witte replaced him as the minister of finance. From this point, a transsiberian railroad would rapidly become a reality. Witte succeeded in converting the Russian ruble to the gold standard, thus inviting foreign investment, particularly from capital-rich France. The French at this time also were actively courting an alliance with Russia as a counter to the Triple Alliance of Germany, Austria, and Italy. Still, there were valid economic reasons, so forcefully defended for so long by Vyshnegradsky, with which Witte had to contend. He managed to find his way around them through financial legerdemain which rested heavily on accounting gimmicks. He ensured that the quality of railway construction would be the cheapest possible in order to meet minimal standards. A national alcohol monopoly became a key source of revenue. He so dominated the Committee of Ministers that there was little effective opposition to his high-handed conduct of railroad policy. Despite the foregoing, Witte's greatest value in support of the railroad was perhaps his role as a dynamic propagandist.

With the full support of Alexander III, rail construction was begun with alacrity. One of the first moves was to establish, in November 1892, the Committee for the Transsiberian Railroad, under the chairmanship of Crown Prince Nicholas. This was an especially wise move since Nicholas, although frequently indecisive, would prove to be a constant and enthusiastic supporter of the project, even after he ascended to the throne in 1894. Witte had already decided that the highest priority would be given to three segments: the West Siberian Railway (from Cheliabinsk, on the eastern slope of the Urals, to the Ob River), the Central Siberian Railway (from the Ob to Irkutsk), and the South Ussuri Railway (from Vladivostok to the upper reaches of the Ussuri River). The deadline for their completion was set at the year 1900.

Simultaneous construction was initiated on separate segments, a factor that exacerbated the problem of moving supplies to the sites. The West Siberian was split into two sections with the city of Omsk on the Irtysh River as the division point. Similarly, Krasnoiarsk was the division point on the Central Siberian Railway. The rail work that was commenced at Cheliabinsk in July 1892 had reached the Irtysh opposite Omsk, a distance of 500 miles, by September 1894, using laborers from European Russia, Persia, Turkey, and Italy. The half-mile-long bridge across the Irtysh to Omsk was completed a year later, and the western section of the West Siberian was considered ready for operation in March 1896. The section east of Omsk was commenced in May 1893 and completed to the Ob, a distance of 384 miles, by August 1895. The decision had been made, based on engineering surveys, to cross the Ob not at the established center of Tomsk but rather at the small village of Novonikolaevsk (modern-day Novosibirsk). With the completion of the bridge over the Ob in April 1897, the entire West Siberian Railway was considered to be operational.

Work on the Central Siberian, from the Ob to Irkutsk, a distance of 1,130 miles, began at the Ob in mid-year 1893. The terrain on this segment was tougher than the semi-steppe to the west. Here dense forests and steeper inclines were involved. Because of the dearth of local population in the region, workers were drawn from the convicts in Irkutsk. The western section, from the Ob to Krasnoiarsk, was opened to rail traffic in February 1897. The eastern section, from Krasnoiarsk to Irkutsk, begun in 1894, became operational in 1898. At this time, the two lines, from Cheliabinsk to Irkutsk (a total distance of 2,014 miles), were amalgamated into one—the Siberian Railway.

The third of the higher priority segments, the South Ussuri, had already been launched by Nicholas in 1891 as noted earlier. The topography proved to be an extraordinary challenge in terms of swamps, forests, basalt outcroppings, and heavy rains, not to mention tigers. One great problem was posed by the unexpected fact that the Ussuri at flood level was thirty-five feet higher than normal. Here, assembling a workforce was extraordinarily difficult. The workers variously comprised soldiers, convicts, and seasonal Chinese labor. Completion of the 250-mile South Ussuri Railway north from Vladivostok to the village of Murav'ev-Amursky (modern-day Iman) was achieved in December 1894. The remaining 225 miles to Khabarovsk, the North Ussuri, was opened in November

1897. By 1898, therefore, well before the 1900 deadline, rails now stretched eastward to Irkutsk and north from Vladivostok to Khabarovsk. Between Irkutsk and Khabarovsk, however, lay some of the most difficult terrain.

The fearsome challenge of the Transbaikal Railway was taken up in 1895. This 687-mile undertaking extended from Mysovsk (modern-day Babushkin) on the east shore of southern Lake Baikal through Verkhneudinsk (modern-day Ulan Ude), across the Yablonovy Mountains, through Chita and Nerchinsk, to Sretensk on the Shilka River. Not only was it necessary to negotiate the Yablonovy Range and steep river valleys and heavy flooding, but also to deal with the intricate problems of construction on permafrost. On this leg, the workforce was made up of exiles and convicts from the mines. Most of the supplies and equipment were shipped from the Pacific up the Amur/Shilka river system. Despite the engineering and personnel problems and extraordinary flooding, which at one point wiped out 230 miles of completed track, the line was declared operational in May 1900.

By the end of the century, therefore, it was possible to travel from Moscow to Vladivostok by taking rail to Irkutsk, a ferry (or sledge) across Lake Baikal, rail to Sretensk, river boat (or sledge) down the Shilka and Amur to Khabarovsk, and rail on to Vladivostok. By this time, understandably, the construction costs were well above estimates despite the ''light construction'' that had been chosen. That stretch from Sretensk to Khabarovsk, known as the Amur Line, was early viewed by Witte as being an excessively costly part of the whole, and he was largely responsible for an alternate solution—the Chinese Eastern Railway. This would be a shorter route (by 500 miles) from Chita to Vladivostok across Manchuria without the challenge of permafrost.

The stage was set for realization of this project by the Sino-Japanese War of 1894–1895 in which the Chinese nation was humiliated by the modernized army and navy of Japan. Part of the settlement agreed to in the Treaty of Shimonoseki was the payment of a huge indemnity in the amount of 200 million taels and the cession of the Liao-tung Peninsula to Japan. Largely at the urging of Witte, France and Germany cooperated with Russia in forcing Japan to retrocede the peninsula to China. Witte then took the lead in arranging a low-interest loan, mostly of French money, to enable the Chinese government to meet its indemnity payments. In the process, he established the Russo-Chinese Bank, which was capitalized primarily by French assets.[2]

The Chinese were grateful for this easing of their desperate situation, but Witte would expect favors for Russia in return. His opportunity came the following year when Li Hung-chang, Chinese elder statesman and hero of the Taiping Rebellion, was sent to Saint Petersburg and Moscow to represent the Ch'ing court at the coronation of Nicholas II. During this visit, Witte was the moving force that engineered an agreement between the two nations, known generally as the Li-Lobanov Treaty for the names of Li and the other signatory, Russian Foreign Minister Prince Aleksei Lobanov-Rostovsky. The treaty provided for a defensive alliance between Russia and China, aimed at Japan, as well as an agreement for the construction of a railroad across Manchuria which would connect Chita and Vladivostok. The document, in its final form, was concluded in September 1896.

The authority to build and operate the Chinese Eastern Railway was vested in the Russo-Chinese Bank, which was to establish the Chinese Eastern Railway Company as the managing institution. Lands necessary for the railroad were to be transferred to the company, which was to have police power over that real estate. It was reluctantly agreed by the Chinese that the line would be built using the wide gauge of the Russian rail system (five feet) rather than the narrow gauge in use in America, Britain, and Continental Europe (four feet, eight and a half inches). It was further stipulated that the entire system in Manchuria would pass to Chinese government ownership free of charge in eighty years or in thirty years upon payment of all construction costs, debts, and accrued interest.

No time was lost in commencing construction of the 1,576-mile railway, which ran from Kaidalovo (fifty miles east of Chita) on the Transbaikal Line to Ussuriisk (fifty miles north of Vladivostok) on the South Ussuri Line. More than 1,200 miles of construction were to be inside Manchuria. The first rails were laid in 1897, and a key center quickly grew to prominence at Harbin, where the railroad would cross the Sungari River. This growth evolved very simply from the fact that the easiest access for supplies to the project was up the Sungari from the Amur River. A new Russian city quickly outpaced the original native town at the site. Despite problems with pirates, disease epidemics, and terrain, good progress was made until the outbreak of the Boxer Rebellion in May 1900. By the time the Russians had mobilized and sent in thousands of troops (ultimately almost 200,000), the Boxer activity had ruined more than 500 miles of railroad. The situation was finally brought under control by the end of the year, and most of the railway was completed in November of the following year— the major exception being the 10,000-foot tunnel through the Ta Hinggan Mountains in northwest Manchuria. This work was finished, and the Chinese Eastern Railway was declared operational, by February 1903.

At this point, the Transsiberian from Cheliabinsk to Vladivostok was a reality, except for the perilous area around the southern rim of Lake Baikal. This comprised a distance of only 162 miles, but it entailed such precipitous cliffs, broken by capes, ravines, bays, and narrow shelving, that it would require thirty-three tunnels and a combination of more than 200 bridges and trestles. In the meantime, passengers and cargo were ferried across the lake until the ice grew too thick in December. For the next five months, transport was by sledge. An unfortunate experiment at laying rails across the ice for the trains was quickly cancelled when a locomotive plunged into the icy depths of Lake Baikal. Work on the Circumbaikal Railway was actually begun in 1901 but was not complete by the outbreak of the Russo-Japanese War in February 1904. Work then was greatly intensified, and the last link was completed in September of the same year. The Transsiberian now was finally operational, making possible coast-to-coast service, thirteen years and four months from the commencement of the South Ussuri Line by Nicholas in 1891.

As we shall see later, Russia suffered serious setbacks in the Russo-Japanese War; therefore, certain strategic reassessments led to the conclusion that the Amur Line should be built, connecting Chita with Khabarovsk—a distance of 1,200 miles through an awesome environment, including the unique problems of permafrost. Construction, begun in 1908, was mostly completed by 1913, but the final hurdle, building a bridge one and one-half miles long at Khabarovsk, delayed the operational date until 1916.

As indicated earlier, for reasons of economy, Witte had chosen to build a railroad keyed to minimum standards. As a result, the final product was described by one observer as "a first-rate job in building a third-rate railway."[3] Light rails of inferior quality, steep gradients, ties of green wood too widely spaced, tight curves, narrow embankments, and too little ballast—all combined to inhibit speed and load size. To this must be added as well a lack of sidings, marshaling yards, and watering sites. These limitations and the small number of steel bridges (most were constructed of wood) required constant repairs. Although there were no catastrophic passenger wrecks, freight casualties were a regular occurrence. By 1900, the express train from Cheliabinsk to Irkutsk required almost six days, for an average speed of fifteen miles per hour (nineteen between stations), and the regular train required two days longer. Five years later, thanks to improvements stimulated by the Russo-Japanese War, the average speed had been increased to nineteen miles per hour. By the beginning of World War I, the entire trip from Moscow to Vladivostok could be negotiated in nine days. Although the tendency of most observers is to dwell on the Transsiberian's shortcomings, the railroad was a huge engineering achievement, and despite its negative aspects, it was a vast improvement over what had been in place before. The empire was connected by a band of steel, and there was a justified nationalistic sense of pride in the accomplishment.

As described, two Russian rail systems were constructed in Asia: the Central Asian Railway and the Transsiberian. During the period of the empire, despite plans to the contrary, the two remained discrete systems. Even after completion of the Orenburg-Tashkent leg in 1906, there was no netting of the two systems east of the city of Samara (Kuibyshev during the Soviet period) on the Volga. As a result, to travel from Tashkent to Omsk, a distance of 950 miles, a train ride of more than 2,500 miles was required. Work was finally started on the Turk-Sib (Turkestan-Siberia) Line in 1913, but not until Stalin's first five-year-plan would the railroad be completed from Novosibirsk via Semipalatinsk and Alma Ata to Tashkent. Despite their inadequacies, the two rail systems would make possible the movement of troops and colonists to many of the far corners of the empire. They ensured retention of virtually all the nation's Asiatic territories despite the cataclysms of revolution, civil war, and two world wars.

NOTES

1. Although Kuropatkin is usually identified primarily with the Russo-Japanese War, his association with Central Asia was of longer duration. He was the military commander of the Transcaspian Oblast from 1890 to 1898 and the governor-general of Turkestan from 1916 to 1917.

2. It was much easier for Russia to arrange the transactions since no parliamentary debates were involved. The French were not discomfited by the arrangement since they considered the investment safe and their interest assured.

3. Cited in Harmon Tupper, *To the Great Ocean: Siberia and the Trans-Siberian Railway* (Boston: Little, Brown & Co., 1965), 245.

16

Russia, Korea, and the Sino-Japanese War

Korea, the Land of the Morning Calm, has for centuries experienced the advantages and disadvantages of being sited between the empires of China and Japan. Its racial homogeneity and uniqueness are largely owed to the huge peninsula that is home to the nation. This stretch of land, over 700 miles in length, north to south, and more than 200 miles in width, is dominated by high mountains and cold weather fronting on the Sea of Japan in the east. Weather tends to be milder in the south and west; therefore, modern historical development has been concentrated more on the shores of the Yellow Sea. The climate overall, however, owing to the proximity of Manchuria, is essentially continental—cold winters and hot summers. For the last five centuries, the national land boundaries in the north have been well defined by the Yalu River toward the west and the Tumen toward the east. Both flow from the same basic watershed: Mount Paektu in the Changbai mountain range.

The peninsula, which had become a unified nation under the Koryo dynasty by the first part of the tenth century, was overwhelmed by the Mongol conquest 300 years later. Then, after the Yuan (Mongol) dynasty lost the Mandate of Heaven to the Ming in China (1368), the Koryo kingdom was given over to deep splits between pro-Yuan and pro-Ming factions. The Koryo dynasty had lost its dynamism and was overthrown by an astute leader named Yi Song-gye, who established a new dynasty in 1392—the Yi.

The Yi dynasty would continue the tributary relationship *sadae* (''serve the great'') with the Ming, and later the Ch'ing, dynasty in China. Nevertheless, a strong xenophobia developed, stemming from the Mongol incursions in the thirteenth century, the Hideyoshi invasions from Japan (1592–1598), and the advent of Manchu armies in the early seventeenth century. This distrust of foreigners would become intensified by the spread of Catholicism among parts of the pop-

Map 9. East Asia, 1905–1941.

ulation as the result of the missionary efforts of the Jesuits in China and the permanent presence of European power in East Asia from the time of the First Opium War (1839–1842). Indeed, Korea became known as the Hermit Kingdom. An even more poignant example of foreign evil—in Korean eyes—was the opening of Japan, effected by Commodore Matthew Perry in 1854.

One of the great internal problems endemic to Korean political life was intense factionalism. Although the Yi dynasty would survive until 1910, new kings were often chosen from among rather remote relatives of the last previous monarch. Such was the case in 1864 when King Ch'olchong was succeeded by a distant cousin—the twelve-year-old lad who became King Kojong. The new king's father assumed the role of regent and was known as the *taewon'gun* ("Prince of the Great Court"). He was effective in reestablishing royal authority by breaking the power of various factions. A fanatic Confucianist, he set about excising what he considered the pernicious presence of Catholicism from the nation in 1866. This spirited persecution, which lasted for six years, included the execution of several French priests and thousands of Korean adherents. The *taewon'gun* had been deeply affected by what he considered the humiliation of China during the Anglo-French occupation of Peking in 1860 and resolved that the Westerners would be excluded from Korea at all costs. However, the great challenge to his policies would come not from the West but from his neighbor—Japan.

The Japanese, who rapidly industrialized after the Meiji Restoration of 1868, soon looked to Korea as an ideal and convenient market. They therefore wished to open the country and at the same time terminate the special tributary relationship between China and Korea—*sadae*. The initial Japanese overtures in 1870 and 1872 were rebuffed. However, termination of the regency of the *taewon'gun* in 1873, together with Japan's new naval power and sheer persistence, all combined to bring about the conclusion of the Treaty of Kanghwa in 1876. This Korean/Japanese pact was patterned on the unequal treaties imposed on Asian nations by the West, even to the matter of extraterritoriality. The treaty contained the important words that described Korea as a free and sovereign state—clearly aimed at *sadae*.

In May 1882, Commodore Robert Shufeldt succeeded in concluding a treaty opening Korean-American relations. His avenue to Seoul was through Peking. The Chinese leader, Li Hung-chang, had been able to persuade the Korean government that by opening up to the Americans and other Westerners, Korea would then have counterbalances to Japanese influence.

The path of formal Russo-Korean diplomatic relations was tortuous indeed. A common eleven-mile border had resulted from the Convention of Peking negotiated by Nikolai Ignat'ev in 1860, which ceded Amuria and Ussuria to Russia from China (chapter 13). In implementation of the pact, Russian members of the border commission ensured that the Russian coastline would extend to Korea in order to prevent the possibility of a British foothold in any of the excellent harbors along the western shores of the Sea of Japan. As far back as

1715, the Korean and Chinese governments had agreed, in order to minimize the probability of border incidents, that there would be no habitation or tilling of the soil along their common boundaries. The Koreans therefore were discomfited by the appearance on the banks of the Tumen River of a brash new neighbor desiring immediate dialogue. Because of Korean reluctance, a quarter century would elapse from delineation of a common border to conclusion of a treaty establishing formal relations.

Like France and the United States, Russia at first attempted to approach Korea by sea. As early as 1854, Vice Admiral Evfimi Putiatin had attempted to make contact at Port Lazarev on the north shore of Yonghung Bay in eastern Korea, but violence resulted. Thirteen years later, a Russian warship entered the Han estuary, and the upshot was bloodshed and death. Overland, the Russians were not much more successful, but violence was rare. Thousands of Koreans, in defiance of their government's policy, commenced emigrating into Russian territory. There was no attempt by ordinary Russians to move into Korea, but officials would try repeatedly to establish communication with their Korean counterparts. The first major quasi-official contact came in March 1864 when three Russians crossed the frozen Tumen, proceeded to the nearest town, and requested that trade be opened. They returned home without any response. This event took place at the farthest point from the Korean capital, but the central government, upon learning of the matter, took action the following June. This consisted of punishing local Korean authorities, including beheading two officials.

For eighteen more years, the Russians kept trying to establish a dialogue while the Koreans maintained their aloof position. In early 1882, a letter, borne by a Korean emigré, contained a request that Russian authorities be advised in the event of epidemics. Surprisingly, a positive response was received, but the border remained closed to normal intercourse. The final connection, instead, would come via the Chinese capital. The treaty initiating formal Russo-Korean relations was the handiwork of the chargé d'affaires at the Russian legation in Peking, Karl Ivanovich Weber. The initial request for treaty negotiations, forwarded in 1882, was refused. Weber therefore proceeded to Seoul in June 1884 and managed to conclude the agreement on July 7.

The Chinese leader, Li Hung-chang, had sent Paul von Mollendorff from the Chinese Maritime Customs Service to Korea as a royal adviser following rioting in Seoul in the summer of 1882. The young German arrived in December of that year and, although his mission was to further the interests of China, he became more concerned for the welfare of his host country. After a failed coup attempt in Seoul in 1884, he concluded that the future of an independent Korea lay not with either China or Japan but rather with some third power. The logical choice would be the United States since many competent Americans had arrived and seemed to have the best interests of the Korean people at heart. However, official America was singularly disinterested and did not bother to respond to Korean requests for help.

began to pressure the Korean government for immediate economic, political, judicial, and other reforms. They then refused the requests of the Chinese and Koreans to withdraw their forces and shrugged off a Russian offer to act as mediator. Although there was not yet a declaration of war, the gauntlet had clearly been thrown down, and the Chinese reluctantly picked it up.

On July 25, a British transport, the *Kowshing*, which had been chartered by China, was sunk in the Yellow Sea with the loss of the 1,000 troops aboard. Four days later, Japanese troops in the Seoul area struck south and overwhelmed the Chinese force at Asan. Finally, a declaration of war, under the date of August 1, was promulgated in Tokyo on August 3. The ensuing war quickly demonstrated that the Japanese had managed to modernize their military much more effectively than had the Chinese. They possessed superior weapons, discipline, and leadership. This was true both on land and on sea. Peking sent forces overland across southern Manchuria to concentrate at P'yongyang in northwestern Korea where, on September 15, they were attacked and overwhelmed by the Japanese army. When the remnants of the Chinese force retreated rapidly across the Yalu, Korea came under exclusive Japanese control.

Two days later, the major naval action of the war, usually referred to as the Battle of the Yalu River, was fought off the coast of northern Korea. The Japanese victory was complete, and the control of the sea gave them the ability to strike along the littoral at will. The Japanese First Army, under General Yamagata Aritomo, struck across the Yalu into southern Manchuria in October, and other forces, who landed by amphibious operations on the Liao-tung Peninsula the following month, were able to overwhelm quickly the Chinese centers at Talien and Port Arthur (present-day Lushun). In January, Japanese forces in Manchuria captured Haicheng, thereby opening the land approaches toward Peking. At the same time, landings were made on the northern coast of the Shantung Peninsula. This led to the capture, from the land side, of the port of Weihaiwei. The Japanese now controlled the seaward approaches to all of northern China. Two months later, the Pescadores Islands had been taken and landings effected on the island of Taiwan.

At this stage, the Chinese were forced into the ignominy of the Treaty of Shimonoseki. Li Hung-chang, who had been stripped of his authority because of the misfortunes of the war, was recalled to negotiate from a position of great weakness. Indeed, had it not been for loss of Japanese face by an attempt on Li's life in Shimonoseki, his position would have been even worse. By the terms of the treaty, which was signed on April 17, 1895, China was forced to recognize the independence of the kingdom of Korea and to cede Taiwan, the Pescadores, and the Liao-tung Peninsula to Japan. In addition, China was required to pay an indemnity of 200 million taels, a sum amounting to three times the annual national budget of Japan, and to grant certain other economic advantages to the Japanese.

In less than a week, however, Japan would be deprived of part of the fruits of her labors. The so-called Tripartite Intervention was the diplomatic pressure exerted by Russia, France, and Germany to force Japanese retrocession of the Liao-tung Peninsula to China. The Russian government, with prodding from Finance Minister Sergei Witte, had taken the lead in ensuring that Japanese territorial acquisitions not include areas on the mainland of Asia. However, to sweeten this bitter pill, China was compelled to pay an additional 30 million taels to Japan. As mentioned in the previous chapter, China was enabled to pay the heavy indemnity only by the loan engineered by Witte, using mostly French capital. Ironically, these assets would go a long way toward the great military buildup conducted by Japan in the following decade. One may say therefore that Russia and France directly helped to finance the power to be faced by the Russian Empire in the Russo-Japanese War of 1904–1905. Also, the Tripartite Intervention, and particularly Russia's role therein, would be remembered by the Japanese with deep resentment.

17

Russia, Manchuria, and the Boxer Rebellion

China's sovereignty came under increasing attack by the Western powers following the Opium War of 1839–1842. This conflict had resulted in the Treaty of Nanking, which opened China to the outside world and introduced the quaint concept of extraterritoriality. Greater indignities were heaped on the nation by the Anglo-French military invasion in 1860, which not only opened Peking to foreign diplomats but also included the destruction of the Ch'ing Summer Palace. To intensify the woes of the dynasty, the Taiping Rebellion raged during the decade and a half starting in 1850.

By the end of the sixth decade of the nineteenth century, it was becoming clear to many Chinese authorities that, for survival, China must modernize. Thanks to such leaders as Tso Tsung-t'ang and Li Hung-chang, the Self-strengthening Movement was attempted for about thirty-five years—from 1860 to 1895. However, the inertia of the court, personified by the powerful Empress Dowager Tz'u-hsi could not be overcome, and the country failed to take advantage of the opportunity.

During this time, too, the nation was subjected to other indignities. Revulsion against the practices of Christianity led to the massacre of French clerics and officials at Tientsin in 1870. This resulted in payment of compensation and apologies. Four years after that incident, the Japanese wrung virtual recognition of their sovereignty over the Ryukyus, which had been a tributary of China for 500 years. Five years later, they annexed the islands outright. In 1885, after a year of warfare, another Chinese tributary was lost when a French protectorate was recognized over Vietnam to the south. Then, the following year, Burma was lost as a tributary state when the British established themselves as the protecting power in that country. These losses, of course, paled beside those China incurred as the result of her defeat in the Sino-Japanese War of 1894–

1895: a huge indemnity, and cession to Japan of Taiwan and the Liao-tung
Peninsula. The latter loss, as we saw in the preceding chapter, was retroceded
as the result of action not by China but rather by France, Germany, and Russia,
at Russia's instigation.

Events in late 1897 would result in the virtual partition of China into spheres
of influence. Germany, as the growing power on the European continent, was
seeking its "place in the sun." An opportunity was provided by the murder of
two German missionaries on the Shantung Peninsula in November. German
forces quickly seized Kiaochow Bay on the south coast of the peninsula, including the excellent harbor of Tsingtao, and a few months later China was
compelled to grant a lease of the area for ninety-nine years. This action immediately resulted in what is known as the "scramble for concessions" of
1898.

The first moves precipitated by the German action were taken by the Russians.
In November 1897 the new foreign minister, Mikhail Murav'ev, convinced Tsar
Nicholas II that Russia should occupy the Liao-tung Peninsula in order to acquire the two ice-free ports of Talien and Port Arthur. This decision was taken
over the stout remonstrances of Finance Minister Witte, who argued that this
made a mockery of the defensive alliance between Russia and the Chinese
Empire and might impact very unfavorably on the progress of the Chinese Eastern Railway. He further warned that the occupation would unleash forces whose
effect in the Far East would ultimately prejudice Russia's territorial goals. Murav'ev succeeded in selling his position, however, by raising the specter of
British occupation of the Liao-tung Peninsula. Russian naval vessels entered
Port Arthur in December, and pressure was brought to bear on the Chinese to
grant concessions.

The Russian demands were not only for the ports but also for rights to build
a railway connecting the ports with the Chinese Eastern Railway. Witte submitted his resignation, which was refused by the emperor.[1] He thereupon, in his
typically bluff way, ensured that the treaty would become a reality. This meant
heavy bribes to Li Hung-chang and other key ministers in Peking. Still, the
Chinese resisted, and only after their appeals for help from Japan and Britain
were rejected did they acquiesce and sign a treaty on March 27, 1898. The
agreement was not for a cession but rather a leasehold of the peninsula and the
ports, to be in effect for twenty-five years. The treaty, which was couched in
terms of a joint action by two friendly powers, further stipulated that Chinese
sovereignty over the peninsula was not abridged.

The day following the signing of the agreement, Russian naval forces arrived
and occupied Port Arthur without incident, the two Chinese commanders on the
spot having been well bribed. Initially the flags of both China and Russia were
raised, which eased the pain to some local Chinese; however, within a few
weeks, the Chinese ensign was no longer flying. Work was immediately begun
to build the 600-mile South Manchurian Railroad to connect Port Arthur with
Harbin, the main center on the Chinese Eastern Railway. Action was com-

menced as well to expand and improve the harbors of Talien and Port Arthur. The problem up to that time facing the Russian Far East Naval Squadron was that operations from its base at Vladivostok were inhibited by ice each winter. As a result, the practice had been to winter over in Japanese ports. Indeed, the bulk of the squadron was in Nagasaki when it was ordered to Port Arthur.

As Witte had predicted, now that the Germans and Russians had achieved their imperialist ends, other nations made their demands on the corpus of China. The Japanese, who would not forget that the power responsible for pushing them out of the Liao-tung Peninsula now controlled it, acquired a sphere of influence in Fukien Province opposite the island of Taiwan. The French won a port for themselves at Kwangchow-wan on the south China coast and established a sphere in the southern provinces of Yunnan, Kwangtung, and Kwangsi. The British received, in addition to a sphere deep into central China up the Yangtze River, a twenty-five-year lease to the port city of Weihaiwei on the northeastern coast of the Shantung Peninsula. They also acquired the so-called New Territories on a ninety-nine-year lease to expand their toehold on the Chinese mainland opposite Hong Kong.

The scramble for concessions in 1898 so exposed China's vulnerability that even the empress dowager realized some sort of action was required. However, being loath to implement the reforms that were proposed, she turned to and supported a movement that was a sure loser—the Boxers. The Righteous and Harmonious Fists, a society usually known as the Boxers, was an offshoot from the White Lotus Secret Society and as such was basically opposed to the Ch'ing dynasty because of its foreign origin. However, by the last decade of the nineteenth century, it had altered its focus so that its slogan now supported the Ch'ing and called for the annihilation of foreigners from overseas. The Boxers claimed that their devotions earned for them superhuman qualities—that they could become immune to bullets and, even, acquire the power of flight. This appealed to parts of the population, particularly in Shantung where the Germans had forcibly taken Kiaochow.

By early 1900 the Boxers had begun to destroy railroads and telegraph lines, and the court took no action against them. Indeed, their status was dignified by being designated the Righteous and Harmonious Militia. By May the foreign legations were beginning to sense danger, and a force made up of 350 Russian, British, French, American, Italian, and Japanese troops was sent to Peking and arrived in early June. Reinforcements were requested from Tientsin, and British Admiral Edward Seymour led an international force out of Tientsin toward the capital on June 10. Boxers destroyed portions of the railroad and the telegraph line along Seymour's line of advance, and Chinese troops forced him to retire toward Tientsin. On the thirteenth, Boxers swarmed into Peking and the following day clashed for the first time with the legation guards. Thus started the two-month siege that was the core of the Boxer Rebellion.

One week later, the empress dowager, now totally dominated by the most conservative elements at court, and placing great trust in Boxer potential, declared war on the foreign powers. In quick response, an international force of approximately 20,000 troops, mostly from Japan, Russia, Britain, America, and France, was able to lift the siege on August 14, and the court, including the empress dowager, fled to Sian, not to return until early the following year. Chinese self-respect was shattered.

The Boxer Rebellion was not confined to the Peking-Tientsin area. Disturbances broke out in Manchuria at Mukden on June 30, and four days later the South Manchurian Railroad was savagely assailed at all stations south of Mukden. On July 7, Peking ordered regular Chinese troops in Manchuria to unite with the Boxers in action against the Russians. This precipitated attacks on Hailar in the west of Manchuria and on Harbin in central Manchuria as well as the railroad in between. Initially, the rail workers had only the Chinese Eastern Railway guards to defend them although the guards, many of whom were military veterans, made excellent account of themselves. By July 9, Russian War Minister Aleksei Kuropatkin had ordered military forces into Manchuria. Before their arrival, however, there was great concern over the large numbers of Chinese subjects living in towns in the Russian Far East. It was this fear that precipitated what is known as the "Blagoveshchensk Incident." On July 14, Chinese troops commenced an artillery bombardment aimed at the town from the other side of the Amur River. Although the cannonade was ineffective, most of the rounds falling harmlessly into the water, the local Russian military authorities of Blagoveshchensk feared an attack might be launched across the river. They therefore decided to deport the Chinese residents of the town—who numbered over 3,000 persons—by the simple expedient of driving them into the Amur. The majority of them perished since the river is half a mile wide at that point.

Late in the month, Russian forces began to pour into Manchuria from various directions. From Transbaikalia they came on the Transsiberian Railway. Others from Sretensk came down the Shilka and Amur to Blagoveshchensk where they crossed the river and attacked Chinese positions. Other forces moved northward from Port Arthur, while still others from Khabarovsk ascended the Sungari, arriving just in time to save the besieged defenders at Harbin on August 2. Control of the full length of the Chinese Eastern Railway had been reestablished by the end of August, and the capture of Mukden (modern-day Shenyang) a month later restored the entire South Manchurian Railroad to Russian hands. No time was lost in repairing the hundreds of miles of damage done the rail system, and both the Chinese Eastern Railway and the South Manchurian Railroad were provisionally opened for traffic in November 1901.

By the time the railroad rights-of-way had been recovered, the number of uniformed Russians in Manchuria had grown to almost 200,000. Despite affecting the role of China's sole friend among the Great Powers (only Russian troops had been withdrawn from Peking after the siege of the legations had been lifted), Saint Petersburg now attempted to capitalize on the situation in the northeast. War Minister Kuropatkin envisioned Manchuria as another Bukhara (which still was a protectorate, in name, in Central Asia). On November 30, 1900, Admiral Evgeni Alekseev, who had been given plenipotentiary powers, coerced Tseng-ch'i, the Chinese military governor at Mukden, to sign an agreement that virtually stripped Manchuria from Chinese sovereignty. This document required the Chinese to disarm and disband all troops in Manchuria, to turn over all ammunition, and to dismantle all fortifications. In addition, it called for the appointment of a Russian agent to be installed at Mukden to provide liaison between the governor-general and the Russian military authorities. The agreement was vague as to the duties and authority of the agent and as to the duration of the arrangement. In Peking, Li Hung-chang was most unhappy at this turn of affairs, and he refused to approve the document on the premise that Tseng was not authorized to negotiate on China's behalf.

The Russians, of course, were totally in charge in Manchuria and resolved still to make the most of their advantage. Therefore, by early February 1901, the Russian government had prepared a draft treaty which was put forward. This paper, although claiming to recognize Chinese sovereignty in Manchuria, contained the following provisions: (1) "temporary" Russian military occupation; (2) Chinese demilitarization in Manchuria until a later, unspecified time; (3) establishment of an indigenous police force of limited numbers; (4) stipulation that China not engage foreign instructors for its army and navy in northern China; (5) compensation to private Russian subjects, to the Chinese Eastern Railway, and to the Russo-Chinese Bank for losses resulting from the Boxer Rebellion; (6) authority for the Chinese Eastern Railway to build a branch from its rail system to the Great Wall; and (7) China's agreement not to grant any concessions to foreign powers for mining operations, industrial enterprise, or railway construction in Manchuria, Mongolia, or Sinkiang without consent of the Russian government.

Now that negotiations for the final settlement of the Boxer matter by the powers involved had been brought to a conclusion, the concern of those nations came to be centered increasingly on this newest territorial grab by Saint Petersburg. There was real fear that, if Russia were able to convert Manchuria into a veritable protectorate, China would be literally broken up. Li Hung-chang was therefore emboldened to reject the proposed Russian treaty out of hand despite the offer of a large bribe. Although there was a desire for annexation of Manchuria in certain offices in Saint Petersburg, it became evident that such a course might result in conflict with Japan. Witte, especially, counseled evacuation of the province. Nevertheless, matters remained unresolved by the time Li died in November 1901. Russia's occupation came under increasing international pressure, including that from the United States.

Russian intransigence was overcome by the sudden announcement of the Anglo-Japanese treaty of alliance, which was concluded on January 30, 1902. Now Russia faced not only the prospect of war against Japan but against a Japan supported by Great Britain. As a result, the Russo-Chinese Convention for the evacuation of Manchuria was concluded on April 8, 1902, in Peking. This doc-

ument provided for a three-phase withdrawal of Russian troops in time incre-
ments of six months. That is, evacuation was to be effected in the area west of
the Liao River (southwest Manchuria) by October 8, 1902, the rest of the southern province (modern-day Liaoning Province) and Kirin Province by April 8,
1903, and the rest of Manchuria by the following October 8. Thus China was
to regain sovereignty over the greater part of her northeast territory. The Russians withdrew from the southwest as scheduled. The second phase was circum-
vented by moving the troops into the sovereign areas of the railway system,
thus technically making them guards; and the third phase was disregarded altogether. Therefore, within a year of the outbreak of the Russo-Japanese War,
Russia controlled northern Manchuria, the Liao-tung Peninsula, and the right-
of-way of the South Manchurian Railroad connecting the two.

NOTE

1. It was not that Witte was a less ardent imperialist. Rather, he preferred that Russia's
territorial aggrandizement be done in a less confrontational way. As he states in his
memoirs:

Given our enormous frontier with China and our exceptionally favorable situation, the absorption
by Russia of a considerable portion of the Chinese Empire is only a question of time, unless China
succeeds in protecting herself. But our chief aim is to see that this absorption shall take place
naturally, without precipitating events, without taking premature steps, without seizing territory, in
order to avoid a premature division of China by the Powers concerned, which would deprive Russia
of China's most valuable provinces. (S. Y. Witte, *Memoirs of Count Witte*, trans. Abraham Yarmolinsky [New York: Doubleday, Page & Co., 1921], 122)

18

Korea and the Russo-Japanese War

While the attention of the European and American powers seemed to be focused on China, and especially on Manchuria, fateful events had been unfolding in the kingdom of Korea. As the result of the Sino-Japanese War and the Treaty of Shimonoseki, which concluded it, the Japanese seemed to hold forth in the country with a free hand. Even as early as the first month of that war (August 1894), the Japanese minister to Korea, Otori Keisuke, had already successfully imposed a formal treaty of alliance on the former Hermit Kingdom. This, of course, facilitated the movement of troops, munitions, and supplies through Korea for the prosecution of the war against China.

During the next few months, Otori attempted to force the implementation of reform measures. King Kojong was compelled to appoint a special council which proclaimed a series of social changes, including the prohibition of such institutions as slavery, the caste system, and childhood marriages. This effort was generally unsuccessful since the Korean bureaucracy managed to circumvent the directives through either ineptitude or petty intrigues. Thus frustrated, the Japanese government recalled Otori and replaced him with a former minister to Korea, Inoue Kaoru. By late November 1894, Inoue had presented the king with a list of twenty-one reforms designed to modernize the governmental structure of the country. To optimize the chance of implementation, he compelled Kojong to appoint certain ministers who were partisan to Japanese policies. Then, on January 7, 1895, the king was forced publicly to inaugurate the new series of changes, including a declaration ending *sadae*—the old tributary system with China.

Shortly after conclusion of the Treaty of Shimonoseki in April, currents began to militate against Japanese efforts to dominate Korean internal affairs. First, the reformers in the government began to meddle with such intimate matters as the topknots worn by the men and even the length of the stems of the pipes they smoked. This merely succeeded in inspiring widespread resistance to any reform. Second, on the international scene, certain of the maritime powers, notably Russia, became increasingly concerned over Japanese activity in Seoul. It appeared to them that Japan had indeed succeeded in freeing the Koreans from their tributary status under China only to subjugate them to Japanese domination. Further, the Japanese suffered considerable loss of face from having to retrocede the Liao-tung Peninsula in the face of the Tripartite Intervention of Russia, France, and Germany. One outcome of this event was the gradual rise of a faction in Korea favoring cooperation with Russia, a faction that tended to align itself with Queen Min (the consort) and the power-hungry Min family.

As a result of these currents, Inoue found his influence sagging. The king therefore was able to dilute any efforts at further reform and to replace those ministers who had been imposed by the Japanese. The government in Tokyo then decided to abandon reform and recalled Inoue. He was replaced in September 1895 by Lieutenant General Miura Goro, a career soldier with no previous diplomatic experience. Upon his arrival, Miura carefully denied any Japanese imperial designs, protesting that his only interest was in a free and independent Korea. He maintained that the continued presence of Japanese troops was essential, however, to protect the telegraph lines to the Liao-tung Peninsula but that they would be withdrawn once that area was evacuated. Miura felt frustrated by the bland policy he was directed to follow, and this sense was exacerbated by the seeming growth of Russian influence at the increasingly independent Korean court. Indeed, Karl Weber, the Russian chargé d'affaires, was making progress in his quiet way in furthering Russia's interests. His wife became a close associate of Queen Min, who was expanding her clout in political affairs and whose faction was decidedly anti-Japanese. Miura therefore decided that vigorous and firm action was called for, and he began to plan for the assassination of the queen.

The deed was carried out in the early hours of October 8, 1895, by a combination of Japanese civilian extremists, Japanese troops, and the *kunrentai* (Japanese-trained Korean troops who were fearful that they were about to be disbanded). The assassins overpowered the palace guard, stabbed the queen, and immediately burned her body. At the same time, King Kojong became a prisoner in his own palace which was controlled by the *kunrentai*. Miura professed to be shocked by the murder and offered condolences. Tokyo, which was taken by surprise, initially was convinced that it was the work of disgruntled Koreans. Gradually, however, the real story of the scope of Japanese involvement began to emerge from the accounts of eyewitnesses. Miura was recalled on October 17, and Komura Jutaro was appointed in his place. Tokyo announced an investigation and promised punishment of any who might be found guilty.

Although the Japanese were not in direct control of the court, the king was pretty much at the mercy of the *kunrentai* and of the new ministers who were carrying out policies that coincided with Japanese aims. He made quiet pleas to the foreign diplomats for help, particularly to Weber and the American minister, John Sill. Their concern and the constant presence of American missionaries in attendance on the king, including sleeping in the palace, were measures that did ensure some degree of safety. However, although Sill was doyen of the diplomatic community, he was given explicit orders from Washington not to interfere in any way. Ultimately, it would be left to Weber and the Russians to provide a different solution.

In January 1896 Korean sensibilities were offended by the announcement that Miura and others had been let off by the special court in Shimonoseki for lack of evidence. Seoul grew increasingly tense, and King Kojong became fearful. Weber was convinced that the time had come to remove the king's jailors. The question simply was by what means. The final answer would be the removal of the king himself from his jailors.

Whether the initiative came from the Russians or King Kojong is not entirely clear, but it was a premeditated event. On February 10, 1896, a Russian landing force of more than 100 naval personnel, with a field piece, were moved from two Russian warships at Chemulpo (modern-day Inchon) to the Russian legation. The reason given for such an action was added security against the unrest in the capital. Early the following morning, the king and the crown prince were spirited past the palace guards in closed sedan chairs, normally used by ladies of the court, and were taken directly to the Russian legation. Deprived of the legalizing presence of the royal authority, the Korean ministers now were suddenly rendered powerless, and those who were not fortunate enough to escape to Japan were brutally murdered by the mobs in Seoul.

In the Russian legation, King Kojong reconstituted his court and appointed new ministers, taking as his advisor in this matter Dr. Horace Allen of the American legation rather than any of the Russians. For more than a year, the center of government for the nation would be on Russian sovereign territory. Immediately after the king's escape, Weber had notified the other legations and knew his actions would cause many questions concerning his aims. His purpose was to keep up the appearance of altruism while, at the same time, ensuring that Russia's interests certainly would not be neglected.

During the time the king held court in the Russian legation, Weber's lack of interference was remarkable. In fact, it caused him to be the target of the Russian nationalist press. However, Weber's conduct was such as to soften whatever response might have been entertained by the Japanese who suddenly had lost their position of influence at the court but who still had the lion's share of foreign troops in the country. Komura pressed for the return of the king to the royal palace, but Kojong had no desire to oblige, and Weber left any such decision to his royal guest.

The crisis would finally be solved three months after the king's escape as the result of negotiations conducted by Weber and Komura, each of whom was in receipt of considerable guidance from his superiors. The Komura/Weber Memorandum of Understanding, also known as the Seoul Memorandum, was signed on May 14, 1896. The document contained four principal provisions in which it was agreed between the two representatives that (1) they would advise the king to return to his palace but leave the timing to his discretion, and the Japanese side would provide assurances that Japanese civilian extremists would be controlled; (2) they were favorably impressed by the high quality of the officials appointed by the king and would recommend in the future that appointments be similarly made; (3) the current state of affairs might require Japanese guards for the protection of Japanese telegraph lines, but the total number was not to exceed 200 and to be withdrawn when conditions improved; and (4) there would be stationed in Korea, for the protection of Japanese settlements, two companies of Japanese troops in Seoul, one in Pusan, and one in Wonsan, each company not to exceed 200 men—and Russian guards were authorized not to exceed in number those of the Japanese. The net result of the agreement was to reduce the Japanese presence and increase that of the Russians to an equal level. It appeared that the murder of Queen Min had cost the Japanese dearly. The memorandum was not published, although its contents became generally known through conversations by diplomats.

The Komura/Weber Memorandum was designed as an interim accommodation, and both nations looked forward to the time of Emperor Nicholas II's coronation in May as an opportunity to achieve an improved modus vivendi. It will be remembered that the coronation was the occasion utilized by Witte to set up the Li-Lobanov Treaty for the East China Railway. The Japanese representative at the coronation was the top military figure and influential member of the *genro* (elder statesmen who dominated the Meiji period)—Yamagata Aritomo. The coronation was held in Moscow on May 26, and on the sixth of June a protocol was signed by Yamagata and Foreign Minister Aleksei Lobanov-Rostovsky. The Lobanov/Yamagata—or Moscow—Protocol contained four open articles and two secret ones.

The first article had to do with the Korean economy. Korea was encouraged to curtail excessive expenditures, but if needed, loans could be arranged from the two powers in a common effort. Second, the two powers would attempt to leave it to the Koreans to form their own defense and police forces. The third article recognized the Japanese right to retain its telegraph lines and the Russian right to establish a telegraphic connection with Seoul; however, Korea could purchase such lines when able to in the future. The final open article was a catchall in which the two nations agreed to handle any unforeseen problems in an amicable manner. The first of the secret articles provided that, in case it became necessary for the two nations to send in forces to maintain the peace in Korea, spheres of activity of the two nations would be defined in order to prevent any collision of their forces. The final article of the protocol confirmed those parts of the Seoul Memorandum dealing with the numbers of troops and the security of the king.

This seemingly rather clear arrangement would become muddied very shortly, thanks to another honored visitor at the coronation. King Kojong had taken advantage of the opportunity to send Prince Min Yong-hwan to ask for Russian aid. Specifically, the king desired Russian protection until he was able to provide for his own defense, Russian instructors to train his forces, Russian political and economic advisors, a Russian loan, and, finally, direct telegraphic communications with Russia. Except for the telegraph lines, Lobanov gave a very vague response to Min, but the young Korean prince was persistent and finally received Russian concurrence to send Colonel Putiata as a military advisor and Dmitri Pokatilov, director of the Russo-Chinese Bank, as an interim financial advisor. At Putiata's urging, the Saint Petersburg government finally authorized the dispatch of two officers, ten noncommissioned officers, and a doctor as military instructors. The group arrived in Seoul on October 1, 1896. This, of course, violated the spirit of the Lobanov/Yamagata Protocol, but the Japanese were forced to put the best face on the matter. Min Yong-hwan was made Korean minister of war.

King Kojong was still resident in the Russian legation, and since Weber maintained a remarkably objective attitude, many concession seekers successfully secured audiences with the king. One such was the Swiss businessman, Jules Bryner,[1] who had established himself as a successful merchant in Vladivostok by the early 1880s. On September 9, 1896, he succeeded in obtaining a concession to exploit timber resources along the Yalu and Tumen rivers, concerning which we shall have more later.

Putiata's instructors set about training an 800-man palace guard: the King now was sufficiently reassured about his safety and agreed to return to Dongbok palace on February 20, 1897. He was accompanied by an honor guard under the leadership of Russian noncommissioned officers who were billeted in the palace compound not far from the king's quarters. The question now was the training of a larger military force. Putiata and Min Yong-hwan favored additional Russian instructors, but such action would be contrary to the Seoul Memorandum. Nevertheless, Saint Petersburg reluctantly approved the favor requested by Weber, and an additional thirteen instructors arrived in Korea on July 29. Still, though, fearful of the Japanese reaction, the Russian government forbade the actual training; none would be done until the arrival of Aleksei de Speier to replace Weber. This change occurred in early September 1897.

The remainder of the year would be dominated by the aggressive actions of Speier. Almost immediately upon his arrival, he demanded that the new Russian instructors commence the work of training Korean troops, and measures were taken to identify the new recruits. On September 30, Kir Alekseev arrived to take on a position as commercial agent with the Russian legation, but it was Speier's opinion that Alekseev should play a more exalted role. So, without consulting with Saint Petersburg, he pressured the Korean government to appoint Alekseev as chief advisor of all financial and related customs affairs of the nation. This action was finally approved in Saint Petersburg only at the insistence of the tsar. Other complications arose, however, since the director of the Korean Customs Service, a Briton by the name of John McLeavy Brown, had been the top foreign economic advisor. Therefore not only the Japanese but now the British were concerned. Nevertheless, Speier was able to force the issue with the Korean government and worked out an accommodation at the end of the year whereby Brown retained his official position with the customs but was supplanted by Alekseev as the senior financial advisor to the government.

By the end of January 1898, the Russo-Korean Bank had been founded to facilitate trade between the two countries, and it appeared that the growth of Russian influence was unstoppable. However, events that would suddenly bring down Speier's house of cards were under way. First, he was alienating the Koreans by his high-handed conduct by such actions as browbeating Korean ministers into accepting Russian desires to establish a storage depot on Deer Island in Pusan harbor in an area that had been earmarked by Seoul for a foreign settlement. Second, his principal interpreter, an illiterate former coolie, made himself most unwelcome to the Korean nobles by his arrogance. Last, events in Manchuria, particularly in the Liao-tung Peninsula, were rapidly displacing Russian interest in Korea. The prospect of a warm-water port in Manchuria had become more appealing and likely than one in Korea.

Aleksei de Speier still believed firmly that Russia's golden future in Korea relied on his tough tactics. Convinced that the king and government were totally dependent on the Russian presence for survival, he submitted—on his own initiative—what amounted to an ultimatum on March 7, 1898. If the Korean government no longer wished military training and economic direction from Russian advisors, it was to advise him in twenty-four hours. Five days later, his bluff was called when the Korean reply asserted that no foreign advisors were desired. A stunned Speier immediately terminated Russian activity. The soldiers left the palace compound on March 18; Alekseev was transferred to the legation in Tokyo; and the Russo-Korean Bank was closed in mid-April.

This cessation of Russian dominance in Korea in March 1898 somewhat softened Japanese chagrin over the Russian lease of the Liao-tung Peninsula in the same month. Tokyo suggested a policy of Japanese recognition of Russian primary interests in Manchuria in return for Russian agreement to Japanese paramount concerns in Korea. Some Russians, such as Roman Rosen, the minister to Tokyo, strongly supported this approach; however, military concern in Saint Petersburg militated against such recognition. As a result, the agreement effecting detente in the Far East was considerably different. On April 25, 1898, Rosen and the Japanese foreign minister, Nishi Tokugiro, signed a convention (Nishi/Rosen) that pertained only to Korea. A very brief document, it consisted of three articles. The first asserted that both countries would carefully observe Korean sovereignty. The second stated that, in the event of a Korean request for advice and assistance, neither nation would take action without mutual agreement. The last article provided that Russia would not impede the development of commercial and industrial relations between Korea and Japan.

Since the Napoleonic Wars in the early nineteenth century, Great Britain had adopted an international policy often described as ''splendid isolation,'' that is, avoiding alliances while trying to control the balance of power of the other European nations. The one exception, of course, had been the Crimean War. The international tapestry had changed dramatically by the end of the century, particularly because of the rise of Germany as the strongest power on the continent of Europe and the one desirous of playing a larger role on the world scene. The Boer War (1899–1902) made the British acutely aware of just how splendidly they were isolated as other powers made sport of the effort required to complete the taming of those fiercely independent Boers in South Africa, and the idea of an alliance became more attractive.

In the Far East, the Japanese had learned from the Tripartite Intervention, to their sorrow, the need of strong friends and allies when confronting other Great Powers. As time progressed, pressures continued to mount in Japan toward settling the Korean problem in a manner in the best interests of the empire. Ito Hirobumi, the great statesman of the Meiji era, generally favored accommodation with Russia and, after the fall of his cabinet, traveled to Saint Petersburg in late November 1901 as a private citizen. He unsuccessfully sought an arrangement whereby Japan would be given a free hand in Korea in commercial, industrial, *and* political matters. Even if Ito had received a positive response, his unofficial trip would have been rendered useless since the government concluded an Anglo-Japanese treaty of alliance on January 30, 1902. Tokyo had grown increasingly uneasy as it watched the Russians proceed toward completion of the South Manchurian Railroad and boost their military presence to almost 200,000 troops in Manchuria during the Boxer Rebellion.

The terms of the Anglo-Japanese alliance provided for the recognition of the sovereignty of China and Korea. More specifically, the British recognized Japan's paramount commercial, industrial, *and* political interests in Korea. Further, it was agreed that, in the event either party became involved in war with a third party, the ally would observe a benign neutrality; if, however, either party became involved in war with two other nations, the ally was obliged to join the conflict. Finally, both powers pledged not to enter into a separate agreement with a third nation without consulting its ally. Japan now had support for its Korean policy, and Great Britain could concentrate more of her fleet closer to Europe.

The Russian government, somewhat taken aback, attempted to expand the application of its Dual Alliance of 1894 with France, which had been designed as an answer to the threat of the Triple Alliance in Europe. In this effort, Saint Petersburg was unsuccessful; however, a Franco-Russian declaration was issued on March 16, 1902, which asserted that the two powers reserved the right to arrive at a preliminary understanding in the event a third nation might, by its actions, threaten the status quo in the Far East.

As noted in the preceding chapter, Russia had agreed to remove its troops from Manchuria in three separate six-monthly stages, commencing on October 8, 1902. The first stage, evacuation of southwestern Manchuria, was accomplished on schedule. However, based on a conscious decision made on February

7, 1903, the other two phases were not carried out. Sergei Witte was adamantly for evacuation, but by this time his position of strength had begun to erode, and other voices were receiving more attention from the vacillating Tsar Nicholas II. One of the voices against evacuation was that of Minister of War Kuropatkin. As long as the railroad to Vladivostok ran through Manchuria, he reasoned, the defense of the Maritime District could be ensured only by asserting hegemony over northern Manchuria. He saw a serious threat to such control in the large number of Chinese living in Vladivostok and other parts of the Russian Far East as well as the accelerating migration of Chinese into Manchuria itself. The Russian government, in April 1903, therefore demanded a series of guarantees in return for evacuation, such as nonalienation of the land to any other nation. The Chinese rejected the proposals out of hand, and the occupation of Manchuria continued.

But other factors impacted on Russian policy as well. The tsar increasingly came under the influence of others who were not ministers of state, notably Aleksandr Bezobrazov, who might be described as an articulate bureaucratic dilettante. What made matters seem even worse was the connection among some of these advisors, the tsar, and timber concessions in the Tumen and Yalu river valleys. It will be remembered that Jules Bryner had elicited timber concessions on the Korean side of the two rivers from King Kojong while the latter was in the Russian legation. Bryner had tried to interest the Russian Finance Ministry in the concession but was turned down. Bezobrazov, on the other hand, was intrigued and successfully promoted the idea of an East Asiatic Development Company to exploit the resources; it was even subscribed to by the private imperial purse. The scheme came to nothing in early 1902, however, thanks to the opposition of Witte, and the tsar directed Bezobrazov to liquidate the scheme. The finance minister thereby earned the intense hatred of Bezobrazov.

Witte was already under fire for such valid reasons as the condition of the nation's finances. The great expenditures for armaments and railroads, together with a crop failure in 1901, gave cause for deep concern. It was probably his more measured position on Far East policy, however, that led to his political demise. In the summer of 1902, the Yalu timber concession reared its head again, this time expanded to include claims of dubious validity on the Manchurian side of the Yalu River. Bezobrazov convinced the tsar to overrule Witte's suggestions for exploitation by private entrepreneurs; instead, Witte was directed to make 2 million rubles available to Bezobrazov to set up a government-sponsored enterprise. To provide labor for the undertaking, Bezobrazov recruited members of the military whose term of active service was expiring and who therefore were technically military reservists. The tsar approved the plan, and the Russian Timber Company of the Far East was formed in Saint Petersburg. Witte's loss of support became evident to all when he was suddenly ''kicked upstairs'' on August 28, 1903, to the essentially honorary post of chairman of the Council of Ministers. He was replaced by a virtual nonentity.

The great hopes for the Russian Timber Company of the Far East came to naught. Its employees were dismissed in October 1903, and the following January the tsar provided 200,000 rubles for the liquidation of the company's debts. The concession, though modest and unsuccessful, was the major Russian commercial enterprise in Korea. Despite this fact, considerable concern was expressed in the international press since what little was known included the fact that the concessions were under governmental aegis and employed military reservists. Japan, in the meanwhile, continued to assert an ever-growing dominance over the economy of the entire Korean nation.

Just two weeks before Witte's dismissal, a fateful decision had been taken by the tsar. This provided for the establishment of a viceroyalty to handle matters in the Far East. Appointed to the position of viceroy was Admiral Evgeni Alekseev, the handsome but incompetent illegitimate son of Alexander II. Alekseev since 1899 had been the commander of Russian naval forces in the Far East and, from his headquarters in Port Arthur, the senior commander of troops in Manchuria. As part of the plan, a Special Committee for Far Eastern Affairs was created to supervise the activity of the viceroyalty. The tsar was the chairman, and the four senior ministers of state were members. The secretary was one of the "Bezobrazov group"—Admiral A. M. Abaza, a cousin of Bezobrazov. This new arrangement of viceroyalty and special committee, in addition to the normal ministerial structure, proved to be an unfortunate move since it complicated the decision-making process at a time when Russian overall policy was not clearly defined. Further, the terms of reference under which the viceroy was to operate were not clearly delineated.

In August 1903, the same month that Witte was dismissed from his ministry and the viceroyalty was established, Tokyo sought new talks with Saint Petersburg in order to sort out the two nations' respective interests on the mainland of East Asia. The ensuing exchanges were rendered cumbrous on the Russian side by the necessity of constantly having to pass commentary back and forth between Saint Petersburg and Alekseev in Port Arthur. Over the ensuing five months, the Japanese would offer four different sets of proposals, and the Russians would respond with their counterproposals. Although compromise was achieved on certain questions, the extended negotiations gelled into two firm and conflicting positions. The Japanese wanted the freedom to intervene in the political affairs of Korea and demanded that Russia acknowledge Chinese sovereignty over Manchuria. The Russians, on the other hand, insisted that Japan should agree not to use Korea for strategic purposes and that a neutral zone should be established in Korea north of 39° north latitude.

The Japanese were deadly serious in their objectives whereas Saint Petersburg seemed not to evince a sense of urgency. The Russian leaders were convinced that Japan would not hazard war, but that if she were to, the outcome would not be to Russia's disadvantage. Further, some thought a small war might be good for the nation. The final Russian counterproposals, dated February 2, did not arrive in Tokyo until February 7, but by that time the die had been cast. The Meiji emperor sanctioned war on the fourth of February, and troops were en route to west Korean ports by the sixth. On that day also, Japan broke off diplomatic relations with the Russian Empire. Two days after that, the Japanese launched a naval attack, and forty-eight hours later they declared war.

The time picked for the opening of hostilities was the result of careful planning. The harbor of Vladivostok was frozen, and the unfinished Circumbaikal Railway acted as a severe bottleneck for the transport of Russian troops and supplies across the Asian mainland. Both sides knew that control of the sea was essential if Japan were to succeed in moving her troops from Japan to the mainland. However, while the Russian fleet was on paper the equal of that of the Japanese, its crews were not well trained or alert to the present danger. Admiral Togo Heihachiro, on the other hand, commanded a force that was well disciplined and drilled for combat. On the night of February 8–9, Togo's fleet appeared off Port Arthur, and a torpedo attack was launched against the Russian ships which were at anchor outside the harbor. Two battleships and a cruiser were put out of action but not sunk. Despite the fact that a sizable force remained, Alekseev ordered the fleet to remain in harbor—in effect blockading his own forces while the Japanese proceeded to transport tens of thousands of troops into Chemulpo. By March, Vice Admiral Stepan Makarov had arrived to take command of the fleet under the overall authority of Alekseev. Makarov's dynamic presence began to breathe life into his force, but he was killed on April 13 when his flagship, the *Petropavlovsk*, hit a mine and sank. Bereft of his energetic presence, the Pacific Squadron, for all practical purposes, ceased to exist.

The Japanese ground forces poured into western Korean ports unopposed. They quickly moved toward the Yalu River which would be the site of the first land battle of the war. On the last day of April and first of May, the Japanese, greatly assisted by gun boats, easily crossed the river into Manchuria. The rest of the land war would be fought in territory that nominally belonged to China. By June the Japanese had landed on the Liao-tung Peninsula north of Port Arthur where they severed the South Manchurian Railroad. One army turned south to commence the siege of Port Arthur while the main force commenced attacking along the railroad to the north. The important center of Liao-yang was taken on September 3 after a battle that lasted ten days. Port Arthur surrendered after a seven-month siege on January 2, 1905, and the old Manchu capital of Mukden was taken by a battle that ended on March 10.

Things had gone from bad to worse for the Russian naval force in the Far East. The small division at Vladivostok did not play an important role; after receiving a drubbing off Pusan, Korea, on August 14, 1904, its ships limped back to port where they would remain for the duration. Four days earlier, the Port Arthur squadron had been forced to depart its base as the Japanese besiegers were coming close to artillery range of the harbor. The plan was to make a run for Vladivostok; in the effort, however, the flagship was damaged, the commander was killed, and the battleships returned to port while a cruiser division dispersed to various neutral ports where the ships were interned. Therefore, the sorry ultimate fate of the Pacific Squadron was destruction by artillery pieces of the Japanese army.

The last dismal chapter of Russian naval power in the Pacific was yet to be played out. As early as June 1904, it had been decided in Saint Petersburg to augment the Pacific fleet with ships from the Baltic which were to be named the Second Pacific Squadron. It took four months for the squadron to get under way under the command of Vice Admiral Zinovi Rozhestvensky. No sooner had the squadron ships exited the Baltic than they mistook British fishing vessels for Japanese craft and blew several out of the water. This, the famed "Dogger Bank Incident," strained relations with the British and rendered refueling en route to the Far East very difficult. Rozhestvensky would have to rely on German and French resources. The remarkable fact is that he was able to shepherd all his motley armada, which included the oldest and the newest fleet units, successfully to the Far East although it did require seven and a half months. Rozhestvensky decided to attempt to make Vladivostok by the most direct route, that is, through the Korea Strait although there was little doubt that Togo's fleet would try to stop him. Thus, as the Second Pacific Squadron steamed into the strait on May 27, the battle was joined just east of Tsushima Island. The result was one of the worst naval disasters in history. Of the fifty-three Russian ships involved, three made it to Vladivostok.

It would seem that the Russians had lost the war; however, the Japanese were greatly overextended in terms of all their assets while the Russians continued to build up their ground forces, now with greater ease since completion of the Circumbaikal Railway. While the Japanese were reaching the end of their tether in terms of manpower and finances, Russia was beginning to feel the pain of revolution back in Europe. For these reasons, both sides were willing to accept the offer of President Theodore Roosevelt to broker a peace treaty. Therefore Sergei Witte and Komura Jutaro were dispatched to the U.S. Naval Shipyard in Portsmouth, New Hampshire, as plenipotentiaries.

The American attitude during the conflict had generally favored the Japanese side. Witte, however, by adroit use of the American press, tended to even out the diplomatic playing field. The Treaty of Portsmouth was signed on September 6, 1905. It was generally a punitive treaty in the sense that Japan was awarded territory at the expense of Russia. This included the Liao-tung Peninsula—the site that Japan had originally won as a result of the Sino-Japanese War but lost through the Tripartite Intervention—and the southern two-thirds of the South Manchurian Railroad, that is, from Changchun to Port Arthur. Also, Sakhalin Island south of 50° north latitude was ceded by Russia to Japan. In addition to this loss of territory, Russia recognized Japan's paramount *political* interests in Korea—the point that had been fundamental to the outbreak of war. Both sides agreed to remove all troops from Manchuria, except railroad guards. Although Japan received territory, one of its primary aims was to collect a massive indemnity. In this matter the Russians were adamant—and so there was none. Roosevelt, trying to be an honest broker, succeeded in alienating both parties:

the Russians because of their territorial losses and the Japanese for failure to receive an indemnity. Japan now, of course, had a free hand to institute a protectorate in Korea, and just five years later the Hermit Kingdom was annexed and became an integral part of the Japanese Empire.

NOTE

1. He was the paternal grandfather of the actor Yul Brynner, whose first name is an adaptation of his grandfather's.

19

War, Revolution, and Reconquest

China continued to sink ever deeper into an abyss of despair and helplessness. The Russo-Japanese War was mostly fought on territory nominally under the sovereignty of the Ch'ing dynasty. Indeed, it took place on land the Manchus considered their patrimony. By the end of the war, although lip service was paid to the integrity of the Chinese Empire, Russia controlled the northern part of Manchuria, and Japan controlled the southern part. By this time, China had been stripped of her tributary suzerainty over the Ryukyus, West Turkestan, Vietnam, Burma, and Korea. Her territorial integrity had been eroded by cessions of land to Russia in Ussuria, Amuria, and Ili; the British in Hong Kong and Weihaiwei; the Germans in Kiaochow; the Japanese in Liao-tung and Taiwan; and the French in Kwangchow-wan. The nation had been divided into spheres of influence. The time was ripe for change, and certain efforts to alter the state of things were made at this time.

There was much support among the literati for a constitutional monarchy, but a leader from southern China named Sun Yat-sen had set as his goal a republic. After finally creating an effective party organization in the Kuomintang (Nationalist Party), Sun realized his dream on January 1, 1912, when the Republic of China came into existence. However, he was forced from power by conservative elements under Yuan Shih-k'ai in 1913.

Yuan appointed loyal followers to the position of governors of provinces, and in the year 1915 he became obsessed with the idea of having himself installed as the first emperor of a new dynasty. There was a certain amount of resistance to this ambition, but the matter became moot when he died the following year at the age of fifty-seven. With his departure, there was a yawning void at the nation's political center, and from that time the provincial governors, whose sense of loyalty was to Yuan the man, not to the office of the presidency, tended to go their own individual ways and initiate that sad period in modern Chinese history known as "warlordism." There would be a pretense at central government in Peking, but in fact the Republic of China would continually be under the influence of some warlord or clique.

In the meantime, revolutionary currents had been on the move in Russia. The eastern Slavs had been far removed from the Renaissance, and the impact of the French Revolution was largely restricted to the abortive Decembrist uprising in 1825 at the death of Alexander I. The Russian "revolutionary tradition" had been largely that of peasant uprisings, usually under Cossack leaders, such as Stenka Razin in 1670–1671 and Emelian Pugachev in 1773–1775. The Polish insurrections of 1830 and 1863 had been quickly suppressed, and it was Russian troops that preserved the throne of the Hapsburgs in Vienna during the revolutions of 1848 to 1849.

As the nineteenth century wore on, however, pressures for change began to build. Defeat in the Crimean War (1853–1856) convinced Alexander II to implement such reforms as elimination of the institution of serfdom and the creation of the *zemstva* (elected bodies to administer rural Russia). His reforms, top down as they were, did not satisfy the small but growing radical revolutionary movement.

The gradual growth of such activity, perforce centered abroad, led to abortive uprisings following the Russo-Japanese War in 1905. Then, nourished by the failures of World War I, the momentum of change resulted in the abdication of Emperor Nicholas II on March 15, 1917, the establishment of a provisional government, and the deluge of the Bolshevik Revolution on the following November 7.

Although hesitant at first, the Bolsheviks showed that they could wield power in a way Nicholas II and the Provisional Government had not been able to. The executive arm of the new government was called the Council (Soviet) of People's Commissars. Vladimir Lenin (real name Ulianov) was the chairman, Leon Trotsky (real name Bronstein) the commissar for foreign affairs, and the Georgian Yosif Stalin (real name Dzhugashvili) the commissar for minorities. In two days the government had closed all hostile newspapers and then proceeded to confiscate all newsprint and ink. On December 20, the *CHEKA* (an abbreviation consisting of the initial letters of two Russian words representing "Extraordinary Committee"), the first designation of the secret police, was established under the leadership of a Pole, Felix Dzerzhynski. Numerous changes in all aspects of existence took place in Russia, such as conversion to the Gregorian calendar, a new orthography for the Russian language and many others of a socioeconomic nature. Also, the name of the party was changed to the RKP(b) [Russian Communist Party (of bolsheviks)].

The various factions opposed to the revolutionary government began to coalesce quickly in the south, northwest, north, and east. The Eastern Front, the one of primary interest to us, was in many ways the most complex facing the Bolsheviks. The principal military threat to Moscow (the new capital in place

of Saint Petersburg) from the east grew out of a phenomenon known as the
"Czech Anabasis." In the course of World War I, many Czechs were captured
by Russian forces or else willingly gave themselves up rather than fight for the
detested Hapsburg emperors of Austria-Hungary. They had been organized by
the Russians into discrete military units to fight the Central Powers. After the
Bolsheviks withdrew Russia from the war in March 1918, the Czech presence
was somewhat of an embarrassment; therefore, an agreement was made with the
French for the Czech Legion to be withdrawn across the Transsiberian Railway
for further transportation to the Western Front. Misunderstandings ensued between the Czechs and the Soviet government with the result that on May 25,
Trotsky, now the war commissar, ordered the entire group, more than 40,000
men, to be disarmed. The Czechs, by now spread all along the Transsiberian
eastward from the Volga city of Samara, quickly responded by taking control
of the cities and towns they were in and displacing the local Soviet governments,
whether of Bolshevik or other political stripe.

Later in the year Admiral Alexander Kolchak, who had commanded a de-
stroyer at Port Arthur during the Russo-Japanese War and served as commander
in chief of the Black Sea Fleet during World War I, became the leader of
"White" forces east of the Urals. With the help of Czech General Rudolph
Gajda, and relying on the nucleus of the Czech Legion, Admiral Kolchak's
forces now appeared to have the brightest prospects for success of any of the
White armies in the civil war. By December 1918, Ufa had been taken in the
south, and the White forces captured Perm in a move toward the northwest.
Kolchak's achievements were rewarded by the other White leaders who agreed
to recognize him as the supreme ruler of Russia. His success, however, was
fleeting. He opted to try to join up with the White forces in the north rather
than with the much larger force in the south. Another factor was that the Czechs
were not eager to continue supporting his aims after the armistice ended World
War I in November 1918. Also, his supply line, promised by the Allies, did not
materialize in the quantity he had anticipated. Indeed, the Japanese played a role
in restricting the flow which perforce had to cross Asia from Vladivostok. As
a result, Kolchak began to suffer reverses.

A Red offensive in May 1919 pushed Kolchak's forces beyond the Urals so
that any chance of linking up with the southern White forces, whose main offensive would not start for another month or two, was lost. The White capital
of Omsk was taken by the Reds in November, and Kolchak was forced to retreat
to Novonikolaevsk (now Novosibirsk) in December. He was pushed even farther
east, and when his train arrived in Irkutsk in January 1920, he was accompanied
still by many Czechs as well as French officers who were his advisors. Irkutsk
itself was very shortly taken over by Socialist Revolutionaries who demanded
that Kolchak and his state treasury be handed over in return for a safe passage
for the others to the east. The Czechs and French agreed. Kolchak was subjected
to a kangaroo court, found guilty of treason, and shot on February 7, 1920. His
body was thrown into the ice of the Angara River.

So the Russian civil war, which lasted from mid-1918 to late 1920, ended in total victory for the Soviet government of the Bolsheviks. The Reds, although initially restricted to an area quite similar to that of the fifteenth-century principality of Muscovy, had the advantage of interior lines of communication. Among the many reasons for their success was their claim to all Russians that they were Russia's bulwark against foreign intervention.

There was indeed foreign intervention, primarily stemming from fear on the part of the Allies that, after the Bolsheviks withdrew Russia from the war in March 1918, munitions that had been shipped to Russia to assist in the war would fall into the hands of the Germans. Also there was a resentment that the Bolsheviks had withdrawn Russia from a war for which she was largely responsible. Other reasons included the British anger over the murder of the imperial family which had a close kinship to the British Crown. French investors, being Russia's leading creditors, experienced a strong urge to intervene after the Bolsheviks repudiated all indebtedness of the predecessor tsarist government.

There was limited participation by the allies on the southern, northwest, and northern fronts, but there was a serious and extended period of foreign intervention directed at Russia from the east. This was due principally to the massive involvement of Japanese troops and the territorial designs of the Japanese Empire. Vladivostok was a major delivery point for Allied munitions. Therefore, British, French, and U.S. forces were sent to prevent the flow of these arms to the Central Powers. The Americans had another concern in that the Russian Provisional Government had contracted, in the summer of 1917, for American engineers and mechanics to operate and maintain the Transsiberian Railway and its rolling stock. Further, the United States was committed to ensuring the safe departure of the Czech Legion. Actually, the Americans had no special brief, as did the British and French, to fight Bolsheviks but rather to look out for the interests of the Russian people—not specifying, however, which Russian people. The United States was opposed to large-scale intervention and the creation of a front at the Ural Mountains. The British, on the other hand, spooked by concern over the thousands of prisoners of war from the Central Powers in Central Asia (a perceived threat to India), favored a force of 100,000 and viewed the Japanese as a splendid source of such military manpower.

The Japanese viewed the revolution in Russia as a sign of weakness that would enable them to pursue their continental ambitions, building on their past successes. Thus Japanese plans were formulated for intervention in the summer of 1917, and the planners were unhappy when they learned of the American involvement in the operation of the Transsiberian Railway.

The path for intervention in the Far East was prepared by the Czech Legion whose detachment in Vladivostok seized the city from the Reds on July 29, 1918. Early the following month, Allied and Japanese troops commenced streaming into the port. The number of Japanese exceeded 70,000 within a period of three months, and the Americans landed somewhat over 7,000. There were also about 1,000 British troops and a lesser number of French and Canadians. The key to control of the eastern parts of Russia was the Transsiberian Railway; therefore, an Inter-Allied Railway Committee was established and guard responsibility was allocated to the participating powers.

The Chinese Eastern Railway, which cut across Manchuria from Manchouli in the west to intersect with the Ussuriisk Line in the east (which connected Vladivostok and Khabarovsk), was assigned to the Chinese. The Japanese were given responsibility for most of the Ussuriisk Line and the Transbaikal Line, which connected Manchouli and Verkhneudinsk (now known as Ulan Ude) via Chita. They were allocated as well the Amur Line, running between Khabarovsk and Chita. The Americans manned fewer, but more strategic, points such as the southern end of the Ussuriisk Line, including Vladivostok, and the Circumbaikal Line linking up Verkhneudinsk and Irkutsk. The Americans also stationed a force in excess of 1,000 men at Harbin, the headquarters of the Chinese Eastern Railway. All guards west of Lake Baikal were under French General Janin, advisor to Admiral Kolchak, although this became academic after Kolchak's demise in February 1920.

During the period of foreign intervention, the Japanese succeeded in alienating a large segment of the local Russian population—to a large degree by the choice of local leaders they supported. These included Grigori Semenov in Transbaikalia and Ivan Kalmykov in the Amur region. Both were extraordinarily cruel, psychopathic killers. Kalmykov was an obscure anti-Bolshevik fighter in the Ussuri valley until the advent of the Japanese in the summer of 1918. He ingratiated himself into their good graces and, by devious means, managed to be elected Ataman of the Ussuri Cossacks. He centered his activities in Khabarovsk, and his brutality became legendary both in the treatment of his own men and in witch-hunts for supposed Bolsheviks. In 1920 he fled into Manchuria where he was arrested and shot by the Chinese.

Grigori Semenov became renowned for his cruelty and casual murder of civilians. He was of Buriat ancestry on his mother's side and for that reason had been sent from the Caucasus to attempt to build an anti-Soviet movement among the Buriat Mongols in Transbaikalia. He was only minimally successful until the Czech takeover of the Transsiberian, at which time he began to operate freely in the area from armored cars on the railroad. When the Japanese arrived, he quickly cast his lot with them and managed to indulge his penchant for killing, torturing, and looting. In January 1920, when the Japanese put down a socialist coup attempt in Vladivostok, they turned the leader over to Semenov. He in turn had the man bound and thrown into the firebox of his locomotive to augment his fuel supply. Semenov was of great value to the Japanese in that his activities hindered the movement of supplies to Admiral Kolchak's army in western Siberia despite the fact that Kolchak was his nominal superior. The Japanese viewed the Omsk government as the more probable threat to their designs in East Asia and therefore had no desire to contribute to its success. Despite all this, Semenov was designated the successor to Kolchak when the latter was killed.

With the death of Kolchak and the collapse of the White forces in Siberia, the rationale for foreign intervention came totally to an end. Therefore, the American forces were withdrawn the first week of April 1920. The Japanese now were left as the only foreign interventionists, a fact they justified on the basis of the need to maintain order in the chaotic Russian Far East. This stand seemed vindicated, on May 25, when the local Bolshevik authority in Niko-laevsk, on the lower Amur, carried out the massacre of every Japanese soldier and civilian in the town, almost 700 people. This event was used as well by the Japanese to justify their seizure of the northern, that is the Russian, half of Sakhalin Island.

The Japanese then were subjected to considerable international pressure to withdraw from the Russian Far East. The Washington Naval Conference of 1921–1922, which we shall discuss later, worked against Japanese interests and saw the dissolution of the Anglo-Japanese Alliance. One development definitely not in their favor was the creation, on April 6, 1920, of the Far Eastern Republic, to include Russian territory from Lake Baikal to the Pacific. Moscow had sup-ported and adopted the suggestion of such a state from Aleksandr Krasnosh-chekov, a man of Ukrainian birth who had become an American citizen. The Far Eastern Republic, with Krasnoshchekov as its president, was touted as a truly democratic country. A constituent assembly was convened, which adopted a Western-style constitution. Its capital at first was Verkhneudinsk and was moved to Chita after Semenov had been forced back to Manchuria in October. Moscow, of course, immediately recognized the new regime. The device of the Far Eastern Republic actually served as a face-saving means for a less awkward withdrawal by the Japanese. Tokyo recognized the new state as early as July 15, 1920, and commenced a measured drawdown of forces which continued until the departure of the last units on October 25, 1922. To the surprise of very few observers, the Far Eastern Republic, at its own request, was incorporated into the Soviet state just twenty-five days later.

There still remained the matter of northern Sakhalin. Initially, in 1921, only such new regimes as those of Ataturk in Turkey, Pahlevi in Teheran, and Emir Amanullah of Afghanistan were desperate enough to exchange recognition with the Bolshevik government. In 1924, however, several European nations, includ-ing Britain and France, extended recognition. Japan therefore felt that her com-petitiveness would suffer if she did not follow suit. Accordingly, on January 20, 1925, the Soviets agreed to mutual recognition, dependent on the return of north-ern Sakhalin. In the meantime, however, the Japanese had been feverishly ex-ploiting the natural resources of the north and succeeded in convincing the Soviets to grant them extensive concessions in the development of the oil and coal deposits even after the restoration of sovereignty.

Despite invading White armies and foreign intervention, the Bolsheviks had pretty well recovered most of the territory predominantly inhabited by Russians by the year 1920, with the exception of the Far East where the process required another two years (and not until 1925 in northern Sakhalin). However, much territory of the former Russian Empire was lost permanently, and other areas had to be recovered by military means. Most of the permanent losses were in Europe; virtually all of the former Russian territories in Asia were retrieved.

In the Transcaucasus, between the Black and Caspian seas, Georgia, Armenia, and Azerbaijan broke away from Russia in the wake of the Bolshevik Revolution. Initially, they constituted a Transcaucasian Federative Republic, but this had dissolved into three separate sovereign countries by May 1918. In less than three years, they had been overrun by the Red Army and in 1922 were organized into the Transcaucasian Federative Soviet Republic. As such they were inducted into the Soviet Union by the Constitution of 1923. Thirteen years later, the Trancaucasus Republic was subdivided into the Georgian, Armenian, and Azerbaijanian Soviet Socialist Republics.

The situation in Central Asia presented a more complex aspect than most other border areas. By World War I, the land of the Kazakhs had been organized into (1) two provinces, Uralsk and Turgai, in the western end of the Kazakh steppe; and (2) the Steppe Governate-General in the eastern Kazakh steppe, comprising the provinces of Akmolinsk and Semipalatinsk. To the south of this lay the Governate-General of Turkestan, which was made up of the provinces of (1) Transcaspia in the west, (2) Semirechie in the east along the Chinese border, (3) Syr Darya between those two, (4) Samarkand to the south of it, and (5) Fergana in the southeast. Also included in the Turkestan Governate-General were the powerless vassal khanates of Bukhara and Khiva.

Since the conquest of Central Asia, described in chapter 14, Russian sovereignty had not been seriously challenged. At the time of the 1905 revolution, disturbances were caused only by Russian garrisons and railway personnel. Yet the constant immigration of Russians and Ukrainians into these Muslim lands, especially in the steppe, caused a gradual heightening of resentment. Not until 1916 did a major outbreak occur, however, and it was related to World War I. From the time of the conquest, the native population had not been subject to induction into the Russian military, but a decree of June 25, 1916, called up non-Russians for labor duties in the rear of the front lines; the quota for Central Asia amounted to half a million men. Not only did the inhabitants resent the imposition but were especially humiliated that they were being called to dig ditches rather than to fight. The rebellion was quashed finally by the end of the year, thanks in part to the firm but reasonable leadership of General Aleksei Kuropatkin who was governor-general of Turkestan at the time.

With the abdication of the tsar in March 1917, a Soviet of People's and Workers' Deputies was established in Tashkent. At the same time, various Muslim congresses were convened in such areas as Kazan, Bashkiria, Azerbaijan, and Central Asia. Among the Kazakhs a moderate national political party was formed as well, called the *Alash Orda*. Then, by the time the Bolshevik Revolution took place in November 1917, the Ural, Orenburg, and Semirechie Cossacks had seized power in their regions, thus sealing the Kazakh steppe from the Bolsheviks. In December a congress in Orenburg proclaimed an autonomous

Kazakh region under the *Alash Orda*. Red forces initially overran the northwest section, including Orenburg, but by the spring of 1918 Ataman Aleksandr Dutov of the Orenburg Cossacks, who later would be commander of the left wing of Kolchak's army, was able to seal off the region again. Unfortunately for the population of Kazakhstan, factionalism prevented constructive progress so that by March 1919, when Kolchak's front collapsed, the Red Army was able to overwhelm Dutov's Cossacks and open the road to Kazakhstan. The following August, the Kirgiz (Kazakh) Soviet Socialist Republic was created.

Most of the political activity in Russian Central Asia, whether on the part of the imperial government or the Tashkent Soviet, was conducted by the Slavic elements rather than the indigenous Muslim population. An exception, in early December 1917, was an Extraordinary Regional Muslim Congress convened in the town of Kokand where it declared itself to be the government of an autonomous Turkestan. This action was branded as "counterrevolutionary" by the Tashkent Soviet under the leadership of Fedor Kolesov, and two months later Red troops surrounded Kokand. The ill-armed defenders were quickly overwhelmed; the city was sacked and thousands massacred by the victors. This ill-advised event was done without instructions from Moscow, and it would harden a large segment of Muslim resistance into the Basmachi movement, discussed later. It would thereby complicate and lengthen the Bolshevik attempts to secure Turkestan.

For the next year and a half, the Soviet government in Tashkent would be in a veritable state of siege because of Ataman Dutov's closure of the Orenburg-Tashkent Railway, the virtual lifeline of Turkestan. The alternative route, via the Caspian Sea and the Central Asian Railway from Krasnozavodsk, would be at the mercy of the British, who had moved onto the Caspian Sea from Persia, until mid-1919. It was from this direction that the Tashkent Bolsheviks saw one of their principal threats, unaware of the paucity of support actually provided by Britain. Another cause for concern was the Bukharan protectorate, which had a lengthy common border with Afghanistan. It was Bukhara that revealed the basic weakness of the Soviet. Just after destruction of the Muslim government in Kokand in March 1918, Kolesov led a small force against Bukhara on the assumption that it would quickly fold. To his surprise, he discovered that the emir had imported arms and knew how to use them. Kolesov narrowly averted a disaster, and Bukhara retained its autonomy for the time being.

Matters brightened considerably for the Tashkent Soviet in the summer of 1919. Kolchak was pushed back beyond the Urals, Dutov was defeated, and the railroad was opened for Red supplies and troops from Orenburg. At the same time, withdrawal of the British from northern Persia and the Caspian opened up that route. Accordingly, Transcaspia (mostly Turkmens) was brought to heel. The protectorate of Khiva, which was compressed along the lower reaches of the Amu Darya, was now ripe for plucking. The invasion commenced on December 25, 1919, and resistance ceased after a month. After communist-style elections were held in May 1920, the new government abolished the khanate and proclaimed the establishment of the Khoresmian People's Soviet Republic.

Because of the Kokand massacre in 1918, Moscow entertained doubts about the Tashkent Soviet's handling of affairs in Turkestan and so, the following year, established the Turkestan Commission. At about this time, concern was growing in Tashkent that Bukhara was rapidly becoming a threat to be reckoned with, thanks to increased aid from Afghanistan. An important member of the new commission was the successful Bolshevik General Mikhail Frunze. He and his chief political commissar, Valerian Kuibyshev, made plans to handle the problem and convinced the commission and Moscow to approve their recommended solution. As a result, on August 28, 1920, in coordination with an uprising by the Bukharan Revolutionary Committee, a military attack was launched. Success was achieved by the second of September, and a month later the Bukharan People's Soviet Republic was proclaimed.

By the end of 1920, Russian Central Asia consisted of the Kirgiz (Kazakh) Autonomous Soviet Socialist Republic, the Bukharan and Khoresmian People's Republics, and, for the rest of Turkestan, the Turkestan Soviet Republic. However, there was still considerable unrest, most of which was provided by the Basmachi, whose activity was concentrated in the former Fergana Oblast. As mentioned, the group grew out of the destruction of the Muslim government and massacre in Kokand in March 1918. The members were quite active and successful for almost two years. Then the arrival of Frunze and the formation of the Turkestan Commission heralded a ''soft'' policy that would reduce grievances, but the subjugation of Khiva and Bukhara the following year heightened fears. Indeed, many more recruits flocked to the Basmachi when the emir of Bukhara fled to the east and joined one of their leaders, Ibrahim Beg. Fighting was hot and heavy for the next year, and the Bolsheviks committed two divisions to the task of rooting out the organization.

The last phase commenced in October 1921 when the charismatic figure of Enver Pasha appeared on the scene. Enver had been a leader of the Young Turks in the eventful years in Turkey before World War I. Then, during the war, he was war minister for the Ottoman Empire. After Turkey's defeat he was forced to flee and sought refuge in Russia. Lenin saw in him a possibility of bringing peace to Central Asia which, except for the Tajiks, was made up of Turkic-speaking peoples. When Enver arrived on the scene, however, he threw his lot in with the Basmachi instead. Despite several early successes, Enver and the Basmachi just did not have the resources to resist the Red Army. His death in battle in August 1922 was a sharp blow, and although the Basmachi continued in existence, they were pushed deep into the Pamirs in what is now Tajikistan. Ibrahim Beg fled to Afghanistan in 1926, and the movement was reduced to border raids until Ibrahim was caught and executed in 1931.

In September 1920 the Turkestan Commission promulgated a constitution which created the Turkestan Autonomous Soviet Socialist Republic (ASSR) within the Soviet Russian state. This included all of the former governate-general except Khiva and Bukhara. In Khiva, certain elements were unhappy with their status. The result was a Red purge of all disaffected entities and the creation of the Khoresmian Soviet Socialist Republic. This pattern was then repeated in Bukhara. The problem here was more complex since Bukhara was larger and closer to the operating areas of the Basmachi; therefore, the Bukharan Soviet Socialist Republic was not proclaimed until September 1924.

Another dimension had now to be considered in view of Lenin's Nationality Policy which provided for national delimitation. Although there was very little sense of nationality among the peoples of Central Asia, the basic loyalties being to clan or family, there were discrete linguistic groups. As a result, the Kazakhs were defined as a group, as were the Turkmens, Kirgiz, Uzbeks, and Tajiks, and the borders were redrawn to reflect this linguistic distribution. All were considered to be parts of the Russian Soviet Federated Socialist Republic until the Constitution of 1936 raised them all to the status of Soviet socialist republics within the Soviet Union.

A major problem encountered by the Bolsheviks in their conquest of border areas with non-Russian populations was reconciling such action with their earlier criticism of tsarist imperialism. The fact was that the Bolsheviks were realists when the chips were down. They realized Russia's vulnerability—the age-old problem—to attack on her periphery. In particular, there was concern that, if Central Asia were not brought into the fold, extensive territory might very well become aligned with and dependent on the British in India acting through Afghanistan. In a more ideological vein, the hoped-for world revolution had not materialized; therefore, the continuing struggle would require a firm base for operations, namely Russia. Accordingly, it was reasoned, it was only right in the meantime that peoples on the border of the Russian state be given the blessings of bolshevism rather than to be subjected to exploitation by the evils of external capitalist influences. Also, the rationale provided that the cultural and ethnic identities of these peripheral peoples were recognized by the new system of Soviet socialist republics, which comprised a union of republics of supposedly equal status. This would be a strength of the Soviet state as long as the central authority was all-powerful. However, when decay set in at the center, the arrangement would hasten and facilitate the breakup of the Soviet Union.

20

Mongolia:
The First Soviet Satellite

While revolution and civil war were taking their toll on China and Russia in the first two decades of the twentieth century, interesting developments had been taking place in Mongolia. When we speak of Mongolia generally, we are addressing that part of the Ch'ing Empire which comprised the region containing the Altai Mountains, the Gobi Desert, and the steppe land on either side of the desert. Addition of this vast region to the Chinese Empire was owed to the omnipotence of the early Manchu emperors. Even before the Manchus came to power as the Ch'ing in 1644, the Eastern or Khalka Mongols had been brought under their control and organized into eight banners. By the terms of the Treaty of Kiakhta of 1728, a Sino-Russian border was delineated, and Russia recognized Mongolia as Chinese territory. Within three decades, thanks to this agreement, the Ch'ien-lung emperor was able to complete the subjugation of all the Mongol clans resident therein. The close relationship between the Manchus and Mongols was reflected in the veritable records of the Ch'ing dynasty which were maintained in the Chinese, Manchu, *and* Mongol languages. In the twentieth century, the area south of the Gobi has come to be designated Inner Mongolia and that to the north as Outer Mongolia.

Despite inroads made by Russia into China after the Peking Convention of 1860, Chinese sovereignty over Mongolia did not come seriously into question, although many Russian writers took the view that it was just a matter of time until the area should logically join the Russian Empire. It would not become a major issue, however, until after the Russo-Japanese War of 1904–1905. Less than two years after the conclusion of the Treaty of Portsmouth, Saint Petersburg and Tokyo came to an agreement on the state of affairs in the region. By the Russo-Japanese Convention of July 30, 1907, southern Manchuria was recognized as a Japanese sphere of influence and northern Manchuria as a Russian one. Additionally, Korea was acknowledged to be an area of exclusively Japanese influence while Outer Mongolia was assigned as a Russian sphere. Note that Inner Mongolia was not mentioned.

The Japanese moved swiftly in Korea, annexing that unfortunate country as an integral part of the Japanese Empire on August 22, 1910. The Russians entertained the urge to act similarly in Outer Mongolia, partly as a measure to ensure the security of the Transsiberian Railway and partly yielding to the imperialistic thrust of the times. Saint Petersburg was deterred, however, by the international realities in Europe where Russian security depended on special relationships with France and Britain provided for in the Dual Alliance and the Triple Entente. Russia did not wish to harm these relationships by precipitate action in Mongolia. There were other forces at work that would increase pressure for Russian involvement, however. In July 1911 the spiritual leader of the Mongols, the Jebtsundamba Khutukhtu ("Living Buddha"), gave his blessing to a congress of Mongol lamas and princes. This action had been in reaction to a new Ch'ing policy of moving Chinese peasantry into Outer Mongolia and augmenting troop strength to ensure a tighter hold on the area. These actions exacerbated a situation already rendered tense by the universal indebtedness of the Mongol population to usurious Chinese merchants. The congress of lamas sent a delegation to Saint Petersburg to request support from the "White Khan." For the reasons given, Russia felt constrained in its actions and therefore responded only by augmenting the Cossack guard in the capital city of Urga (modern-day Ulan Bator or Ulaanbaatar).

Matters took a sudden turn after the Chinese Revolution erupted on October 10, 1911. The new Chinese government would proclaim no change in its nation's territorial integrity, but the Mongols declared their independence on November 3 on the basis that their allegiance had been to the emperors of the Ch'ing dynasty rather than to the Chinese state. At this time, the commander of the Cossack guard in Urga was Grigori Semenov, the half-Buriat officer we encountered in the preceding chapter in relation to the Russian civil war. This worthy took it upon himself to disarm the Chinese guard in Urga, but his actions were disavowed by the Russian authorities, and he was reassigned. The following month, on December 6, the Jebtsundamba Khutukhtu was declared head of the new Mongol state and twenty-two days later was hailed as the Great Khan of the Mongol Empire in the grand tradition of Jenghis Khan and his successors. By this time the Russians had provided sabers, rifles, and ammunition so that the Mongols themselves were strong enough to defeat the local Chinese forces. The highlight of the struggle was the successful siege of Kobdo in August 1912 by Mongol troops under command of a controversial figure, Ja Lama. The Russians now sent in troops sufficient to discourage a Chinese response.

Since eastern Mongolia abutted directly on lands dominated by the Japanese in Manchuria, an understanding was necessary to prevent any untoward incidents. Thus a secret protocol was signed on July 8, 1912, which divided the two spheres of influence at the longitude of Peking (116°27'E): the area to the west was assigned to Russia; the east, to Japan. The Russian Empire now posed as the champions of Mongol autonomy and self-determination and managed to conclude the Russo-Mongol Treaty of November 3, 1912. This pact recognized the autonomy of the new state but at the same time created a virtual Russian protectorate. Outer Mongolia was to make no treaty without Russian approval, and special privileges were granted to Russian subjects.

International pressure still prevented Saint Petersburg from going too far; a Sino-Russian treaty was therefore acceded to on November 5, 1913, recognizing Chinese suzerainty over an "autonomous" Outer Mongolia. This agreement also clearly implied that Inner Mongolia was a separate issue altogether. The matter would not rest there long since the outbreak of World War I brought about a new set of circumstances, particularly after Russia began to suffer military reverses. Talks among Russian, Chinese, and Mongol delegates, which commenced at the border town of Kiakhta in September 1914, resulted in a treaty the following June. This understanding recognized Chinese sovereignty over Outer Mongolia and provided that the ruler of the land would be invested by Chinese authority. Mongolia was to exercise internal autonomy but was to have no treaty-making power. The agreement also recognized the special privileges granted to Russian nationals in 1912.

All this changed considerably with the onset of revolution and civil war in Russia. With the new power vacuum to the north, the government in Peking attempted to reassert control over all of Mongolia and actually announced total reincorporation of the area into the rest of China in November 1919. Outer Mongolia was spared harsh measures, however, by virtue of the weakness of the Chinese central government. Indeed, what authority did exist in Peking was sharply undercut by a change of regime in June 1920, which was engineered primarily by the warlord of southern Manchuria, Chang Tso-lin.

Nevertheless, China was the nominally sovereign authority in Outer Mongolia in 1920, at which time the balance of strength began to swing back to the north. The current of the Russian civil war in Asia shifted in favor of the Bolsheviks as they pushed Admiral Kolchak and his White forces eastward during 1919 and destroyed him in February 1920. It will be remembered that, in April 1920, the Far Eastern Republic was proclaimed and that foreign intervention in the Soviet Far East came to an end, except for the Japanese presence. Grigori Semenov, who was an agent for the Japanese and nominally was the successor to Kolchak, was quickly pushed out of Transbaikalia into Manchuria. Despite the fact that the half-Mongol Semenov had been an ardent proponent for a Greater Mongolia, it was not he but rather his extraordinary deputy, Baron Nicholas von Ungern-Sternberg, who now would enter the scene in Outer Mongolia.

Ungern-Sternberg was originally from the Baltic region but by 1908 had been commissioned in a Cossack cavalry regiment. He first arrived in Outer Mongolia as part of the Russian military augmentation in late 1911. While there he acquired a fascination with the Mongols and their Lamaist Buddhist beliefs. He always seemed a bit strange and wild, but his ferocious valor in battle managed

Eastern Destiny

to keep him from being cashiered for bizarre behavior. It seems that his family was wiped out by Bolsheviks, and he developed a pathologic hatred for them—as well as for other groups such as Jews. Thus he ended up fighting Red forces with Semenov during the civil war. When Semenov retired to Manchuria, Ungern-Sternberg collected a ragtag bunch of followers with the aim of ejecting the Chinese from Outer Mongolia and organizing it as a base for continuing the fight against the Bolsheviks.

Ungern-Sternberg's initial attack on Urga, launched in October 1920, was beaten off by the Chinese defenders. These same Chinese troops then went on a looting spree in the Mongol capital, further alienating the local population. When the baron returned to the attack three and a half months later, after great suffering occasioned by a fierce Mongolian winter, he had the support of the Mongol populace and succeeded in capturing the town. His troops now indulged in an orgy of killing and rape that destroyed his popularity with the very people he sought to enlist in his grand anti-Bolshevik designs. He did envision a Greater Mongolia and even seemed to be convinced that he was the reincarnation of Jenghis Khan himself, but he would have to launch his program without any enthusiastic Mongol support.

As we know from chapter 19, the Far Eastern Republic (FER) had been in existence for almost a year by the time Ungern-Sternberg took Urga. The very experienced and capable Bolshevik warrior, Vasili Blucher, had been appointed minister of war of the FER and commander in chief of its armed forces. Therefore, when the baron attempted to invade northward through Kiakhta in May 1921, he encountered troops that were well armed and disciplined. He was thrown back into Mongolia by these Red forces which then followed up their advantage by occupying Urga on July 6. Ungern-Sternberg was captured in August while trying to escape to Sinkiang. He was taken to Novonikolaevsk (Novosibirsk) where he was given a pro forma trial and executed on September 22, 1921.

In the meantime, a Mongol communist movement had been gaining strength under the leadership largely of Sukhe Bator and Khorlain Choibalsan. A Mongolian People's Party had been loosely formed in January 1920, and just over a year later, in the FER town of Kiakhta, this political organization was transformed into the Mongolian People's Revolutionary Party. On that occasion (March 1) a Provisional Revolutionary Government of Mongolia was formed as well as a Mongolian People's Revolutionary Army under Sukhe Bator. This army invaded with the troops from the FER when they pursued Ungern-Sternberg, and the provisional government was transferred from Kiakhta to Urga, and the word "provisional" was dropped in the process.

The Ungern-Sternberg episode worked greatly to the advantage of Moscow's designs. In its initial overtures to the nations of Asia, the Bolshevik government struck the pose of a force for reform. It decried the imperialistic ventures of the former tsarist regime and promised to treat all nations great or small with respect. In particular, Lenin desired to be on good terms with the Republic of

China. He desperately sought recognition by as many nations as possible, especially those sharing a common border with the Russian Federation. The Soviet foreign commissar, Georgi Chicherin, who had replaced Trotsky, sent a circular note throughout Asia with the message of a new Russian attitude toward its neighbors. It would have been very difficult therefore for Red troops to enter Mongolia to help set up a new regime. However, the gamble of Ungern-Sternberg provided a logical cause for military action from FER territory. Thus, at the invitation of the Mongols, an essentially Russian force was able to enter in company with the Mongolian People's Revolutionary Army (all 700 members) and run the renegade baron to ground.

When the Mongolian People's Revolutionary government was proclaimed on July 10, 1921, it was termed a "constitutional monarchy," with the Jebtsundamba Khutukhtu serving in the role of monarch. Russian experts from the Communist International (COMINTERN) headquarters in Moscow arrived to assist the new government in creating a Mongol clone of the Russian Soviet form of government. This, of course, included the apparatus of compulsion (secret police), known in Outer Mongolia as the GVO. When the Jebtsundamba Khutukhtu died in 1924, he was never replaced. Instead, a Mongolian People's Republic was proclaimed. In this fashion, the second viable communist regime in the world was successfully established in rural Outer Mongolia rather than in one of the industrialized nations of Europe. A Sino-Soviet treaty was finally concluded in the same year whereby the Chinese were accorded sovereignty over Outer Mongolia but at the expense of having to recognize the very special Soviet interests therein. An indication of Moscow's confidence in the viability of the new regime in Ulan Bator was the removal of the last Russian troops from the country in March 1925.

Bilateral Soviet-Mongolian relations had been established by a secret treaty in November 1921. This agreement provided for mutual recognition, diplomatic representation, and a clear means of communication. It also granted the Soviets certain special rights such as cession of land needed for railroad construction. Despite the fact that the Bolsheviks were in essence setting up a brother state, they withheld from Outer Mongolia a piece of territory, named Urianghai, which amounted to more than 68,000 square miles, or about the size of the American state of Washington.

Urianghai, also called Tannu-Tuva or just plain Tuva, was a remote land in the northwestern corner of Outer Mongolia dominated by the upper reaches of the Yenisei River. By the early twentieth century, several thousand Russians had settled in the region so that they accounted for 15 percent of the population. By 1910, despite the desire of many high-ranking bureaucrats in Saint Petersburg to annex Urianghai, no sound legal basis could be generated since the Treaty of Kiakhta had rather precisely defined the border, and the Treaty of Tarbagatai of 1864 had further refined the westernmost frontier delineation. With the advent of the Chinese revolution and the Mongolian declaration of sovereignty in 1911, however, a new sense of urgency impelled annexationists to push their case lest Urianghai automatically become part of an autonomous Outer Mongolia. Although the Russians supported Mongolian autonomy by the treaty of November 3, 1912, they viewed Urianghai differently. The tsar sided with the expansionists, and after some of the local leaders were prevailed upon to submit a formal request for inclusion in the Russian Empire, a protectorate named "Tuva" was established in July 1914.

The protectorate came to an end when the Chinese, who returned to rule Mongolia in 1919, also reasserted their control over Urianghai. However, when the Red troops entered Mongolia to deal with Ungern-Sternberg in 1921, they came as well into Tuva. The Soviets announced that the former protectorate status of Tuva had been abolished forever, to be replaced by a free and independent state. Suiting action to the words, they convened a congress in Kyzyl, the Tuvinian capital, which proclaimed the newly independent nation of Tannu-Tuva. Just as in Mongolia, a Soviet-style state was created with the advice of the COMINTERN and the stimulus provided by the presence of Russian troops. Tannu-Tuva's sovereign status would be recognized only by Soviet Russia and Mongolia, and the new "state" was more completely dominated by Moscow than it had been by Saint Petersburg while in its earlier role as an official protectorate. During World War II, any ambiguity about the status of the area was resolved when it was incorporated into the Russian Federation as the Tuvinian Autonomous Soviet Socialist Republic.

21

Russians, the Chinese Eastern Railway, and Sinkiang

Vladimir Lenin, Leon Trotsky, and most of the avid older Bolsheviks viewed Russia primarily as a power base from which to launch a world revolution since Karl Marx had taught that a communist society would logically come into existence in a highly industrialized nation such as Germany. Contrary to expectations, those movements that made a pretense at revolution in Central and Western Europe rapidly perished.

In order to promote progress toward the ultimate goal of world revolution, the Third Communist International (COMINTERN) was formed March 2, 1919, with headquarters in Moscow.[1] Although it was dominated by Lenin and the Russian Bolsheviks, the COMINTERN was made up initially of Communist party members from most Central and Eastern European countries. The Second Congress of the COMINTERN, held in July 1920, established the organizational framework and adopted the "21 Conditions," which detailed the tight discipline to be demanded of all participating parties in order to achieve revolution in their respective countries. The controlling voice naturally was that of the only party to have attained such an end—the Russian Bolsheviks.

When Trotsky was named the people's commissar for war and commenced building the Red Army in 1918, he was replaced as people's commissar for foreign affairs by Georgi Chicherin. Chicherin, whose origins were in the gentry, had actually started his career in the tsarist foreign service. A former Menshevik, he was never part of the inner Bolshevik circle, but he served his nation well. Soviet Russia now had the advantage of a two-level apparatus for the exercise of foreign policy: the effective diplomacy of Chicherin and the influence of the COMINTERN on the leftist parties in many countries.

Looking toward Asia, the Bolsheviks felt they had to eradicate Russia's imperialistic image. The tsarist archives were opened and texts of "secret" treaties published. On July 4, 1918, Chicherin renounced the special rights and interests that had been unfairly exacted by previous Russian regimes. This announcement, directed at China, elicited very little response from Peking although, in Canton, Sun Yat-sen reacted positively. Interestingly, just one year later Lev Karakhan, Chicherin's deputy, made a similar but less general declaration of goals to China. He specifically promised the nullification of *certain* treaties, termination of the Boxer indemnity, and cancellation of extraterritoriality. He stressed the claim that Russia was China's only ally. When examined closely, Karakhan's declaration reveals that the Soviets were ready to give up privileges, concessions, and indemnities—but not territory. At no time, for example, was there a specific proposal to return Amuria and Ussuria, and we have seen how Soviet policy was adamant that Mongolia not be returned to Chinese control. The rationale, of course, was that any former part of China that came under Soviet (Russian) control was free from imperialism whereas under China, such areas would be subjected once again to capitalistic exploitation by the Great Powers. In other words, the expansion of the Soviet state was a means of spreading social revolution.

A major bone of contention, which developed between Russia and China during the period of the Bolshevik Revolution and ensuing civil war, was the Chinese Eastern Railway (CER) which was built by the Russians across Manchuria in accordance with the treaty negotiated by Sergei Witte in 1896. It will be remembered that the railroad, its equipment, and even control over the right-of-way were vested in the Russo-Asiatic Bank (Russo-Chinese Bank until 1910), an institution dominated by Russia and funded by French capital. At the time of the abdication of the tsar in March 1917, Dmitri Horvath, who had been general manager of the CER since 1902, seized control of the railroad and declared himself head of a new "All-Russian Provisional Government," with its capital in Harbin.

Very quickly, however, socialist activity increased in Harbin, and, as in other Russian cities, a Soviet of Workers' and Soldiers' Deputies was established. The following December 12, in the wake of the Bolshevik Revolution, the soviet seized power and commenced to rule through a revolutionary military committee. This action alarmed the foreign powers, especially France, and at French instigation, China sent troops into Harbin on Christmas Day. The Chinese captured and expelled the Bolshevik guards and, the following month, closed the railroad at the Russo-Manchurian border. Then, as we saw in chapter 19, the Chinese were assigned guard responsibilities for the CER as part of the foreign intervention in the Far East which commenced in August 1918. Horvath now reasserted his "government," with the support of the entente powers and was rewarded when the Russo-Asiatic Bank was declared to be independent of Soviet Russia and became the recipient of the Russian share of the Boxer indemnity payments. Horvath was also designated acting general director of the bank. Toward the end of the year 1918, when Aleksandr Kolchak took over as the supreme ruler of all White Russian forces, Horvath immediately recognized the action and threw his support behind the admiral.

After the fatal reverses suffered by Kolchak and his armies in late 1919 and early 1920, Horvath once again attempted to assume political responsibility over all Russians in the CER, but he was frustrated by a general strike among the employees. He was finally forced to leave, and the Chinese asserted increased control over the management of the railroad. Finally, in the summer of 1920, China discontinued making the Boxer indemnity payments (to tsarist representatives, of course—one reason why the Soviets had so graciously offered to suspend the requirement for the payments). At the same time, China refused any longer to recognize any pre-Bolshevik representatives, thus setting the stage for direct negotiations with the Soviet state.

Very little significant change in Sino-Soviet relations took place in the course of the next two years. This was a period whose focus was blurred by the existence of the Far Eastern Republic (FER), that device of Lenin's to squeeze the Japanese out of the northeast Asia mainland. With the demise of the FER in November 1922, following the withdrawal of Japanese troops, the greatly intensified Soviet presence caused the Chinese government to pay more heed to Soviet demands for resolution of problems, including mutual recognition. Despite its altruistic stand on tsarist imperialism, Moscow still laid claim to a huge interest in the Chinese Eastern Railway, namely its ownership. On the other hand, Western powers (particularly France, which had the greatest financial interest) tried to pressure China into avoiding any action that might threaten the position of the Russo-Asiatic Bank as the controlling financial authority of the CER.

Despite intense Soviet desires, the skilled negotiator Adolph Joffe was unable to achieve an agreement with the Chinese; instead, the talents and prestige of Lev Karakhan were required before a treaty could finally be hammered out and agreed to on May 31, 1924. This pact, as mentioned in the preceding chapter, was the basis for the resolution of the problem of Outer Mongolia. It provided as well for the very basic matter of mutual recognition of sovereignty. In addressing the knotty problem of the CER, it was agreed that there would be equal representation of the two countries in the management and direction of the railway. For example, the board of directors would comprise five Russians and five Chinese with a Chinese president and Russian vice president. A Russian was to serve as general manager with a Chinese and a Russian assistant. All profits were to be split evenly.

The treaty also recognized Chinese sovereignty over and responsibility for security of the real estate involved. On the other hand, Russian ownership of the railroad was tacitly assumed with the reaffirmation that it would revert to China automatically eighty years after its completion date (calculated from 1903). Also, as provided for in the treaty of 1896, China could *purchase* the CER in 1956 if she so opted. The agreement further asserted that the future of the railroad would be determined by the two contracting parties without interference from any outside interests. This cut out the Russo-Asiatic Bank, which would be liquidated two years later. Other provisions of the pact included a Russian agreement to a conference to review all previous treaties and to replace them with new, more friendly documents. This meant, among other things, the renunciation of special privileges and extraterritoriality. The treaty also stipulated that neither side would permit activities within its borders whose purpose might be the overthrow of the government of the other side.

The realities of the Chinese political scene threw into question the ability of the Peking regime to deliver on its commitments in that the de facto authority in Manchuria, the site of the CER, rested with the warlord Chang Tso-lin. It became necessary therefore for Moscow to negotiate separately with Chang's power center in Mukden. The result was the conclusion, on September 20, of a treaty essentially the same as the Sino-Soviet pact except that the time frame for restoration of the CER to Chinese ownership was reduced from eighty to sixty years. Since Chang Tso-lin and his fellow warlord Feng Yu-hsiang were able to engineer a coup in Peking a month later, the new "national" regime had no problem in approving Chang's treaty.

The pact's effectiveness would be regularly challenged. The Chinese accused the Soviets of trying to "bolshevize" the CER Company and at the same time were resentful of the very fact of the Russian presence. In less than two years, matters had come to a virtual impasse. In this instance, the cause was related to Chang Tso-lin's struggle with two other warlords. In January 1926 his troops refused to pay for their transit on the railroad and actually commandeered a train. General Manager A. N. Ivanov thereupon closed down the line, and the local Chinese commander promptly arrested and jailed him and other Russians. The matter was finally cleared up when Foreign Commissar Chicherin advised Peking that if the Chinese were unable to police the line properly, the Soviet Union would be happy to handle railway security. Later in the year other incidents, such as the Chinese seizure of CER company boats on the Sungari, spiced up management problems.

Misunderstandings were not limited to the CER, particularly after Chang Tso-lin took direct charge of the Peking government at the end of the year. On February 28, 1927, the Soviet ship *Pamiati Lenina* was seized in Nanking, and the crew and diplomatic couriers were incarcerated. Propaganda and official documents were confiscated. Chang's concern over communist penetration of the areas he controlled led next to a raid on the Soviet mission compound in Peking on April 6. Chang had received permission (required at the time from the doyen of the foreign community) for his agents to enter the legation compound but only to enter the offices of the Soviet Far Eastern Bank and those of the CER, which were adjacent to the Soviet mission compound. The 500 police officers involved were carried away by enthusiasm and extended their search to the quarters of the military attaché in the mission itself. They confiscated cartloads of propaganda and official documents and arrested a total of eighty people, a quarter of whom were Russians. Among those taken was Li Ta-chao, one of the founders of the Chinese Communist party (CCP). He and several other Chinese were executed. Despite Soviet protests, Chang refused to make amends; instead, he published documents taken from the mission and from the *Pamiati Lenina*. Moscow was not in a position to do more at the time and withdrew all its diplomatic personnel, effectively severing relations. Yet the CER continued to function.

It will be remembered that the Kuomintang (KMT) party was the creation of Sun Yat-sen, who became the first provisional president of the Republic of China. He then stepped aside in favor of Yuan Shih-k'ai, and a year later he was forced to flee the country. After the demise of Yuan in 1916, Sun returned to his roots in Canton where he was, in effect, the warlord for Kuangtung Province. Here he commenced to carry out reforms, attempting to set up a model government. Sun became disenchanted with the lack of support from the West, as epitomized by the decisions of the Paris Peace Conference which were inimical to the interests of China. He was deeply disappointed by the results of the Washington Naval Conference of 1921–1922 (discussed in the following chapter) as they pertained to China. On the other hand, he watched with wonder and admiration as Lenin launched a revolution and retained power with his program in Russia. He realized that his party (the KMT) needed revamping and looked to the Bolsheviks for inspiration.

When the COMINTERN took a careful look at a revolutionary future for China, it saw in the CCP only an embryonic instrument. A Marxist study society, organized in 1920, had given birth in July of the following year to the CCP with the COMINTERN serving as midwife. In view of the party's anemia and the preponderance of peasants in the Chinese population, it was decided in Moscow that the united front approach would be appropriate in China. It was also concluded that the CCP should be allied with the KMT since the KMT seemed to offer the best possibility for success in the Chinese political scene. The ultimate goal, of course, would be to subvert the KMT from within at the appropriate time.

The catalytic agent for the melding of perceived COMINTERN and KMT needs was the COMINTERN representative, Adolph Joffe. After five months of negotiation and discussion, the Sun/Joffe Manifesto was signed in January 1923. This document contained four basic elements. Three of them were similar to items we have encountered in other Sino-Soviet negotiations: Soviet renunciation of special rights, principles to guide relations in the operation of the CER, and the assertion that there were no Soviet imperial designs on Mongolia. The fourth, and most important, element was a statement that it was not possible to carry out communism or the Soviet system in China at the present time. The practical result of this declaration was a close cooperation among the COMINTERN, the KMT, and the CCP. There was no fusion of the CCP and KMT; rather, communists were permitted to join the KMT as individuals. Sun was still in total charge of his party.

A special COMINTERN advisor, Mikhail Borodin (real name Gruzenberg), who had emigrated to the United States but returned to Russia after the revolution, was sent to advise Sun Yat-sen. He was accompanied by forty other advisors. The KMT was reorganized along the lines of the Communist party of the Soviet Union whereby national party congresses would be held periodically, with power in the meantime vested in a Central Executive Committee. Of the twenty-four members of this committee, three were communists. The first national congress would convene on January 20, 1924, the day before Lenin's death.

In the summer of 1923, the young (in his thirties) Chiang Kai-shek was sent to Moscow to study Soviet military organization and particularly the system of political indoctrination. He also was to observe the disciplinary system of the Soviet Communist party. After three months he returned and by the following summer had established the Whampoa Military Academy near Canton. In the fall of 1924, a General Galen (it was really General Vasili Blucher, who had been the minister for war of the Far Eastern Republic) arrived to become the top advisor to the academy. A member of the Political Education Department was the communist, Chou En-lai. As classes passed through the academy, a deep feeling of loyalty was carefully fostered toward the commandant, Chiang.

Sun Yat-sen died on March 12, 1925. Without Sun's prestige at the center, a rather shaky political alliance of left and right wings of the party evolved. Insofar as the military arm was concerned, Chiang was the unchallenged leader, for the new Nationalist army had done well in local operations with the help of Russian materiel. The following year, Chiang considered his new army ready for the test of the long-awaited Northern Expedition, which commenced on July 27, 1926. Three columns pressed northward: the western one through Hunan Province to the city complex of Wuhan on the Yangtze; the eastern through Fukien Province to Shanghai; and the central thrust, led by Chiang himself, through Kiangsi Province to Nanking. The undertaking was highly successful, thanks in no small part to the actions of local communists whose propaganda and agitation prepared the larger towns and cities for conquest.

Strains in the CCP/KMT marriage were becoming gradually more pronounced, however. One of the chief reasons stemmed from the struggle between Stalin and Trotsky back in Moscow. Trotsky's position was that communist participation in the KMT should be only as a group whereas Stalin pushed for continuation of the existing system but calling for more radical activity. The nominal head of the KMT, Wang Ching-wei, was at Wuhan with Borodin and the left-wing leadership of the KMT. The right-wing leaders were in Nanking with Chiang. There was disillusionment and suspicion in both camps, and Chiang became convinced that the COMINTERN goal was to seize power now that the KMT was enjoying successes. So deep was his concern that he ordered a massacre of all known communists commencing on April 12, 1927. This resulted in thousands of deaths in Nanking, Shanghai, and other major centers in the eastern part of China controlled by Chiang.[2] This action sharpened the differences between the communists and the left-KMT elements in Wuhan with the result that the communists were ousted on July 27. Borodin and his fellow advisors departed for Moscow via Mongolia.

By the end of the year, the two KMT factions had resolved their differences. Chiang Kai-shek became the commander in chief of the armed forces and henceforth would be the dominant figure in the Kuomintang. Chiang now was ready to continue the Northern Expedition. The forces in the north were more challenging than those his troops had encountered thus far. He therefore was required to accept as allies certain warlords, but the campaign achieved its principal objective on June 4, 1928, when Peking fell and Chang Tso-lin was forced to flee toward Manchuria. (It was his last ride since he was killed in an explosion, arranged by the Japanese, when his train neared Mukden.) Chang Tso-lin was succeeded by his son Chang Hsueh-liang. The younger Chang professed to support Chiang's Nationalist government, and by the end of 1928 most of the international community had recognized the new Republic of China regime. Chiang's weak position in northern China was reflected in his choice of Nanking as the national capital.

Chiang Kai-shek's negative attitude toward the Soviet Union and what he considered their imperialist aims caused him to entertain the possibility of removing the Russians for good from the Chinese Eastern Railway. His partner in this effort was the Manchurian warlord, Chang Hsueh-liang. The first moves were made as early as January 1929 when Chinese authorities in Harbin confiscated the CER company's telephone system. In May, the Soviet consulate general was raided; Russians were arrested and documents seized. Ignoring Russian protests, the Chinese the following month took over the CER telegraph system and operation of the railroad, dismissing Russian employees and replacing them with Chinese. In a bold move, Chang Hsueh-liang deployed 60,000 troops in the region, including some White Guard Russian units.

The Soviets had had enough. On July 13, a strong note was issued by the acting commissar of foreign affairs, Karakhan, which was a virtual ultimatum to return immediately to the conditions as provided for in the 1924 treaty. The Chinese response was not considered satisfactory, and on August 6 a special Far Eastern Army was authorized, to be under the command of General Blucher. Exchanges of notes between Mukden and Moscow failed to make any dent in the stalemate, and skirmishes became more frequent along the Soviet-Manchurian border. The prevailing opinion in Nanking, partially due to evaluations made by German advisors, was that the Soviet Union was too weak to take effective military action. It was believed further that world opinion would support the Chinese position. Both evaluations were in error.

The Soviet attacks came from three quarters: at the west end of the CER, the east end, and at the confluence of the Sungari and Amur rivers. The first warning action was the bombing of Suifenho in eastern Manchuria opposite the border town of Pogrannichny on September 7. A month later Soviet ships destroyed Chinese gunboats on the Sungari, which had been floating mines down the Amur. The main attack was reserved for Manchouli, the western terminus of the CER. On November 17, Russian infantry and cavalry, supported by aircraft and tanks, rapidly seized the town. Within ten days they had occupied Hailar, about 125 miles into Chinese territory. Chang Hsueh-liang's forces were in disorder, and he sent an urgent message to the Russians that he was willing to negotiate on the basis of Karakhan's note of the preceding July 13. Chiang Kai-shek was singularly unsuccessful in obtaining support from the signatories of the Kellog-Briand Pact for the Renunciation of War. As a result, on December 22, 1929, the Khabarovsk Protocol was promulgated. This document, signed by a plenipotentiary representing both Mukden and Nanking, restored operation of the CER to the conditions established by the treaty of 1924. As will be shown in the following chapter, this equilibrium would be destroyed shortly by the entry of the Japanese into the Manchurian equation.

In addition to the vast border provinces of Mongolia and Manchuria ringing China proper were Tibet and Sinkiang. Of the four, Tibet enjoyed the greatest degree of autonomy from China and was never a serious goal of Russian expansion although concern over rumors of Russian interest occasionally caused considerable paranoia in British India. Sinkiang, or Chinese Turkestan, on the other hand, played an important role in Russo-Chinese relations by virtue of the lengthy border it shared with four Soviet republics.

In Sinkiang, as in the other border regions, Chinese central control was weakened by the Chinese revolution and the abdication of the last Ch'ing emperor. The area of this huge province, taken together with that of Manchuria, Outer Mongolia, and Tibet, amounted to more than 2.5 million square miles. That means that ties were suddenly loosened between the Chinese capital and more than half of the territory that had been in the Ch'ing empire. Sinkiang was very different from Tibet and Mongolia in that, instead of being devotees of Lamaistic Buddhism, the inhabitants were predominantly Muslim.

At the time of the Chinese revolution, a very shrewd Chinese named Yang Tseng-hsin was appointed governor, or *tuchun*. Yang was able to rule without any fatal Muslim outbursts while paying only lip service to direction from the central Chinese government. He managed to do this despite imperial Russian designs on his province and an influx of Russian settlers into the Ili valley. Russian pressure was eased with the outbreak of World War I, but even graver difficulties confronted Yang as a consequence of the Bolshevik military operations in Russian Turkestan.

As noted in chapter 19, Mikhail Frunze arrived in Tashkent in late 1919 to win back the area by persuasion of disaffected Muslims and the annihilation of any surviving White Army elements. These latter included forces under atamans Aleksandr Dutov and Boris Annenkov as well as an Admiral Bakich. By the spring of 1920, the remnants of these troops, numbering only from about 4,000 to 5,000, straggled into Sinkiang. Yang initially gave them refuge, but when these White forces, somewhat augmented by other stragglers, began to use Sinkiang as a safe haven from which to take part in uprisings across the border, he decided it would be wiser to be on good terms with the Bolsheviks.

Yang Tseng-hsin therefore concluded a treaty with the Soviet representatives, signed on May 27, 1920. This document provided for local trade, specifically for the Ili valley but inferentially for all of Sinkiang. The new spirit of cooperation then led to a campaign by Soviet and local Chinese troops to rid the huge province of the White refugees in the spring and summer of 1921. Bakich and Annenkov both ended up in Outer Mongolia where they were apprehended, returned to Russia, and shot. Dutov was assassinated by Soviet agents in the Sinkiang town of Kuldja later in the year. His deputy, Colonel Papingut, would survive to play a future role in Sinkiang.

Despite the regularization of Sino-Soviet relations by the central governments of China and the Soviet Union in the treaty of 1924, Yang Tseng-hsin continued to rule essentially as an independent head of state until he was assassinated in 1928. His successor was the corrupt opportunist Chin Shu-jen whose inept rule totally alienated his predominantly Muslim population. His actions elicited a military invasion by the Tungans (Chinese Muslims) from Kansu Province, under the leadership of a young warrior named Ma Chung-ying, in late 1930. In the course of the operation, Ma was seriously wounded and his followers decisively defeated by Chin's troops, which were dominated by White Russian expatriates. These same forces, under the leadership of Colonel Papingut, then turned on Chin and supported a successful coup which replaced him with the figure of Sheng Shih-ts'ai. Sheng, a product of the Whampoa Military Academy, had taken part in Chiang Kai-shek's Northern Expedition; therefore, it would seem that the provincial government of Urumchi would now move closer to Nanking, but quite the opposite would come to pass.

It was during Chin Shu-jen's period of rule that Soviet propinquity had become much more palpable to the leaders of Sinkiang by virtue of the completion in 1930 of the Turkestan-Siberia (Turk–Sib) Railway. This line, which divided from the Transsiberian at Novosibirsk, ran south through Semipalatinsk. Then, for the stretch between Ust-Kamenogorsk and Alma Ata, a matter of 600 miles, the railroad parallelled the Soviet-Sinkiang border at a distance averaging just over 100 miles.

Ma Chung-ying, by now recovered from his wounds, and although advanced in rank to general in the Nationalist army, commenced the invasion of Sinkiang once again. At this stage he had larger ambitions, reminiscent of Yakub Beg, of a pan-Turanian state in Central Asia. Such intent did not favorably impress the Soviet authorities, and there were many rumors rampant that Ma was backed by the Japanese. The Soviets responded to a request for help from Sheng Shih-ts'ai, thereby choosing to back a representative of the KMT government in China rather than a "revolutionary." Ma confidently commenced the investiture of Urumchi in January 1934. To his great shock, his forces were decimated by two Soviet brigades of "volunteers" (actually *OGPU*[3] troops) in unmarked vehicles and aircraft which invaded Sinkiang on January 24.

The scene in the province provided a series of ironies. After defeat by Soviet forces, Ma Chung-ying accepted the hospitality of the Soviet Union and disappeared from the scene. As Sheng warmed to the Soviets, he jailed the remaining White Russians, including Colonel Papingut, who had made possible his ascent to power; it is presumed that they died while incarcerated. Then Sheng, who had been so well identified as a creature of the KMT, asserted his independence from Nanking and converted his province into a veritable Soviet protectorate.

By May 1935, Sheng Shih-ts'ai had concluded a secret agreement with the Soviet Union whereby he was advanced a loan of 5 million gold rubles and the promise of munitions as well as Soviet forces as necessary to quell any disorders in Sinkiang. He agreed to receive Soviet technicians and advisors into key elements of his government and enterprises. This even included the creation of a Soviet-style secret police. Virtually all of Sinkiang's trade was with its huge neighbor. Sheng had occasion soon to avail himself of Soviet commitments. A Turkic uprising in 1936 and another the following year were both put down only after Soviet troops and war planes came to his aid. After the second action, a reenforced Soviet brigade remained in garrison in Hami—the *eastern* gateway city to Sinkiang. Sheng therefore was a "kept man" of the USSR although outwardly he gave lip service to Chinese sovereignty.

NOTES

1. It was known as the *third* Communist International since it was reckoned to have been preceded by two very similar associations. The First International Workingmen's Association was established by Karl Marx himself in 1867 and collapsed in 1879. It was headquartered initially in London and later in New York. The Second Workingmen's Association, centered in Paris, was established in 1889 but gradually dissolved during the course of World War I.

2. It must be remembered that communist revolutionary documents had been confiscated by the authority of Chang Tso-lin six weeks earlier from the *Pamiati Lenina* in Nanking and just four days earlier from the Soviet mission compound in Peking. A historical footnote is that Borodin's wife, an American woman named Fanny, was captured aboard the *Pamiati Lenina*. The saga of her trial and escape from China is one of the more fascinating stories of the period.

3. The title of the secret police was changed periodically. As noted in chapter 19, it was originally (1917) CHEKA. That was followed by GPU in 1922 and shortly thereafter, following the formation of the USSR, by OGPU. In 1934 the institution was redesignated NKVD. Later, it would be known successively as MVD and KGB.

22

The Soviet Union and Japan in the 1920s and 1930s

In the history of Russo-Chinese relations, Russia was consistently the more aggressive nation of the two. By comparison, Japan was, in the first half of this century, the more active player in her strategic relationship with her huge Slavic neighbor. This was clearly reflected in the sequence of events leading to the Russo-Japanese War in 1903–1904 as discussed in chapter 18. In 1910 Japanese annexation of Korea was decisive, whereas Russian actions in Outer Mongolia following the Chinese revolution a year later were tenuous at best. Then, in the wake of the Bolshevik Revolution, Japanese intervention in the Russian civil war was more extensive in terms of troops and duration than that of any other country involved. Indeed, they were withdrawn in 1922 only after the formation of the Far Eastern Republic and after other pressures were brought to bear by the Western powers at the Washington Naval Conference of 1921–1922.

Although termed a "naval" conference, the gathering in Washington, D.C., addressed a wide range of subjects dealing with Pacific Ocean problems. The meeting, called in July 1921, convened the following November. Nine nations took part: Great Britain, France, China, Japan, Italy, Belgium, the Netherlands, Portugal, and the United States. Germany and the Soviet Union were not invited. On December 10, the powers did not cancel extraterritoriality in China but did agree to examine the existing Chinese legal system toward that end. Three days later a four-power treaty was signed by Britain, France, Japan, and the United States which confirmed their respective holdings of Pacific islands, many of which were League of Nations mandates. Thereby, Japanese occupation of the former German colonies of the Marshalls, the Carolines, and Marianas (less Guam) was given Great Power approval. This would be in return for Japanese accession to later agreements respecting China.

On February 1, 1922, the British officially gave up their lease to Weihaiwei on the northern coast of the Shantung Peninsula, and the French gave up their concession in Kwangchow-wan. Three days later two treaties were signed. In one, the nine powers agreed to respect Chinese sovereignty and territorial and administrative integrity. In the other, Japan agreed to withdraw from the former German concessions in Kiaochow with the stipulation that China pay for the assets received and for Japanese improvements thereto. On February 6 was concluded the most widely known agreement: the Naval Armaments Treaty, which called for a limitation on the number, tonnage, and armament of capital ships and assigned the ratios governing the size of the major navies of the world.[1]

A casualty of the Washington Naval Conference was, understandably, the Anglo-Japanese treaty of alliance of 1902. Indeed, in the course of the decade, forces were at work in Japan which fostered the growth of virulent anti-Westernism and inspired an intense ultranationalism. Although the nation had succeeded in industrializing, modernizing, and successfully competing with Western countries, Japan felt excluded from the real concert of nations, essentially on the basis of race. This perception was intensified at the Versailles peace conference held in 1919 when the United States and Britain successfully torpedoed the Japanese proposal to include a clause on racial equality. The resentment would be further heightened by the American Exclusion Act of 1924 which rendered Japanese immigrants ineligible for American citizenship.

The first telling incident to indicate the trend of Japanese actions in the future was the bombing of a train in Manchuria which resulted in the death of the Chinese warlord Chang Tso-lin in 1928. This assassination was not the result of Japanese national policy but rather the work of middle-grade officers of the Kwantung Army.[2] The new Showa emperor (Hirohito) was appalled and directed the prime minister, General Tanaka Giichi, to ensure that the culprits were disciplined. Despite the fact that Tanaka was formerly its chief, the army refused to comply on the basis that it would injure the prestige of the organization. The army leadership further took the position that the head of the civilian government, although a military man, had no authority to call for such disciplinary measures; rather, such power was vested solely in the emperor. The irony here, of course, is that the emperor desired the measures be taken.

Just over three years later, on September 18, 1931, the Kwantung Army again acted independently of Tokyo in perpetrating the famous Mukden Incident. This event, again the work of middle-grade officers, was an explosion that destroyed a tiny section of the South Manchurian Railroad (SMRR) just outside Mukden, the Manchurian capital. Before the night was over, Japanese troops had breached the city walls and occupied the capital, thereby commencing a systematic occupation of all of Manchuria. Just five months later, the sovereign state of Manchukuo was proclaimed to be under the rule of Emperor P'u-i, who as a child had been the last Manchu ruler of the Ch'ing dynasty in China. In reality, P'u-i was nothing more than a puppet, and the only nation voluntarily to grant full recognition of Manchukuo's sovereignty would be Japan.

The Soviet Union, now in the throes of collectivization and the first five-year plan, was hardly in a position to stem the Japanese tide, and Tokyo for its part initially assured Moscow that no action would impinge on the Chinese Eastern Railway (CER). However, such assurances came from the diplomatic corps, not from the Kwantung Army. Japanese troops entered Harbin as early as March 1932 and soon laid demands on the CER for the transportation of combat forces. With the assertion of Japanese control over Manchuria, the boundary between Japan and the Soviet Union had suddenly expanded from the ten miles along the Tumen River (Soviet border with Korea) and the sixty-five miles across Sakhalin to almost 2,000 miles stretching from Outer Mongolia to the Pacific Ocean. The CER soon was an elongated island in a land dominated by Japanese military forces. Soviet concern was reflected in the resumption of diplomatic relations with China in December 1932 after a hiatus of five years.

Pressure on the CER intensified in early 1933 when the Japanese closed both ends of the railway. The Soviet response in May, out of weakness, was an offer to sell the Russian half ownership of the railroad's assets. After nineteen months of wrangling, a contract of sale was agreed to in a treaty signed on March 23, 1935. At Japanese insistence, the agreement was concluded between the Soviet Union and Manchukuo, with Japan as an interested ally of the latter. The Soviets therefore were forced into a reluctant recognition of the puppet state. The agreement called for the payment of 140 million yen plus another 30 million to cover the retirement costs of Soviet workers. One third was to be paid in cash installments over a period of three years with the balance to be provided in goods. As it turned out, the last payment was not made until 1940. A final proviso was that Japan would guarantee payment by Manchukuo. The Japanese renamed the CER the North Manchurian Railway.

Japan now had the option of extending her mainland empire at the expense of the Soviet Union or of China. It was decided to be more feasible to push south. Thus Japanese pressure was increasingly exerted against Inner Mongolia and northern China. This effort would be pursued until the Marco Polo Bridge Incident of 1937 near Peking precipitated the Sino-Japanese War, considered by many to be the opening round of World War II.

The Japanese assertion of authority over Manchuria and the acquisition of the CER were factors considered in the second five-year plan of the Soviet Union. The result was a special five-year plan for the Far East itself. Not only did it provide for acceleration of development in Siberia and the Far East but also included double-tracking the Transsiberian throughout the length of the railroad and the beginning of the Baikal-Amur Mainline (BAM) around the north of Lake Baikal toward Sovetskaia Gavan on the Tatarsky Strait. Special benefits were offered to colonists from European Russia to settle in the region. The entire population of the Soviet Far East at the time amounted to only 2.5 million souls; therefore, an important factor in the development plans was an expanded use of the system of concentration camps known as Gulag. The plan called as well for the creation of military ground forces comprising 350,000 troops and an air arm of 2,000 aircraft.

In Japan, militarism increasingly was in the ascendancy. Extremists committed outrages such as the assassination of the foreign minister in February 1932 and the prime minister three months later. Although the senior officers of the military did not approve of such conduct, they were able to exploit the emotional fallout to their own advantage. The most extraordinary terroristic outburst occurred on February 26, 1936, when teams of the First Division in Tokyo, under the command of young officers, succeeded in assassinating several senior officials in the name of a "Showa restoration," including former prime ministers Takahashi Korekiyo and Saito Makoto, as well as an army general. This time the military, now well ensconced in power, took quick and decisive action and meted out punishment to 103 culprits and issued seventeen death penalties.

At the same time that the military was gaining control of policy in Japan, a new phenomenon was rearing its head in Central Europe—national socialism. In 1933 the Nazi party stormed to power in Germany on a program that appealed to the Germans' fear or resentment over the Treaty of Versailles, Jews, and communism. The Soviet Union therefore found itself between two hostile authorities: militaristic Japan and Hitler's Germany. The two powers began in short order to coordinate foreign policy vis-à-vis Moscow. Such efforts reached fruition in the Anti-COMINTERN Pact of November 1936 (which included Italy as well). Both Germany and Japan were quick to assure the Soviets that their understanding was directed against the COMINTERN itself and *not* against the Soviet Union. However, the treaty included a secret provision committing the two to confer on policy toward Moscow.

The Soviet Union therefore found itself in a most awkward position and pursued the dual goals of not offending the two nations and of trying to divert their expansionist energies toward targets other than itself. The Soviet foreign commissar, Maxim Litvinov, was quick to renew Japanese concessions in northern Sakhalin and the fishing agreement for Far Eastern waters. Russian nerves were therefore quieted substantially when the Sino-Japanese War erupted in July 1937, and Moscow concluded a nonaggression pact with China in Nanking the following month. The Russians also commenced sending arms to the Chinese.

From the time of the Japanese subjugation of Manchuria in 1932, with the extraordinarily long border now shared between Japanese and Soviet control, border incidents gradually developed and increased in frequency. As the Japanese began to penetrate Inner Mongolia, they were increasingly tempted to push into Outer Mongolia, an autonomous region nominally under Chinese sovereignty but one that owed its autonomous state to Russian interest. The apparent Japanese border violations that shortly began to occur were to a degree excusable. Since Manchuria and Mongolia both had, until 1911, been integral to the Chinese Empire, the boundary between them had never been delineated with any great precision.

As border incidents continued to flare and the Japanese began to claim certain lands on the Mongolia/Manchukuo border, Russian concern resulted in a "gentlemen's agreement" of November 1934 with the Mongols in which the Soviet

Union promised to defend the Mongolian People's Republic (MPR). So, for the first time in nine years, Russian troops reentered Outer Mongolia. Two months later, the first major military clash occurred between Mongolian and Manchukuoan troops in the general region of the lake named Buir Nor (now called Buyr Naar). Here the western border of Manchuria (currently part of the Inner Mongolian Autonomous Region) and eastern Outer Mongolia meshed like two pieces of a jigsaw puzzle. This action led to a conference between the two "nations" at Manchouli, located at the western end of the Chinese Eastern Railway. During the conference, in the summer of 1935, the Japanese levied demands on the representatives of the MPR for a series of concessions, such as the stationing of Japanese military advisors in the Mongol capital. This the Mongols firmly rejected.

Japan, while pushing for "autonomy" of regions in northern China and Inner Mongolia, viewed Outer Mongolia with a mixture of curiosity and greed since, in their view, it was an international anomaly: autonomous but still nominally under Chinese sovereignty. They therefore declared the Manchouli conference inconclusive, and in February 1936 an even fiercer Manchukuoan/Japanese attack was launched in the Buir Nor area, which was beaten back but only with considerable bloodshed. In Moscow, Stalin publicly announced that the Soviet Union would help defend Mongolia, and on March 12 the two countries signed the Protocol of Mutual Assistance. In other words, the Mongolian People's Republic became the first of the Soviet satellite nations and entered an understanding whereby both parties pledged that in the event of a military attack on one, the other would render any assistance, including military. This treaty, however, raised questions of propriety with China, the sovereign authority in Mongolia. The matter would fester for another decade.

Such border activity was not restricted to the Buir Nor region. Between 1932 and 1936, 250 separate incidents were recorded between Manchukuo on the one hand and Mongolia or the Soviet Union on the other. In May 1936, as a "peace move," Japan suggested a neutralized belt around the Manchurian perimeter, similar to what had existed for centuries between China and Korea. Soviet rejection of this suggestion was prompted by fear for the security of the Amur Line segment of the Transsiberian Railway which in places was within thirty-five miles of the border. Incidents continued and came to number more than 500 by 1938. In June 1937, just weeks before the outbreak of the Sino-Japanese War, the most serious confrontation yet occurred on two islands in the Amur River. While the Red Army leadership was undergoing a bloodletting in the purge trials in Moscow, Soviet troops established themselves on the two islands. Skirmishes ensued, and the Russians, in response to Japanese demands, withdrew; the Japanese then, contrary to pledge, occupied the same islands and refused to budge when the Russian side protested. It now appeared to several Japanese military leaders that the purge trials had inflicted great damage on leadership effectiveness in the Red Army.[3] This attitude understandably led to further border adventurism on the part of Japan despite her deepening involvement in trying to bring China under her control.

In the meantime, the Soviet Union's second five-year plan was rapidly building a military force-in-being in the Far East and Transbaikal areas. This fact, taken together with the Japanese decision to launch war against China in July 1937, combined to ensure that future Soviet responses to probing would be less measured or timid. The first test came in July 1938 at Changkufeng, a hill on the Soviet-Manchurian border located in the tight corner where the territories of Korea, Manchuria, and Russia meet, near Lake Khasan. The crisis occurred during a tense period of Russo-Japanese diplomatic activity touching upon Sakhalin and the Chinese Eastern Railway, as well as Soviet military support to China.

Changkufeng has a clear view of Pos'et Bay where the Soviets had begun building an airfield and a submarine servicing facility. By July 18, the Russians were in position on the heights. The Japanese attacked in force and were astonished at the toughness of their adversary. In the course of the fighting, which involved units at the battalion level and continued until the second week of August, casualties amounted to well over 1,000, with more than 500 Japanese and 250 Russian troops killed in action. Japan received very little diplomatic support from Germany at this juncture since Germany was in the delicate process of *anschluss* with Austria and negotiating the Sudetenland crisis. As a result, the matter of Changkufeng was resolved in favor of the Soviet Union, which remained "king of the hill."

The following year would see the heaviest fighting between the two Asian powers since the Russo-Japanese War of 1904–1905. The Soviets as usual were deeply concerned about asserting the military principle of defense in depth. In this instance, the fear was the vulnerability of the Transsiberian in the Transbaikal region. This meant ensuring the inviolability of the borders of Outer Mongolia. Moscow had cause for worry since the Kwantung Army was still intent on pushing its advantage as far as possible. On May 11, 1939, Japanese/Manchukuoan troops launched an attack in the region just to the east of Buir Nor near the river known as the Khalkhin Gol, which was a few miles west of the border claimed by the Mongols. The ensuing fracas is referred to as Nomonhan, the name of a small town on the claimed borderline. The Mongol and Soviet troops put up a firm resistance, and the new Soviet foreign commissar, Viacheslav Molotov, declared that the Soviet Union would come to the aid of the Mongols in accordance with the Protocol of Mutual Assistance of 1936. Indeed, on the following day, June 1, General Georgi Zhukov was ordered to the MPR with instructions to take over military operations. Both sides now upped the ante. Zhukov requested and was provided three rifle divisions and ample reinforcements of tank, aircraft, and heavy artillery units. The Japanese ordered additional troops and created the Sixth Army command in the area.

General Zhukov, who would rise to be the top Soviet military leader during World War II, massed his forces and supplies with utmost secrecy until he was ready to launch his attack on August 20. In this rehearsal for the upcoming war in Europe, he succeeded in crushing his adversary through the careful coordination of the total firepower of his armor, aircraft, and heavy artillery. Although statistics for Soviet/Mongol casualties are not available, we can guess that they were considerable but nothing like the losses absorbed by the other side. Of the more than 75,000 Japanese/Manchukuoan troops involved in the small war at Nomonhan, more than 8,500 were killed and more than 9,000 wounded. This venture by the Kwantung Army was costly indeed. It would discourage the Japanese from further probing the borders around Manchukuo.

To add to Japanese chagrin, it was during the final battle at Nomonhan that Tokyo had to absorb the great shock of the Russo-German Non-aggression Pact, signed on August 23, 1939. This action would be followed nine days later by the German invasion of Poland and the declaration of war by France and Britain. The Soviet Union now seemed to be free from any threat in the West; she had succeeded in diverting German avarice instead toward the rich democracies of Western Europe. This dramatic development was a factor in defusing the situation on the battlefield at Nomonhan and led to a Russo-Japanese border understanding that was announced on June 9, 1940.

NOTES

1. In the course of the Washington Conference, the United States was able to drive tough bargains with the Japanese with confidence. This stemmed from the successful American cryptanalysis of the Japanese diplomatic cipher systems in use at the time. Such success remained a national secret until the publication in 1931 of the book *The American Black Chamber* by Herbert O. Yardley, who was in charge of the cryptanalytic effort against Japan in 1921 and 1922.

2. Not to be confused with Kwangtung Province in southern China. It was the title of Japanese forces in Manchuria and meant "east of the pass" in reference to Shanhaikuan at the eastern end of the Great Wall.

3. Marshal Vasili Blucher who, as we have seen, played a major role in war and politics in the Far East, was a judge early in the trial but then he himself fell to the purge. He was executed in November 1938.

23

World War II and Settlements

As we have seen, from the time of the Mukden Incident in 1931, Japanese expansionist pressure on mainland Asia was sustained. Whereas their efforts to penetrate the borders of the Soviet Union or Outer Mongolia would be met with stiff and often dangerous resistance, the Japanese had found China to be a much softer and inviting target. As they extended their influence farther into northern China and Inner Mongolia, they used the device of insisting on ''autonomy'' for the regions they sought to detach from the Republic of China. One of their aims was to dominate Inner Mongolia, thereby isolating China from possible Soviet influence and assistance. To be totally successful in this, however, they would have had to dominate Sinkiang as well, but, as suggested in chapter 21, their prospects in that quarter dimmed when Ma Chung-ying was defeated in 1934 at Urumchi.

In northern China, the combustible situation was ignited on July 7, 1937, at a site somewhat to the southwest of Peip'ing (Peking) known as the Marco Polo Bridge (Lukouch'iao). The local Japanese commander demanded access to the nearby town of Wanping to search for a soldier claimed to be missing; when refused, he ordered the bombardment of the town. As the result of this ''Marco Polo Bridge Incident,'' Japanese troops poured into northern China. Peip'ing and Tientsin were soon occupied, and the Japanese hoped for a quick termination of the ''China affair.'' Within a year, however, it became increasingly clear that they would not easily deliver a knockout punch to China.

Meantime, in Europe, early steps toward World War II were in progress. The conquest of Ethiopia by Fascist Italy in 1935 was followed a year later by the reoccupation of the Rhineland by Nazi Germany—an action in contravention of the Treaty of Versailles. In that same year, the world was further polarized by the outbreak of the Spanish civil war and the conclusion of the Anti-COMINTERN

Map 10. Soviet Union / Commonwealth of Independent States, post–World War II.

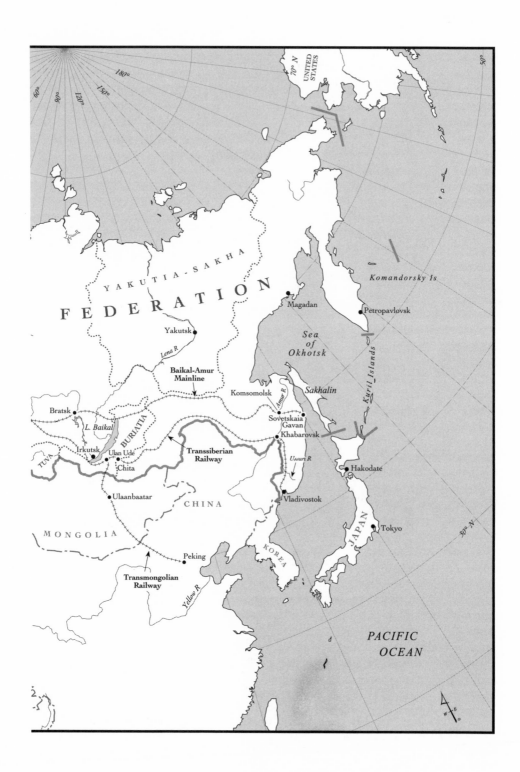

Pact between Japan and Germany, to be joined later by Italy. In 1938 Adolph
Hitler succeeded in absorbing Austria into his Third Reich and gaining the
capitulation of France and Britain to his demands for the Czech borderlands.
This quickly led to the partition and demise of Czechoslovakia.

On August 23, 1939, the Russo-German Non-aggression Pact stunned the
world. Yosif Stalin, who was so paranoid in his relationships with other nations,
felt he could more easily trust a fellow, all-powerful dictator like Hitler. The
agreement provided that each side, in addition to refraining from aggression
against the other, would remain neutral in case the other engaged in hostilities
with a third party. In addition, a secret protocol agreed to the partition of Europe
from the Baltic to the Black Sea: a reprise of the Tilsit Agreement between
Napoleon and Alexander I in 1807. The Soviet Union provided Germany with
raw materials, military exercise areas, and—to evidence good faith—even
names of Austrian and German communists, who were immediately arrested.
The Moscow propaganda thrust now was directed at the democracies as the
prime enemies of socialism. The Japanese were caught completely by surprise.
The war in Europe began with the German invasion of Poland on September 1,
1939.

While Japanese Foreign Minister Matsuoka was visiting Berlin in March
1941, Hitler decided, in the interest of security, not to acquaint him with the
ambitious German plans to invade Russia: code name BARBAROSSA. As a
result, while Matsuoka stopped in Moscow the following month on his way
back to Tokyo, he concluded the Russo-Japanese Neutrality Treaty. This document would have much greater impact on the Soviet fortunes in World War II
than any other. The agreement, signed on April 13, 1941, provided for friendly
relations and territorial inviolability as well as neutrality in case either power
were to become involved in hostilities with a third nation. The treaty was to be
valid for five years and was to be automatically extended for an additional five
years unless one side declared, a year before the expiration date (that is, in April
1945), a desire not to extend.

Just two months later, on June 22, the greatest land invasion in history was
launched as 190 Axis divisions invaded the Soviet Union along a front 2,000
miles long. Stalin was in a state of shock, having disregarded warnings from
Winston Churchill in Britain and from one of the most effective Soviet spies of
all time: Richard Sorge in Tokyo. The Soviet western defenses crumbled, and
German troops were within thirty-five miles of Moscow by October. At this
point a key decision, made possible by the Russo-Japanese Neutrality Treaty,
brought half of the 350,000 troops from Transbaikalia and the Far East to the
defense of Moscow. This force, conditioned to winter warfare, was invaluable
in the successful defense of the Soviet capital.

Although Japan had signed the neutrality pact with Moscow, once the German
invasion of Russia had begun, there was pressure in some quarters of Tokyo to
seize the opportunity presented for expansion of the nation's mainland empire.
This led to a fateful debate in Tokyo on July 2 as to whether the future pointed

north or south—reminiscent of the Chinese debate of 1875 over the priority of defense by land or by sea. Despite the fact that the Kwantung Army was at its peak of 600,000, supported by the Army of Korea at a strength of 50,000, the decision was to look southward. Such an option was prompted by several factors, not the least of which was the experience of the small war at Nomonhan in 1939 that showed a successful conflict against the Soviet Union would require a major military effort. Also, the presence of Soviet bombers in Vladivostok threatened to bring the war too close to the home front. Although Sakhalin produced oil, the Japanese Imperial Navy was convinced that it was insufficient to its needs, preferring the more plentiful source of the East Indies. Besides, it was reasoned, if Germany were able to overwhelm Russia, Japan could always change its decision later. For these reasons, Stalin's gamble in denuding his Asiatic military cadres proved sound. This time he listened to the intelligence provided by Richard Sorge.

The Japanese attack on Pearl Harbor on December 7, 1941, galvanized the United States into creating a military force that Japan could not withstand. Also, the Germans made the great mistake of declaring war on the United States, thereby pushing America and the Soviet Union into an anti-Axis alliance. This meant that Russia would share in the Lend-Lease largess of the United States; indeed, it would come to command the lion's share. Routes for forwarding Lend-Lease materials to the Soviet Union were tortuous and limited. The one most frequently described in the press was the "Murmansk Run," which moved through the Norwegian Sea and was subject to deadly air attacks from the Luftwaffe in Norwegian bases. A second was through the Persian Gulf, across Iran, the Caspian, and up the Volga. This would be one of the vital reasons for the desperate and ultimately successful Russian defense of Stalingrad on the Volga. The third route for Lend-Lease, which carried 75 percent of the materials moved, was across the Pacific in ships given to the Soviet Union by the United States and manned by Russian crews trained by Americans. This movement, which connected with the Transsiberian Railway in Vladivostok, was made possible by the Japanese observance of the Russo-Japanese Neutrality Treaty. At the same time, the United States was sending thousands of aircraft via Alaska and Siberia to help the Russian struggle against Germany.

Despite the official peace existing between the Soviet Union and Japan, there was constant tension. Blackouts were enforced in the Russian cities at night. Based on the tragic experience of the German siege of Leningrad, dependents were evacuated from border areas. As early as 1937, Stalin had decreed that the considerable Korean population (roughly 250,000) in the Soviet Far East be forcibly relocated to Central Asia, and in 1941 those Orientals left were sent to Gulag camps. At the same time, White Russian officers in Gulag were released. Russians up through age fifty-five were mobilized.

As the war went increasingly in favor of the Allies, certain key conferences of heads of state were held. The first of these to deal with East Asia, held in Cairo in November 1943, involved Franklin Roosevelt, Winston Churchill, and

Chiang Kai-shek. The leaders announced that they would pursue the war until they gained victory over Japan. They declared that Korea should regain its independence and that China should have returned to her the lands taken by violence and greed, including the Pescadores Islands in the South China Sea.

Churchill and Roosevelt then proceeded to Teheran where they met for the first time with Yosif Stalin. Here, the first Russian claims to the lands of eastern Poland were broached as well as Stalin's vague claim to lands in the Far East that had been taken through treachery, presumably an allusion to the loss of southern Sakhalin to Japan by the Treaty of Portsmouth in 1905. Stalin very reluctantly agreed that China should be given the status of a Great Power in the postwar settlements. At this time, the first delicate mention was made of the possible involvement of the Soviet Union in the Pacific war, a subject the Russians were reluctant even to mention for fear that compromise of the information to Tokyo might impact the flow of U.S. aid across the Pacific.

Just over a year later (February 1945), the Big Three met again, this time at the Crimean resort of Yalta on the shores of the Black Sea. On this occasion, in addition to matters dealing with postwar settlements of the war in Europe, such as occupation zones in Germany, Russian participation in the war against Japan was an important subject. In return for Russian entry into the Pacific conflict two or three months after Germany's surrender, Churchill and Roosevelt agreed that the Soviet Union should receive that which had been taken from Russia before. This was detailed in the Yalta agreement as southern Sakhalin, the Chinese Eastern Railway, the South Manchurian Railroad, and the use of Port Arthur and Talien in the Liao-tung Peninsula. Also included were the Kuril Islands, none of which had been under Russian sovereignty since the Treaty of Saint Petersburg of 1875 assigned all of them to Japan in return for designating Sakhalin part of the Russian Empire. President Roosevelt was totally uninformed on the matter of the Kurils, as was his secretary of state, Edward Stettinius, although the latter's briefing book contained a memorandum detailing the history of the islands and suggesting an optimum future solution. It is probable that Roosevelt would have taken no other action even if he had known the background since the specter of having to invade the Japanese homeland loomed, and he was eager to have help in facing the high casualty rate expected.

The Yalta agreement also addressed matters concerning Sino-Soviet relations. It was agreed that Manchuria was to be under Chinese sovereignty but that the Manchurian railroads were to be operated jointly by the Chinese and Soviets. It further provided that the status quo would continue in the Mongolian People's Republic; that is, Mongolian autonomy with a recognition of Chinese sovereignty. Finally, Stalin's principal concession was that he would conclude a pact with Nationalist China. Chiang Kai-shek was not privy to the Yalta Declaration, but Roosevelt took it upon himself to seek Chinese accession thereto.

The last of the Big Three conferences would be held at Potsdam, Germany, in late July 1945, some ten weeks after the end of the war in Europe. Roosevelt, who had died in April, was replaced by President Harry Truman, and in the very course of the conference, Winston Churchill was unseated as prime minister of the United Kingdom, to be replaced by the leader of the Labour party, Clement Attlee. Whereas the conferees concerned themselves primarily with European matters and the fate of defeated Germany, they did briefly address the situation and goals in the Far East. The Potsdam Declaration stated that the terms of the Cairo Declaration (November 1943) would be carried out, that Japan was to surrender unconditionally, with her sovereignty limited to the four major islands of Honshu, Hokkaido, Kyushu, and Shikoku as well as such minor islands as would be determined by the allies. This declaration was signed by Britain and the United States on July 26 but not by the Soviet Union until August 9, the day Russia would commence hostilities against Japan.

On April 9, 1945, as U.S. forces were storming ashore on the island of Okinawa in the Ryukyu chain and just two months after the Yalta conference (whose instrument of agreement was secret), the Soviet Union denounced the Neutrality Pact with Japan. Such an action, however, merely meant—in terms of the treaty and as interpreted by the Japanese—that the Soviets were opting not to renew it after its expiration on April 12, 1946. In actual fact, however, from the end of the war in Germany (May 5, 1945), the materials reaching Vladivostok by ship from the United States were being stockpiled for Russian entry into the Pacific war.

The apocalyptic moment came on August 6, 1945, when an atomic bomb was dropped by the United States on the city of Hiroshima on the main Japanese island of Honshu near the Inland Sea. Half the city's buildings and inhabitants were destroyed. Two days later the Soviet Union declared war, and on August 9 the second atomic bomb was dropped, this time on the port city of Nagasaki on the southern island of Kyushu. The rationale given to the Japanese ambassador in Moscow for the Soviet declaration of war was that it was the duty of an ally in support of the Potsdam Declaration. A perhaps clearer rationale for opening hostilities would come out after the war, during the War Crimes trials, when the Soviet authorities gave vent to a variety of complaints about Japanese transgressions dating back to 1904.

When the Russians attacked on August 9, they had mobilized a force which, including the Soviet Pacific Fleet, totaled 1.6 million men under the command of Marshal Aleksandr Vasilevsky in Khabarovsk. Already in position were 5,000 tanks and 4,000 aircraft. The Kwantung Army in Manchuria was now a shell of its former self, having been raided for troops to stem the American tide in the Philippines and to defend the home islands. It now was subjected to simultaneous invasions from three directions: the Transbaikal Front, attacking eastward from Outer Mongolia; the First Far Eastern Front, invading westward across the Ussuri River; and the Second Far Eastern Front, crossing the Amur River southward from Blagoveshchensk. The Transbaikal Front, by far the largest, consisting of four armies under Marshal Rodion Malinovsky, struck directly east toward Mukden and Changchun and southeast across Inner Mongolia to sever communications between Manchuria and the Japanese forces in China proper. The First Far Eastern Front pushed toward Mukden and, complementing fleet amphibious landings, penetrated southward into Korea. The Second Far Eastern Front, in addition to attacking northern Manchuria, was responsible as well for providing troops for the investment of southern Sakhalin and the Kuril Islands, with transport and other support being furnished by the Soviet Pacific Fleet.

On August 11, two days after the atomic bombing of Nagasaki, Tokyo announced that it accepted the Potsdam Declaration. Four days later, the emperor broadcast a message to his subjects, directing the military to lay down their arms, and on September 2 the official surrender documents were signed aboard the battleship USS *Missouri* in Tokyo Bay.

The Russian phase of the war in the Pacific was short and decisive. Within two weeks, Japanese forces in Manchukuo and Sakhalin were overwhelmed. Soviet landings in the Kurils did not commence until August 17, two days after the emperor's address to the nation, and the southernmost island was not occupied until the end of the month. This brief period of combat resulted in the deaths of 84,000 Japanese and 32,000 Russian troops.

The home islands of Japan were quickly occupied, principally by American forces, and a supreme allied command was set up under the leadership of General Douglas MacArthur. Three months before, Germany had been divided into four occupation zones (American, British, French, and Russian) in accordance with the understandings concluded at Yalta and Potsdam. The Russians therefore proposed that they should take over the island of Hokkaido as their fair share of the occupation of Japan. This was denied them, and the occupation of Japan became an essentially American operation.

The United States, which had been pressuring the Soviet Union to join the war in the Pacific, was almost as stunned as was Japan by the force and celerity of the Russian juggernaut in Manchuria. One of the provisions of the Cairo Declaration had been the independence of Korea. However, Roosevelt believed that Korea should receive tutelage and gradually achieve sovereignty as a trust territory under the Great Powers. Accordingly, at Yalta, an informal agreement had been reached whereby U.S. and Russian forces would occupy the southern and northern parts of the country, respectively. At the Potsdam Conference, the dividing line between the two areas was designated as the parallel of 38° north latitude. Now, as the Red Army was pushing into Korea, the Americans were nowhere to be seen. After President Truman's reminder to Marshal Stalin, Soviet troops halted at the 38th parallel. U.S. forces finally arrived on September 8 to set up a military government.

Moscow, in compliance with the Yalta agreement, concluded a Treaty of Friendship and Alliance with Chiang Kai-shek's Nationalist government on August 15, 1945. The negotiations had commenced in Moscow on June 30, with T. V. Soong as the prime Chinese plenipotentiary. A key figure in the Chinese delegation was Chiang Kai-shek's son, Chiang Ching-kuo. This young man had spent ten years in the Soviet Union, from the Sino-Soviet falling-out in 1927 until well after rapprochement in 1932. He knew Stalin and had private sessions with him at this time. China was in a very weak bargaining position whereas Soviet military power was at its peak. Further, Stalin was armed by the concurrence of Britain and the United States in support of his goals.

The basic Sino-Soviet treaty of alliance, which was directed at Japan, committed the two sides to supporting each other against any future Japanese aggression. It also provided that there would be joint operation of the Chinese Eastern Railway and South Manchurian Railroad (the two in the future to be one system, called the Chinese Changchun Railway), to expire after thirty years, but that Manchuria was under Chinese sovereignty and that China was responsible for the physical security of the railway system. Further, in the Liao-tung Peninsula, Port Arthur was designated a joint naval base for use by both nations, with the responsibility for defense of the base assigned to the Soviets. Talien was to be a free port, open to all nations.

Stalin had been willing to compromise his initially extreme positions (such as exclusive Russian control of the railroads) in Manchuria. However, he was adamant when it came to Outer Mongolia, his rationale being that no major nation should be in a position which could so seriously threaten the Transsiberian Railway. Therefore China had to accede to the agreement which called for a plebiscite of the people in Outer Mongolia to decide their future. Chiang Kai-shek realized that he could gain no more, and the treaty was quickly ratified (August 24) by both nations. The Mongolian plebiscite was held on October 30, and, to nobody's surprise, the Mongols voted unanimously for independence from China. Accordingly, the Nationalist government of China recognized the sovereign state of the Mongolian People's Republic on January 5, 1946.

As the result of World War II, only one nation's territory was expanded appreciably: that of the Soviet Union. In addition to acquiring vast territories in Europe, which approximated the borders of the former Russian Empire, Moscow secured sole possession of Sakhalin and the Kuril Islands in the Far East. The Russians had successfully detached Outer Mongolia from China and had installed a compatible regime in Korea north of the 38th parallel. They had, as well, restored their interests in Manchuria, including the Liao-tung Peninsula. Indeed, as the result of the invasions in August, more than 300,000 Russian troops under Marshal Malinovsky were effectively occupying all of Manchuria.

24

The USSR and the Asian Mainland during the Cold War

Within a very short period after the conclusion of World War II, international politics came to be dominated by that political/ideological standoff known as the Cold War. Although there were no hostilities between the principal powers, hot spots would develop along the perimeter of the socialist camp, notably in Korea, the Indo-Chinese states, and Afghanistan.

As allies during the war, the United States and the Soviet Union were never comfortable bedfellows and were held together only by the shared desire to defeat their common enemies. The shock of the Hitlerian invasion had reenforced the deep Russian concern for secure borders, an anxiety that had been nurtured over the centuries by depredations of Mongols, Lithuanians, Poles, Swedes, and Frenchmen. Thus, immediately after the war in the wake of Red Army advances, a cordon sanitaire of compatible or at least pliable governments was created reaching from Germany on the Baltic to Bulgaria on the Black Sea. Winston Churchill's famous speech of March 1946 described the lowering of an "iron curtain" across Europe, but the existence of a cold war between the Soviet Union and its erstwhile allies was not generally recognized until a year or so later.

Great anxiety grew in the Western nations over the new Soviet political and military dominance in Central and Eastern Europe as well as the threat of communist revolution in other nations outside those countries under direct Soviet control. In 1947, in response to Soviet pressures on Turkey and Greece, U.S. President Harry Truman enunciated the Truman Doctrine, which promised aid to any nations subject to aggression. Western concern over the heavy-handed Soviet treatment of Poland in 1947, the Czech communist coup in February 1948, the isolation of Berlin two months later, and the communist successes in China's civil war would lead to an institutionalization of the estrangement. This took the form of a containment policy that resulted in a series of treaty organizations (with such acronyms as NATO, SEATO, and CENTO) designed to maintain the security of countries in Western Europe, southeastern Asia, and southern Asia. In 1955 the Soviet Union responded with the creation of an alliance with its fellow socialist states known as the Warsaw Pact.

As we have seen, Russian conquests in the late eighteenth and the nineteenth centuries brought into the empire huge areas inhabited by sizable non-Russian and mostly non-Slavic peoples. This was especially the case in Asia. These populations, which could not be easily absorbed into the state, presented special problems of administration. Initially they were held firmly by the autocratic power of the tsar who was the unchallenged head of government and church. When the tentative exercise of such authority by Nicholas II resulted in his abdication and civil war, such peripheral areas attempted to break away. As described in chapter 19, they were forcibly retrieved by the Red Army and organized into the Union of Soviet Socialist Republics (USSR).

After it was created in 1923 (and refined in 1936), the USSR carefully fostered the notion that it was indeed a union of ethnic polities tied together by the common bond of a shared ideology. In fact, the cement holding them together was the Communist Party of the Soviet Union (CPSU) and the tight discipline asserted by its all-powerful leader, Yosif Stalin. Control, which emanated from the center in the Russian capital of Moscow, was exercised through various organs, not the least of which was an apparatus of compulsion—the secret police. Despite the union's multiethnic facade and the fact that the party leader was a Georgian, the instincts and reflexes of the nation were essentially Russian.

With such a hold on its non-Russian Asiatic republics, there was massive defense in depth, but Soviet security concerns in Asia, as in Europe, were of the most sensitive sort. As described in the preceding chapter, Stalin succeeded in ensuring independence from China for the Mongolian People's Republic (MPR) in January 1946, an event that eased some Soviet concern over the security of the Transsiberian Railway. The next nearest threat to the Transsiberian was Manchuria. Here Soviet occupation troops under Marshal Malinovsky numbered over 300,000 after the war, but they were committed to depart after three months in accordance with the Sino-Soviet Treaty of August 15. The Soviet stay was prolonged partly at the behest of the Russians but also because the Chinese government was not prepared to take over from the Soviet occupation forces. Russian withdrawal finally commenced in March 1946.

The postwar situation in China had begun to deteriorate rapidly between the Nationalists, on the one hand, and Mao Tse-tung's communists, on the other. A full-fledged civil war was in progress by 1946. Crucial battles went in favor of the Chinese communists, and Nationalist forces began to crumble. Mao Tse-tung proclaimed the People's Republic of China (PRC) in Peking (renamed from Peip'ing to carry the symbolic impact of "northern capital" once again) on October 1, 1949. He did this from atop the Wu-men, or Meridian Gate, where the emperors of the past had viewed Chinese armies departing to carry out the imperial will. Chiang Kai-shek and his remaining followers were forced to flee to Taiwan where they established a new capital of the Republic of China (ROC) at Taipei.

Although the Soviet Union rendered moral support and provided weapons captured from the Japanese to the Chinese communists, Soviet troops took no direct action in the civil war in China. The new government of the PRC proceeded to exhibit its new power and independence by expelling the consular officials of the Western powers. Such was not the case with the Russian representatives. Mao Tse-tung had pretty well burned all other diplomatic bridges and thus had no one to turn to for help other than the USSR. He therefore had to travel to Moscow, hat in hand, to cut the best possible deal with Stalin. The resulting treaty established what became known as the Moscow-Peking Axis.

The Treaty of Friendship, Alliance, and Mutual Assistance, to be in effect for thirty years, was signed in Moscow on February 14, 1950. It of course invalidated the treaty between the Republic of China (ROC) and the USSR of 1945 although several of the provisions were similar. This agreement was directed not only at Japan but also at any country that might collaborate with her in aggression—a rather thinly veiled reference to the United States, which was the principal occupying power of Japan. Regarding Manchuria, China at this time received lenient terms which were granted largely because she was now a sister socialist state. The USSR agreed to transfer all Soviet rights and property connected with the Chinese Changchun Railway (the former CER and SMRR combined) to China without compensation. This was to be effective upon conclusion of a peace treaty with Japan or the end of the year 1952, whichever came first. The Soviets also agreed to withdraw from the Port Arthur base area although China was obligated to reimburse the cost of base development and improvement. Moscow was committed as well to return to the PRC all property it administered in Talien. Perhaps most important for the immediate future of the PRC, the Soviet Union agreed to assist the Chinese in modernizing their industry and military; however, the amount provided was the relatively modest sum of $300 million.

Turning next to another great border province—Sinkiang—we see that at the beginning of the war, the local warlord Sheng Shih-ts'ai was still in control. He owed his position to military and other support from the Soviet Union, while nominally recognizing Chinese sovereignty over his province. After the German invasion of Russia in 1941, however, Sheng's position became less secure, and he was dismissed by Chiang Kai-shek in 1943. Instability became the order of the day, and conditions after the war bordered on the chaotic until the arrival, in July 1949, of a communist army under command of General P'eng Te-huai, who firmly established the authority of the People's Republic of China in the province. Nevertheless, a Soviet presence of sorts was asserted pursuant to the new Moscow-Peking Axis. By an agreement of March 27, 1950, a Sino-Soviet joint-stock company was created, for a period of thirty years, for the exploitation of petroleum, rare metals, and nonferrous metals. Therefore, although the PRC was unable to reverse the independence of Outer Mongolia and reluctantly embraced the MPR as a sister socialist state, it was able to reassert firm control over Manchuria and Sinkiang, and the same would be true for that other great border area: Tibet.

Less than a year after the formation of the People's Republic of China, the Cold War suddenly became hot—on the Korean Peninsula. As we saw in the preceding chapter, Korea was divided between the military authorities of the Soviet Union and United States at the 38th parallel of latitude. An attempt to install a provisional government for the entire nation was bound to founder on the ideological cleavage between the two major powers; therefore, two very different governments finally developed on either side of the arbitrary border. The Republic of Korea (ROK), with its capital at Seoul and under President Syngman Rhee, was proclaimed on August 15, 1948. The U.S. military government was terminated, and American troops departed the following year. On September 9, 1948, the People's Democratic Republic of Korea (DPRK) was inaugurated, with its capital at P'yongyang, under the leadership of the communist leader Kim Il-song, and three months later the USSR announced the withdrawal of its troops from the new country.

The United States had rapidly disarmed after the end of World War II, and despite promulgation of the Truman Doctrine, did not seem to exhibit the will to back up the doctrine with troops. To add to this, a speech by the U.S. secretary of state defining American vital interests on the rim of East Asia omitted mention of Korea. For these and other reasons, a North Korean gamble was taken, with the full backing of Stalin, it is now known. Korean communist troops, well armed with Soviet weapons, invaded the Republic of Korea in force on June 25, 1950, with no prior indication of intent. The attack was almost completely successful in that only the perimeter about the southeastern port city of Pusan survived until the arrival of U.S. troops from Japan. In the United Nations Security Council, North Korea was branded an aggressor, and what became an overwhelmingly American side in the ensuing war would operate under the aegis of the United Nations (UN).

On September 15, 1950, amphibious landings at Inchon, on the Yellow Sea coast west of Seoul, drastically changed the fortunes of the war. The North Korean forces were sent reeling back northward. In late November, when it appeared the fighting was about to end, 300,000 Chinese troops from the PRC suddenly entered the fray. The age-old Chinese concern for the fate of the Korean "little brother" was now buttressed by ideological kinship between two communist governments. These forces, although regular army soldiers under the command of Marshal P'eng Te-huai, were called "volunteers." The war became a stalemate, and two years later an armistice was finally signed. All during the conflict, as we now learn, Soviet forces played a role, albeit well disguised, especially as fighter pilots. One festering sore in Sino-Russian relations, which would linger after the Korean war, grew out of the fact that, although the Soviet

Union armed the Chinese communists, the weapons were not free; payment was demanded.

While Stalin was still alive, Mao Tse-tung was willing to follow Moscow's lead in affairs of the communist world, but with the Soviet leader's death in March 1953, the situation changed. Mao found himself particularly disenchanted with Nikita Khrushchev, who finally emerged as Stalin's successor in 1955. Khrushchev implemented extensive internal changes, such as dismantling much of the Gulag system. He also, in an impassioned speech to the Twentieth Communist Party Congress in 1956, denounced Stalin and his cult of personality (such action was especially displeasing to Mao). In international affairs, Khrushchev seemed willing to conclude agreements with the West, such as the Austrian Peace Treaty, which terminated the occupation of that country. Indeed, he ushered in the so-called period of Peaceful Coexistence. This action was viewed by Mao as cowardly, particularly since the USSR had announced in 1953 its successful production of a hydrogen bomb. It seemed as if Mao's assessment was correct as uprisings flared in Russia's European satellites; however, the Hungarian revolt in 1956 was more than Khrushchev and the Soviet leaders could countenance, and the uprising was quickly quashed.

Despite such Sino-Soviet discord, it seemed to most Western observers that there was but one great, communistic monolith bestride the greater portion of the Eurasian continent. In 1956 the Transmongolian Railway was completed, tying Russia and China closer together. Plans were announced for the joint exploitation of the Argun and Amur rivers for hydroelectric power. Further, the Sino-Soviet joint-stock companies were liquidated, thus removing a thorn from Chinese sensitivity.

In truth, relations were becoming less harmonious. Two deep rifts began to develop, one economic and the other ideological. China became increasingly indebted to the Soviet Union, which made loans, not grants. By 1957, including the cost of arms for the Korean War, China owed her "benefactor" $2.4 billion. Chinese payment more often than not was in goods, and after the disaster of the "Great Leap," China was hard pressed to meet her obligations. Much dearer to Mao was the ideological struggle with the rest of the world. Not only did he exhibit a cavalier attitude toward nuclear war but, he believed, Soviet achievements in the world of technology spelled a superiority that should be exploited. Moscow did possess nuclear weapons, and by 1957 Russian scientists and engineers had developed an intercontinental ballistic missile; it also had launched the first man-made satellite into orbit about the earth. Mao became disillusioned when the Soviet Union would not back him to the hilt when he precipitated an international crisis in September 1958 by bombarding the Nationalist-held islands of Quemoy and Matsu. This action stiffened American anti-PRC attitudes and elicited a U.S. declaration of support for the ROC on Taiwan.

In implementation of the Moscow-Peking Axis, which came into being in 1950, an army of Soviet military and industrial technicians had come to China to help. They remained even during minor flaps between the two countries, and their numbers would be augmented as late as 1959. It would all come to a stop in 1960, however. By the end of the sixth decade, the Soviet Union had begun construction of its first ocean-going submarine force. Operations of such craft demanded highly dependable communications and other support. Accordingly, the PRC was approached with a request for the right to build a communications station in China as well as repair and resupply facilities. Further, permission for shore leave for the crews was requested. A blunt refusal contributed to a massive falling out between the two largest communist nations. Technicians were re-called to the Soviet Union, including those who had been working with the Chinese to develop a nuclear capability. They took all plans and paperwork with them.

From this point, all attempts to paper over differences were abandoned, and Sino-Soviet relations continued to deteriorate as ideological polemics between the two dominated the communist world. In 1962 China was even further es-tranged when Moscow neglected to consult with her over the Cuban missile crisis and failed to support the PRC side in its border crisis with India. Then, within two years, the Chinese successfully assembled an atomic bomb and scheduled detonation in the test range for October 15. Khrushchev seriously considered a preemptive attack on the installation. Mao, upon learning of this, made plans for the invasion of Outer Mongolia. It is possible that the ouster of Khrushchev, whose future had been sealed by the loss of face over the Cuban crisis in 1962, prevented open hostilities at the time. The Chinese detonated their bomb on October 16. Three years later, they had developed a hydrogen bomb.

The accession of Leonid Brezhnev to power in place of Khrushchev did not lessen tension. Indeed, developments in China ensured increased confrontation. Like Sun Yat-sen, Mao Tse-tung was a more effective revolutionary than man-ager. After the damage of the Great Leap, wiser heads had prevailed, and Mao had given up his position as chief of state to Liu Shao-ch'i in April 1959. For six and a half years Mao chafed as he saw the development of an entrenched bureaucracy. In late 1965, with the solid support of the army under Lin Piao, he commenced what is known as the Great Proletarian Cultural Revolution, which would rock China to its very foundation. Liu Shao-ch'i was destroyed, and gangs of young toughs, designated "Red Guards," terrorized the nation. At the same time, Chinese foreign policy became erratic, and border clashes with the Soviet Union escalated to the point that open warfare appeared possible.

Although the PRC recognized the Mongolian People's Republic, Mao in his heart of hearts was a true irredentist. In 1952 a map first appeared in a history book intended for use in secondary schools which showed China's borders as those during the glory days of the High Ch'ing; it included all the tributary powers of that age, including virtually all of Southeast Asia, the Himalayan countries, and the Ryukyu Islands. The map bore legends indicating how and when certain segments of Greater China had been seized by imperialist powers. A second edition was issued two years later, but the maps created no great stir for almost a decade, until PRC border eruptions occurred, principally along those boundaries shared with India and the Soviet Union. The Russians now viewed the maps carefully and saw in them an implied threat to their security. This derived from noting the inclusion in Greater China of Outer Mongolia, Sakhalin, Amuria, and Ussuria—as well as a huge segment of eastern Kazakhstan and Kyrgyzstan—a segment which, of itself, amounted to some 197,000 square miles.

Actually, the maps reflected a nationalistic view that was very much in accord with the true China as envisaged by the previous regimes as well. Mao Tsetung, as early as 1954, had suggested to Moscow that Mongolia be reunited with China. In March 1963, a Peking editorial featured the "unequal" treaties, including those with Russia. Then, in August 1964, in a talk to some Japanese socialists, Mao said, "About a hundred years ago, the area to the east of Lake Baikal became Russian territory and since then Vladivostok, Khabarovsk, Kamchatka, and other areas have been Soviet territory. We have not yet presented our account for this list."[1] A calculated insult of historical proportions was issued by the PRC on the occasion of the eight hundredth anniversary of the birth of Jenghis Khan. The great Mongol leader's invasion of the West was hailed as a cultural, civilizing force.

On the first two days of March 1969, violence erupted along the Ussuri River on an insignificant island named Damansky. Some 300 Chinese troops dug in on the island and ambushed Russian soldiers, killing seven and capturing nineteen of them. Two weeks later the Russians retaliated in force, an action that resulted in 800 Chinese casualties. Two months after that there were clashes along the Sinkiang/Kazakhstan border and, two months later still, along the Amur at Goldinsky Island near Khabarovsk.

Tempers in Moscow were at the boiling point, to the extent that Minister of Defense Andrei Grechko is said to have strongly recommended terminating the Chinese threat with nuclear weapons. Wiser heads prevailed, however, and Premier Aleksei Kosygin stopped in Peking on September 11 after attending the funeral of Ho Chi Minh in Hanoi. By this time the Great Proletarian Cultural Revolution had begun to run out of steam, and conversations between Chou and Kosygin resulted in an understanding that there would be no war and that the borders would remain status quo until changed by treaty.

Talks in Peking the following year elicited no agreement; the Chinese took the position, which they still espouse, that although they did not demand a change to the borders set by the "unequal" treaties, they sought recognition by the Soviet side that they were indeed "unequal" treaties. The USSR had failed in 1969 and in 1970 to convince the United States to assist in a preemptive attack to destroy Chinese nuclear facilities; so it now began to build up its military strength in Asia. By the end of the decade, fifty-three army divisions were stationed in the Soviet Far East (five of them in the MPR) and another thirty divisions in Central Asia. In addition to this, the Soviet Pacific Fleet grew dramatically to the point where it could boast that it was the largest of the Soviet fleets in terms of surface warships. At the same time, Brezhnev launched his policy of détente in Europe to soften problems on his western flank.

This was the period too when work was going on apace on one of the great undertakings in the postwar Soviet Union related to security (as well as exploitation of natural resources)—the Baikal-Amur Mainline (BAM). As mentioned in an earlier chapter, this railroad was begun in the 1930s as part of the second five-year plan. It was designed to provide a secure route, farther from the Manchurian border, which would reach from the north of Lake Baikal to the port of Sovetskaia Gavan opposite Sakhalin. Although there were claims that the BAM had been completed during the war, the forging of the railroad's final link would not be announced until October 1984, and the BAM would not be officially opened and declared operational until the following year. Even at that it would be a bare-bones installation without needed spurs, stations, and other vital infrastructure. Nevertheless, its construction, over 2,000 miles in length and under some of the most daunting natural conditions, was no mean achievement.

The PRC responded to Russian military deployment by positioning 1 million troops along the border and building massive bomb shelters in the major urban centers. Peking moved its nuclear weapons facilities and developed an intercontinental ballistic missile capability. A significant shift in Chinese strategic thinking was to entertain détente with the United States. In July 1971 Henry Kissinger, national security advisor to President Richard Nixon, made his dramatic, secret visit to the PRC via Pakistan to set up the historic presidential visit to China for the following February. Such a move had finally been made possible by the American realization that Eurasian communism was not the monolith as believed for so long.

Meanwhile, the final dramatic moment of the Great Proletarian Cultural Revolution occurred in September 1971 when Mao's heir apparent and cheerleader for the Mao cult of personality was forced to make a fateful decision. Lin Piao, whose position had been unassailable a year before, now found himself in the difficult position of losing his exalted situation or else implementing a military takeover of power. His indecision and ultimate lack of nerve resulted in a rather ignominious attempt to escape by flight to Mongolia. The plane crashed, thereby neatly ending the threat of military dictatorship. Just five years later, Mao and Chou both left the scene, and after a brief, sharp struggle with Mao's widow and the other three members of the Gang of Four, Teng Hsiao-p'ing would emerge as the paramount leader and launch China on the path of economic reform and the Four Modernizations.

After the communist success in Vietnam in 1975, Sino-Soviet relations deteriorated even further. Now no longer united in supporting Hanoi against Saigon and the Americans, the Soviets and Chinese pursued different aims in Southeast Asia. On November 3, 1978, just three months after the conclusion of the Sino-Japanese peace pact, a Soviet-Vietnamese Friendship Treaty was signed. Article 6 of the document called for consultation in the event either signatory were attacked or threatened and for appropriate measures as necessary to safeguard their security.

China was now largely surrounded by the Soviet Union, Vietnam (including its client state of Laos), and pro-Soviet India. The great naval base built by the Americans at Cam Ranh Bay in Vietnam would become a key support facility for the Soviet Pacific Fleet. The Vietnamese invaded Cambodia, defeated the Pol Pot regime, and installed its own hand-picked Cambodian government. These actions, together with the Vietnamese expulsion of ethnic Chinese, precipitated a short-lived Chinese attack on Vietnam's northern border commencing on February 7, 1979. The Soviet invasion of Afghanistan on Christmas Day of the same year drove an even wider wedge between the PRC and the USSR.

In the Soviet Union, an ever more entrenched bureaucracy and feverish period of arms production would ultimately result in a faltering economy, which was constantly called upon to support various developing nations around the world. An aging and lethargic Leonid Brezhnev died in 1982, to be followed in quick succession by two other leaders of the geriatric set: Yuri Andropov and Konstantin Chernenko. After Chernenko's demise in 1985, the reins of Soviet power fell to Mikhail Gorbachev. Younger and more robust, he attempted to generate energy and implement change through certain reforms, but in the space of six years his failed efforts resulted in the sudden collapse of the Soviet Union and sovereignty for each of its fifteen republics. All the Asian republics but Georgia then opted for membership in the Commonwealth of Independent States which, in many ways, is what the Soviet Union had claimed to be—an association of sovereign nations.

In the final analysis, therefore, the Russian experience on the Asian mainland since World War II has turned out to be one essentially of retrenchment. The earliest territorial change was the granting of sovereignty to Mongolia, which then for decades would be the sole client state committed to the USSR. In China, which for the first time in over a century was ruled by a strong central authority, Soviet interests and influence were gradually eroded to the point where the danger of open conflict along their 4,500-mile border came close to the surface.

For the last century, Russian interest in and influence over the Korean Peninsula have generally been highly exaggerated. In earlier chapters it was shown that, except for a very brief time in 1896–1897, the role of the Russian Empire in Korean affairs was minimal. After World War II, we see a Soviet position of preeminence from 1945 to 1950 north of the 38th parallel. Thereafter, there was a tussle between China and the USSR for the most influential position in North Korea, with the USSR generally gaining ascendancy.

Despite the loss of the Transcaucasian and Central Asian republics, the territorial extent of the Russian Federation in Asia still exceeds that of any other nation in the world—in excess of 5 million square miles, or almost a third of mainland Asia. It amounts essentially to the territory acquired by the expansion of Muscovy in the seventeenth and eighteenth centuries. Still, the security problems are daunting. Not only has the former massive territorial cushion been lost, which provided such defense in depth, but, remarkably, the land borders of the Russian Federation are just as long as were those of the Soviet Union, and defense now must depend on a population little more than half that of the USSR.

The region still is lightly populated and largely dependent on the Transsiberian Railway, that slender umbilicus which now is partly in another nation—Kazakhstan. There is, as well, the not-so-latent irredentist attitude of the PRC toward large segments of the Russian Federation, particularly those areas (Amuria and Ussuria) that were acquired by the Russian Empire in 1860 and contain the largest Russian population centers in the region.

NOTE

1. Harrison E. Salisbury, *War between Russia and China* (New York: W. W. Norton, 1969), 136.

25

The USSR and
the North Pacific
during the Cold War

Russia is historically a land—as opposed to a naval—power. Although the Imperial Russian Navy (IRN) enjoyed success and prestige under Peter I, Catherine II, and her two grandsons (Alexander I and Nicholas I), it was rarely employed other than as a seaward extension of the army. Small wonder, this, considering the geographical realities of the empire with such widely dispersed ocean areas.

Even when the Russians moved across the North Pacific to Alaska in the eighteenth century, they tended to dominate the area only until the arrival of ships of the world's major maritime powers. We have seen how Aleksandr Baranov was frequently forced into accommodations, mostly with American skippers, in order to get the job done for the Russian American Company. Although IRN officers were important in the later administration of that company, there was no appreciable Russian naval presence in the North Pacific. And, as recounted in chapter 11, the decision of Alexander II in 1867 to sell Alaska was based on his conviction that he did not possess the naval power required to defend it.

Not only was the empire thereafter restricted essentially to Pacific waters off Asia, but it suffered devastating naval reverses in the Russo-Japanese War. At the onset of that war, there was a modern Russian fleet-in-being at Port Arthur, but inept naval leaders on the spot failed totally to employ the force in a meaningful way and let it die an ignominious death, literally handing control of the sea environment to the Japanese. This was arguably the major contribution to the ultimate Japanese victory.

Seventy years before the end of World War II, Russia and Japan had divided the territorial spoils of the northwest Pacific by the Treaty of Saint Petersburg. It will be remembered that Russia received Sakhalin Island and Japan all of the

Kuril Islands. At the time it was generally conceded—by Russians and Japanese alike—that the advantage of the outcome went to the Russian side. After all, Sakhalin had natural riches whereas the Kurils were mostly barren isles. Russian writers early in this century, including General Aleksandr Kuropatkin, an important figure in the Russo-Japanese War, defined the eastern limit of Russian concern as the Korean border. They totally discounted the island frontier with Japan.

This attitude did not change essentially with the advent of the Soviet Union—although there was an irredentist theme concerning southern Sakhalin. During the period between the two world wars, the navy was still considered a minor adjunct of the army, and resources were not made available for the capital-intensive construction of a high seas naval fleet. The Soviet Union did commence the construction of a sizable merchant fleet and fishing fleet, however, thereby spawning a considerable seagoing population. But Soviet writers as late as 1939 still echoed the theme that the Treaty of Saint Petersburg was a Russian coup.

Very suddenly, as early as 1945, the same Soviet writers drastically changed their line. Now their position was that the perfidious Japanese had hoodwinked an inept Russian imperial government into parting with the Kuril Islands in 1875. Such a change in attitude was most likely the result of two factors. First, a rationale was needed to justify the Soviet seizure of the Kurils from Japan. Second, for the first time in Russian history, the strategic value of the islands in defense of the motherland was realized.

In the course of the last half century, one of the Soviet Union's principal concerns in the North Pacific has involved relations with its island neighbor—Japan. In that country, after the war, occupation proceeded apace. General Douglas MacArthur was designated Supreme Commander for Allied Powers (SCAP). Although nominally under the general direction of an eleven-nation Far Eastern Commission in Washington, D.C., and a four-power (America, Britain, China, and the Soviet Union) Allied Council in Tokyo, MacArthur operated as a veritable dictator, albeit it a benign one. As mentioned earlier, the Russians were rebuffed in their attempt to play a wider role in Japan at this time.

The period of occupation was shortened by the outbreak of the Korean War in the summer of 1950, which diverted U.S. attention from Japan to the more immediate military challenge on the Asian mainland. Japan now became an important source of goods and services in support of the UN in the Korean War, and preliminaries for a peace treaty were carefully orchestrated by U.S. Ambassador-at-Large John Foster Dulles, which led to a conference convened in San Francisco on September 4, 1951. Four days later, a treaty of peace was signed by forty-eight nations and Japan. On the same day, a mutual security pact was concluded between the Americans and Japanese whereby the Japanese permitted U.S. troops to remain indefinitely on their soil.

The Soviet Union, the People's Republic of China (PRC), and the Republic of China (ROC) on Taiwan were not among the signatories of the peace treaty.

Difficulties between the Japanese and the ROC were finally worked out, and an agreement was signed in April 1952. In the case of the PRC, twenty-seven years would elapse before the conclusion of a treaty of peace, and none has been signed between Japan and the USSR or Russia at the time of this writing (1996).

The San Francisco Treaty of Peace, to which the Japanese had very little alternative, provided that Japan was indeed to lose all territory except the main four islands (Hokkaido, Honshu, Kyushu, and Shikoku), as provided for in the Potsdam Declaration, but the wording of the document did not specify the recipients of the real estate that was ceded. The Soviet representative at San Francisco refused to sign any paper that did not specifically designate to whom the territory would be yielded. In actual fact, American troops occupied the Ryukyus and Bonin and Volcanic Isles, and the Soviet Union was in full possession of Sakhalin and all the Kurils.

At the time of the San Francisco conference, Japanese Prime Minister Yoshida Shigeru, while acceding fully to the text of the treaty, made the plea that the southern four islands of the Kurils were a special case. He claimed that these islands, consisting of Iturup (Japanese Etorofu), Kunashir, Shikotan, and the Habomais, had always been part of Japan, even dating from the first treaty with the Russian Empire—the Shimoda pact of 1855. Going further, he labeled Shikotan and the Habomais as part and parcel of Hokkaido and asserted that they therefore should not even be included in the Kuril Islands. The southern four islands in question, which comprise fewer than 2,000 square miles, have come to be known in Japan as the Northern Territories. Conflicting Russo-Japanese claims over them have continued to be a great stumbling block to the conclusion of a peace treaty.

Except for the four main Japanese islands, therefore, the former empire was dismembered. In addition to the island groups occupied by the United States and the Soviet Union, Korea became two independent states, and the Republic of China was awarded Taiwan and the Pescadores Islands. The former Japanese League of Nations mandates in the mid-Pacific were designated United Nations Trust Territories and administered mostly by the United States. The Americans returned the Bonin and Volcano Islands to Japanese sovereignty in 1968 and the Ryukyus in 1972. The mid-Pacific islands have mostly achieved independence and membership in the United Nations. The Republic of China government continues to control Taiwan, and Russian sovereignty is still asserted over Sakhalin and the Kurils, including all four southern islands.

After the death of Stalin and the rise of Khrushchev in the mid-1950s, the Soviet Union launched a series of efforts to tidy up international relations, such as the Austrian peace treaty and recognition of the Federal Republic of Germany. Included among Soviet goals was a Russo-Japanese peace treaty. Thus Moscow initiated a series of talks with the Japanese, which began in London in June 1955. By this time, the United States, which had insisted on denuding Japan of all but the four main islands in 1951, had come around to the position that there was a sound historical argument in favor of Japanese retention of the southern four islands of the Kurils. During the London talks, although the Japanese side initially laid claim to all the Kurils and southern Sakhalin, the chief negotiator Matsumoto Shunichi was instructed by Tokyo that the final position would be the recovery of Shikotan and the Habomais. In August the Soviet side, led by Yakob Malik, suddenly agreed that it had no objection to returning the two islands, and the Russian side even withdrew its long-standing insistence that Japan dissolve its mutual assistance treaty with the United States At this point, despite the appearance that a settlement was nigh, the Japanese leadership grew timid, primarily because of developments in domestic politics, and they reasserted the demand that all four southern islands be returned. Moscow now reacted coldly, and talks were suspended until the following year.

When the two sides reconvened in Moscow, the differences concerning the Northern Territories could not be bridged, and the declaration made public on October 19, 1956, essentially provided only for diplomatic and economic relations. The declaration did pledge the two nations to continue negotiations toward a treaty of peace, and the Soviet Union agreed to transfer Shikotan and the Habomai Islands to Japan—but only at such future time a peace treaty might be concluded. Twice more during the Khrushchev regime were exchanges made seeking to resume negotiations with the aim of terminating the state of war still existing between Japan and the USSR—once in 1961 and again in 1964. Both exchanges came to naught for the same basic reasons: the Northern Territories and the U.S.-Japanese alliance.

Then, as noted in the preceding chapter, the accession of Brezhnev in Moscow and the onset of the Great Proletarian Cultural Revolution in China strained relations between the USSR and the PRC to the breaking point. Matters between Japan and the USSR became more confusing when the Chinese chimed in on the side of Japan, compelling the Soviets to take a sterner stance on territorial exchange. Moscow, in fact, denied that there was a problem, that it had been solved by the conferences at Yalta and Potsdam in 1945.

In the early 1970s, after Sino-American rapprochement became a reality, Tokyo began to take steps toward an accommodation with China. Prime Minister Tanaka Kakuei made a visit to Peking in September 1972, which caused Moscow to adopt an even tougher stance vis-à-vis the Northern Territories. (This attitude did not, however, preclude informal Russo-Japanese agreements for economic cooperation in Siberia and the Soviet Far East.) By 1975 Sino-Japanese negotiations for a peace treaty were ongoing, but they stumbled over Chinese insistence that any such agreement should contain a clause condemning the efforts of any country to establish hegemony in the Asia-Pacific region—a clear swipe at the Soviet Union.

The year 1975 also saw developments in Europe which would impact on the likelihood of territorial settlement in the Far East. Soviet leader Leonid Brezhnev's policy of détente toward the Western nations paid dividends when, on August 1, the Final Act of the Conference on Security and Cooperation in Europe (CSCE) was signed in Helsinki, Finland. The West German accession to the CSCE act in essence signed away any irredentist goals the Germans might harbor. The effect of the CSCE, in Soviet eyes, was to legitimize by treaty all territorial gains realized by the Soviet Union through the Yalta and Potsdam declarations. Having won such a victory in Europe, Moscow would now be even more reluctant to countenance any exceptions in Asia.

The following year saw the demise of Mao Tse-tung and Chou En-lai in China, which would put the brakes on Sino-Japanese negotiations. There also occurred an event that would further estrange the Soviets and Japanese. A Soviet Air Force pilot, Viktor Belenko, defected and flew his new MIG-25 jet interceptor aircraft into the Hakodate Airport on September 6. Despite Soviet diplomatic pressure, Belenko was granted asylum in the United States, and Japanese and American technicians disassembled and analyzed the plane. Finally, sixty-seven days later, in response to repeated Soviet demands for the return of the craft, all the parts were crated up and loaded on a Russian ship. Early the following year, apparently in retaliation, the Soviet Council of Ministers declared a 200-nautical-mile exclusive fishing zone around the nation, which included all the Kuril Islands, a condition that was reflected in the Russo-Japanese fisheries treaty signed in May 1977.

The Sino-Japanese Peace Treaty was finally concluded on August 12, 1978. This was in spite of, or perhaps even in contempt of, a Soviet air and naval exercise of unprecedented scope conducted in areas adjacent to Japan. The treaty as signed contained the controversial antihegemony clause; therefore, the Soviet reaction could almost have been predicted. Commencing in early 1979, additional troops were ordered into Kunashir and Iturup, and considerable base construction activity commenced. The Russians later set about upgrading military facilities on Shikotan as well.

Since that time, the prospects have dimmed considerably for a resolution of the problem of the Northern Territories. Attitudes have hardened on both sides, and especially since the fragmentation of the USSR into its fifteen component parts in 1991, security concerns in the Russian capital make it highly improbable that any Russian leader would survive were he to agree to the cession of any territory of the Russian federation.

Leonid Brezhnev is remembered for the doctrine of intervention that bears his name, for détente with the West, and for the phenomenal buildup of Soviet military power to make up for the humiliation of the Cuban missile crisis of 1962. The massive Soviet land forces, with their awesome power in tanks and artillery, were augmented by a huge nuclear arsenal, a modern jet fighter and bomber force, and, for the first time in Soviet history, a modern seagoing navy. By the end of the sixth decade, diesel submarines, with all the necessary communications and maintenance support, were operating on the high seas. Very shortly these would be replaced by November-class nuclear-powered attack submarines. Within a decade, at the same time that the Soviet army and air force were ringing China with 1 million men under arms, Yankee-class ballistic missile submarines were on station off the two coasts of the United States. Not only were the Russian shipyards turning out many submarines—they were building an astonishing array of classes of submarines. The Soviet submarine strength grew to be the greatest of any peace-time nation in history.

An interesting stimulus for the development of Soviet sea power was the ideological side of the Cold War. The Soviet Union was a veritable fortress with the satellite states as cushion against containment of the West; however, she carried the ideological struggle to many nations in Asia, Africa, and the Western Hemisphere. The most salient example was Cuba, which even provided proxy military forces in revolutionary movements in several Third World nations. In the case of satellites along the Soviet border, support was easily exerted by the Red Army, but a new dimension of power projection was required for support of those client movements beyond the reach of the Red Army.

The largest Soviet submarine force was logically assigned to the Northern Fleet in Poliarnoe near the Barents Sea, the only Russian littoral granting relatively unimpeded access to the open Atlantic Ocean. This force came to number more than 135, which equaled the entire inventory of U.S. submarines. The Soviet Pacific Fleet came in for its fair share of growth as well. In addition to the ninety-eight submarines assigned to it, there were 205 surface combatant ships, which constituted the largest surface force of any Soviet fleet area. Indeed, this armada exceeded the size of the U.S. Pacific Fleet, in terms of numbers of ships, by a ratio of three to two. Vladivostok was the headquarters and principal operating base for the Pacific Fleet. As such, it furnished the ships to support the large squadrons that were continuously deployed in the South China Sea and the western reaches of the Indian Ocean.

One of the more dramatic aspects of the Cold War over the sea was that of peripheral flights for intelligence purposes. In the mutually assured destruction (MAD) nuclear standoff, early warning of missiles or aircraft, which might be en route with nuclear weapons, was of prime importance. Thus the United States and Canada developed the Defense Early Warning (DEW) Line of land- and ship-based radars as part of the North American Air Defense System. Similarly, the Soviet Union devised its air defense organization known as *Protivo-Vozdushnaia Oborona* (PVO). The game, early on, became one of testing the effectiveness of each other's system by noting the electronic responses to special flights along the perimeters of the other's airspace. Since such flights usually occurred over international waters, they supposedly were not violating a nation's sovereign airspace. However, the opportunity for incidents was high, particularly if an error in navigation occurred. U.S. aircraft were downed in the Baltic, Barents, and Black seas and in the Pacific in the late 1940s and early 1950s. This included a U.S. Air Force RB-29 on June 3, 1952, over the Sea of Japan. No Russian aircraft flying perimeter missions were attacked, but they were regularly intercepted and escorted by U.S. fighter aircraft.

In the Pacific, American peripheral flights were flown not only against the USSR but also against the PRC and the DPRK. One was shot down off Shanghai in 1956, and one was destroyed by North Korean interceptors over the Sea of

Japan in 1969. Although there were no further disasters in this vein for almost the next decade and a half, the continued tension led to the tragic downing of a (South) Korean Airlines commercial flight on September 1, 1983. This Boeing 747 had wandered off course and entered the airspace of the USSR near Sakhalin Island. Improperly identified by the Soviet PVO authorities, it was destroyed on command by antiair fire.

The game played itself out on the ocean as well as above it. When ballistic missiles with nuclear warheads were placed on U.S. submarines in the 1960s, the Soviets sought to monitor the departure of these vessels from their home bases en route to take up patrol stations off the perimeter of the USSR. We therefore saw the appearance of Soviet "station ships" (small vessels with electronic monitoring capability) off Guam, the Hawaiian Islands, and every other point of harbor egress used by U.S. fleet ballistic missile submarines. The United States also was briefly involved in coastal electronic surveillance until the embarrassment of the loss of the USS *Pueblo* in January 1968.

The principal fleet center for the Soviet Pacific Fleet, as stated above, was Vladivostok. With the arrival in the Pacific of their ballistic missile submarines, however, the Soviet authorities established the operating base for them at Petropavlovsk on Kamchatka. This was done primarily for security reasons. Avacha Bay, the harbor for Petropavlovsk, opens into the broad Pacific. If the vessels had been based in Vladivostok, they would have had to exit the Sea of Japan via tightly restricted waters.

A considerable Russian presence in the North Pacific has been a reality now for more than three decades. This is true not just of naval power. It also includes ships of the fishing and merchant fleets as well as sophisticated vessels engaged in pelagic research. This should come as no surprise since the rich fishing grounds are of great importance to the nation, and Russia has the task of defending the longest coastline of any nation in East Asia.

More than 400 years have passed since Yermak Timofeevich first established the sovereign authority of Muscovy east of the Ural Mountains. In that time Russian sway has been extended eastward across the taiga, through the North Pacific, and onto the North American continent. It has also spread across the Caucasus Mountains and deep into the steppe and deserts of Central Asia. Russia's eastern destiny has essentially been one of expanding its borders to the point where the force of expansion meets an equal and opposite political authority, whether Japan, China, or, as often was the case, the maritime power of European nations.

Dominating, as it has, the so-called heartland of Eurasia and threatened, as it has been so often in the past by powerful neighbors, Russia has been driven by the compulsion to achieve its security in territorial depth. Its occasional contractions have been few but notable: the sale of Alaska in 1867, the cession of southern Sakhalin in 1905, and the divorce from the soviet socialist republics in Transcaucasia and Central Asia in 1991.

Although it has realized extraordinary losses of Asian territory in this decade,

Russia has in the meantime asserted a presence in the North Pacific which is unprecedented in its intensity. This massive contiguous polity, which has dwarfed all its modern contemporaries, was held together first by the authority of an all-powerful autocrat and later by the discipline of the dictatorship of the Russian proletariat. Despite its still awesome order of magnitude, Moscow now is in crisis as it seeks a strong center of gravity to provide the cohesion necessary to ensure that there is indeed still a destiny in the east for the Russian federation.

Suggested Reading List

Baddeley, John F. *The Russian Conquest of the Caucasus*. London, 1914. Reprint. New York: Russell & Russell, 1969.

Banno Masataka. *China and the West 1858–1861: The Origins of the Tsungli Yamen*. Cambridge: Harvard University Press, 1964.

Batalden, Stephen K., and Sandra L. Batalden. *The Newly Independent States of Eurasia: Handbook of Former Soviet Republics*. Phoenix: Oryx Press, 1993.

Becker, Seymour. *Russia's Protectorates in Central Asia: Bukhara and Khiva, 1865–1924*. Cambridge: Harvard University Press, 1968.

Bobrick, Benson. *East of the Sun: The Epic Conquest and Tragic History of Siberia*. New York: Henry Holt, 1992.

Clubb, O. Edmund. *China and Russia: The Great Game*. New York: Columbia University Press, 1971.

Collins, Perry McDonough. *Siberian Journey: Down the Amur to the Pacific 1856–7*. Edited by C. Vevier. Madison: University of Wisconsin Press, 1962.

Coox, Alvin D. *The Anatomy of a Small War: The Soviet-Japanese Struggle for Changkufeng/Khasan, 1938*. Westport, Conn.: Greenwood Press, 1977.

———. *Nomonhan: Japan against Russia, 1939*. Stanford, Calif.: Stanford University Press, 1985.

Dallin, David J. *The Rise of Russia in Asia*. New Haven, Conn.: Yale University Press, 1949.

———. *Soviet Russia and the Far East*. New Haven, Conn.: Yale University Press, 1948.

Dawisha, Karen, and Bruce Parrott. *Russia and the New States of Eurasia: The Politics of Upheaval*. New York: Cambridge University Press, 1994.

Deuchler, Martina. *Confucian Gentlemen and Barbarian Envoys: The Opening of Korea 1875–1885*. Seattle: University of Washington Press, 1977.

Dmytryshyn, Basil et al. *The Russian American Colonies: A Documentary Record 1798–1867*. Portland: Oregon Historical Society Press, 1989.

————. *Russia's Conquest of Siberia: A Documentary Record 1558–1700.* Portland: Oregon Historical Society Press, 1985.

Dmytryshyn, Basil et al., ed. and trans. *Russian Penetration of the North Pacific Ocean: A Documentary Record 1700–1797.* Portland: Oregon Historical Society Press, 1988.

Donnelly, Alton S. *The Russian Conquest of Bashkiria 1552–1740: A Case Study in Imperialism.* New Haven, Conn.: Yale University Press, 1968.

Evans, John. *The Russo-Chinese Crisis: N. P. Ignatiev's Mission to Peking, 1859–1860.* Newtonville, Mass.: Oriental Research Partners, 1987.

Fairbank, John K., ed. *The Chinese World Order: Traditional China's Foreign Relations.* Cambridge: Harvard University Press, 1968.

Fisher, Raymond H. *Bering's Voyages: Whither and Why.* Seattle: University of Washington Press, 1977.

————. *The Russian Fur Trade 1550–1700.* Berkeley: University of California Press, 1943.

Foust, Clifford M. *Muscovite and Mandarin: Russia's Fur Trade with China and Its Setting, 1727–1805.* Chapel Hill: University of North Carolina Press, 1969.

Fu Lo-shu. *A Documentary Chronicle of Sino-Western Relations (1644–1820).* 2 vols. Tucson: University of Arizona Press, 1966.

Gibson, James R. *Farming the Frontier: The Agricultural Opening of the Oregon Country, 1786–1846.* Seattle: University of Washington Press, 1985.

————. *Feeding the Russian Fur Trade: Provisionment of the Okhotsk Seaboard and the Kamchatka Peninsula 1639–1856.* Madison: University of Wisconsin Press, 1969.

————. *Imperial Russia in Frontier America: The Changing Geography of Supply of Russian America, 1784–1867.* New York: Oxford University Press, 1976.

Golder, F. A. *Russian Expansion in the Pacific 1641–1850.* Cleveland, 1914. Reprint. New York: Paragon Book Reprint, 1971.

Grousset, René. *Conqueror of the World.* New York: Orion Press, 1966.

————. *The Empire of the Steppes: A History of Central Asia.* Translated by N. Walford. New Brunswick, N.J.: Rutgers University Press, 1970.

Halperin, C. J. *Russia and the Golden Horde: The Mongol Impact on Medieval Russian History.* Bloomington: Indiana University Press, 1987.

Hambly, Gavin, ed. *Central Asia.* New York: Delacorte Press, 1966.

Harrington, F. R. *God, Mamon and the Japanese.* Bloomington: Indiana University Press, 1966.

Harrison, John A. *Japan's Northern Frontier.* Gainesville: University of Florida Press, 1953.

Hsu, Immanuel C. Y. *The Ili Crisis: A Study of Sino-Russian Diplomacy 1871–1881.* Oxford, England: Clarendon Press, 1965.

Hummel, Arthur W., ed. *Eminent Chinese of the Ch'ing Period (1644–1912).* Washington, D.C.: U.S. Government Printing Office, 1943.

Keene, Donald. *The Japanese Discovery of Europe, 1720–1830.* London, 1952. Reprint. Stanford, Calif.: Stanford University Press, 1969.

Kennan, George. *Siberia and the Exile System.* 2 vols. 1891. Reprint. New York: Praeger, 1970.

Kerner, Robert J. *The Urge to the Sea: The Course of Russian History.* Berkeley: University of California Press, 1942.

Khisamutdinov, Amir. *The Russian Far East: Historical Essays*. Honolulu: Author, 1993.

Khlebnikov, Kyrill T. *Baranov: Chief Manager of the Russian Colonies in America*. Edited by Richard A. Pierce and translated by Colin Bearn. Kingston, Ont.: Limestone Press, 1973.

———. *Colonial Russian America: Kyrill T. Khlebnikov's Reports, 1817–1832*. Translated by B. Dmytryshyn and E.A.P. Crownhart-Vaughan. Portland: Oregon Historical Society, 1976.

Kim, C. I. Eugene, and Kim Han-kyo. *Korea and the Politics of Imperialism 1876–1919*. Berkeley: University of California Press, 1967.

Kotkin, Stephen, and David Wolff, eds. *Rediscovering Russia in Asia: Siberia and the Russian Far East*. Armonk, N.Y.: M.E. Sharpe, 1995.

Krasheninnikov, S. P. *Explorations of Kamchatka: North Pacific Scimitar*. Translated by E.A.P. Crownhart-Vaughan. Portland: Oregon Historical Society, 1972.

Kuropatkin, A. N. *The Russian Army and the Russo-Japanese War*. Edited by E. D. Swinton and translated by A. B. Lindsay. New York: Dutton, 1909.

Lantzeff, George V., and Richard A. Pierce. *Eastward to Empire: Exploration and Conquest on the Russian Open Frontier, to 1750*. Montreal: McGill-Queens University Press, 1973.

Lattimore, Owen. *Inner Asian Frontiers of China*. Washington, D.C.: The National Geographic Society, 1951.

Lee, Robert H. G. *The Manchurian Frontier in Ch'ing History*. Cambridge: Harvard University Press, 1970.

Lee Yur-bok. *West Goes East: Paul Georg von Mollendorff and Great Power Imperialism in Late Yi Korea*. Honolulu: University of Hawaii Press, 1988.

Lensen, George A. *Balance of Intrigue: International Rivalry in Korea & Manchuria, 1884–1899*. 2 vols. Tallahassee: University Presses of Florida, 1982.

———. *The Damned Inheritance: The Soviet Union and the Manchurian Crises 1924–1935*. Tallahassee: Diplomatic Press, 1974.

———. *The Russian Push toward Japan: Russo-Japanese Relations 1697–1875*. Princeton, N.J., 1952. Reprint. New York: Octagon Books, 1971.

———. *Russia's Japanese Expedition of 1852 to 1855*. Gainesville: University of Florida Press, 1955.

———. *The Strange Neutrality: Soviet-Japanese Relations during the Second World War 1941–1945*. Tallahassee: Diplomatic Press, 1972.

Lensen, George A., ed. *Russia's Eastward Expansion*. Englewood Cliffs, N.J.: Prentice-Hall, 1964.

Lincoln, W. Bruce. *The Conquest of a Continent: Siberia and the Russians*. New York: Random House, 1993.

Lisiansky, Yuri F. *A Voyage round the World*. London, 1814. Reprint. Amsterdam: Da Capo Press, 1968.

Lobanov-Rostovsky, A. *Russia and Asia*. New York: Macmillan, 1933.

Malozemoff, A. *Russian Far Eastern Policy 1881–1904 with Special Emphasis on the Causes of the Russo-Japanese War*. Berkeley, 1958. Reprint. New York: Octagon Books, 1977.

Mancall, Mark. *Russia and China: Their Diplomatic Relations to 1728*. Cambridge: Harvard University Press, 1971.

Marks, Steven G. *Road to Power: The Trans-siberian Railroad and the Colonization of Asian Russia, 1850–1917*. Ithaca, N.Y.: Cornell University Press, 1991.

Martin, H. D. *The Rise of Chingis Khan and His Conquest of North China*. Baltimore, 1950. Reprint. New York: Octagon Books, 1981.

Mehnert, Klaus. *The Russians in Hawaii 1804–1819*. Honolulu: University of Hawaii Press, 1939.

Pierce, Richard A. *Russian Central Asia 1867–1917: A Study in Colonial Rule*. Berkeley: University of California Press, 1960.

———. *Russia's Hawaiian Adventure, 1815–1917*. Berkeley, 1965. Reprint. Kingston, Ont.: Limestone Press, 1976.

Qasvini, Mirza Muhammad. *The History of the World Conqueror*. Translated by J. A. Boyle. 3 vols. Cambridge: Harvard University Press, 1958.

Quested, Rosemary K. I. *The Expansion of Russia in East Asia 1857–1860*. Singapore: University of Malaya Press, 1968.

———. *Sino-Russian Relations: A Short History*. Sydney: George Allen & Unwin, 1984.

Rice, Don C. *Russia and the Roots of the Chinese Revolution 1896–1911*, Cambridge: Harvard University Press, 1974.

Richardson, Hugh E. *A Short History of Tibet*. New York: E. P. Dutton, 1962.

Rossabi, Morris. *China and Inner Asia from 1368 to the Present Day*. New York: Pica Press, 1975.

———. *Kubilai Khan: His Life and Times*. Berkeley: University of California Press, 1988.

Rupen, Robert. *How Mongolia Is Really Ruled: A Political History of the Mongolian People's Republic 1900–1978*. Stanford, Calif.: Hoover Institution Press, 1979.

Salisbury, Harrison E. *War between Russia and China*. New York: W. W. Norton, 1969.

Sansom, George. *A History of Japan*. 3 vols. Stanford, Calif.: Stanford University Press, 1958.

Sebes, Joseph. *The Jesuits and the Sino-Russian Treaty of Nerchinsk (1689): The Diary of Thomas Pereira, S.J.* Rome: Institutum Historicum, S.I., 1961.

Semyonov, Yuri. *Siberia: Its Conquest and Development*. Translated by J. R. Foster. Baltimore: Helicon Press, 1963.

Sinor, Denis, ed. *The Cambridge History of Early Inner Asia*. New York: Cambridge University Press, 1990.

Spuler, Berthold. *History of the Mongols*. Translated by H. Drummond and S. Drummond. Zurich, 1968. Reprint. New York: Dorset Press, 1988.

Starr, S. Frederick, ed. *Russia's American Colony*. Durham, N.C.: Duke University Press, 1987.

Stephan, John J. *The Kuril Islands: Russo-Japanese Frontier in the Pacific*. Oxford, England: Clarendon Press, 1974.

———. *The Russian Far East: A History*. Stanford, Calif.: Stanford University Press, 1994.

———. *Sakhalin: A History*. Oxford, England: Clarendon Press, 1971.

Stephan, John J., and V. P. Chichkanov, eds. *Soviet-American Horizons on the Pacific*. Honolulu: University of Hawaii Press, 1986.

Tang, Peter S. H. *Russian and Soviet Policies in Mongolia and Manchuria*. Durham, N.C.: Duke University Press, 1959.

Tikhmenev, P. A. *A History of the Russian-American Company*. Translated and edited by R. A. Pierce and A. S. Donnelly. Seattle: University of Washington Press, 1978.

Treadgold, Donald. *The Great Siberian Migration: Government and Peasant in Reset-

tlement from Emancipation to the First World War. 7th ed. Boulder, Colo.: West-view Press, 1990.

Tupper, Harmon. *To the Great Ocean: Siberia and the Trans-siberian Railway.* Boston: Little, Brown & Co., 1965.

Vernadsky, George, and M. Karpovich. *Kievan Russia.* Vol. 2 of *A History of Russia.* New Haven, Conn.: Yale University Press, 1948.

———. *The Mongols and Russia.* Vol. 3 of *A History of Russia.* New Haven, Conn.: Yale University Press, 1953.

———. *Russia at the Dawn of the Modern Age.* Vol. 4 of *A History of Russia.* New Haven, Conn.: Yale University Press, 1959.

Weber, David J. *The Spanish Frontier in North America.* New Haven, Conn.: Yale University Press, 1992.

Westwood, J. N. *A History of Russian Railways.* London: Allen & Unwin, 1964.

Wheeler, Geoffrey. *The Modern History of Soviet Central Asia.* New York: Praeger, 1964.

White, John A. *Diplomacy of the Russo-Japanese War.* Princeton, N.J.: Princeton University Press, 1964.

———. *The Siberian Intervention.* New York: Greenwood Press, 1950.

Widner, Eric W. *The Russian Ecclesiastical Mission in Peking during the Eighteenth Century.* Cambridge: Harvard University Press, 1976.

Witte, Sergei Y. *The Memoirs of Count Witte.* Translated and edited by A. Yarmolinsky. New York: Doubleday & Page, 1921.

———. *The Memoirs of Count Witte.* Translated and edited by S. Harcave. London: M. E. Sharpe, 1990.

Wood, Alan, ed. *The History of Siberia: From Russian Conquest to Revolution.* New York: Routledge, 1991.

Zagoria, Donald S., ed. *Soviet Policy in East Asia.* New Haven, Conn.: Yale University Press, 1982.

Ziegler, Charles E. *Foreign Policy and East Asia: Learning and Adaptation in the Gorbachev Era.* New York: Cambridge University Press, 1993.

Index

Abagaitu Letter, addendum to Treaty of Kiakhta, 66

Abahai, son of Nurhaci and leader of the Manchus (1626–1643), 41

Abaza, A. M., secretary of Special Committee for Far Eastern Affairs (1903), 181

Abbasid Caliphate, 11, 17

Ablin, Setkul, Bukharan caravaneer in service of Muscovy (16th c.), 44, 45

Abulkhair, Khan of Kazakh Lesser Horde (1730s), 139

Achansk, temporary Muscovite encampment on Amur River (1650s), 49

Afghanistan, 145, 150, 192–94, 236

Afognak, Alaskan island, 97

Ahmad, Khan of the Golden Horde (late 15th c.), 21

Aian, Russian port on Sea of Okhotsk, 120, 124

Aigun, Manchu town on Amur opposite mouth of Zeia River now called Heihe, 52, 125

Aigun, Treaty of (1858), 127, 129

Ainu, 69, 71, 76

Akkeshi, *basho* on northeast corner of Hokkaido, 76

Ak-Masdjid, town in Kazakhstan renamed Perovsk and now Qyzylorda, 140, 143

Akmolinsk, town and province in Central Asia, 191

Alash Orda, Kazakh political party (1917), 191–92

Alaska, xv, 82, 95–97, 110, 223, 239, 245

Albazin, temporary Muscovite stronghold on Amur River (17th c.), 49–52, 55, 59

Alekseev, Evgeni, admiral in command of Far East Forces (1899–1904), 170, 181–82

Alekseev, Kir, senior financial advisor to Korean government (1897–1898), 177–78

Aleutians, xv, 82, 97, 110

Alexander I, Emperor of Russia (ruled 1801–1825), 105, 107–10, 117, 123, 185, 239

Alexander II, Emperor of Russia (ruled 1855–1881), xv, 113–14, 124, 127, 140, 145–47, 150

Alexander III, Emperor of Russia (ruled 1881–1894), 150–53, 163

Alexander Nevsky, Prince of Novgorod (mid-13th c.), 19

Alexis, Tsar of Muscovy (ruled 1645–1676) and father of Peter the Great, 52

Allen, Dr. Horace, American missionary

inspecting Russian American Co.
(1861), 113
Kostromitinov, Petr, manager of Fort
Ross (1830–1838), 110
Kosygin, Aleksei, Soviet premier (1964–
1980), 235
Kotsebue, Otto von, Russian naval officer
(early 19th c.), 106, 109
Kowshing, Chinese ship involved in Sino-
Japanese War, 165
Kozyrevsky, Ivan, Cossack leader in
Kamchatka (early 18th c.), 72–73
Krasnoiarsk, major center on Yenisei
River, 85, 102, 154
Krasnoshchekov (true name Tobelson),
Aleksandr, president of Far Eastern
Republic (1920–1922), 190
Krasnozavodsk, town on east coast of
Caspian Sea and base for military
operations into Central Asia, 150,
192
Krusenstern, Adam, leader of first Rus-
sian round-the-world voyage (1803–
1806), 83–84, 101–3, 109, 117, 120
Kubilai, grandson of Jenghis Khan and
fifth Great Khan and founder of Yuan
dynasty in China (ruled 1260–1294),
16–17
Kuchum, khan of Sibir (1563–1582), 28–
30
Kudo Heisuke, influential writer in Japan
(late 18th c.), 80
Kuibyshev, Valerian, Soviet political
advisor to Frunze in Central Asia
(1919–1920), 193
Kuibyshev. *See* Samara
Kuldja (also Ili), 143, 209
Kulikovo, site on Don River of Musco-
vite victory over Golden Horde (1390),
19
Kumarsk, Muscovite encampment on
Amur River (1650s), 50–51
Kunashir, Kuril Island northeast of
Hokkaido, 86–87, 241, 243
Kung, important Manchu prince in
Chinese government (1860s), 129
Kunrentai, Japanese-trained Korean
troops (1890s), 174

Kuomintang, 185, 205–7
Kuril Islands, xv, xvii, 6, 69–72, 81–90,
110, 224–27, 240
Kuroda Kiyotaka, leader in colonization
of Hokkaido (late 19th c.), 90
Kuropatkin, Aleksei, important figure in
Russo-Japanese War and Central Asia,
150, 158 n.1, 170, 180, 191, 240
Kuskov, Ivan, founder and first manager
of Fort Ross (1812–1821), 102–3, 106,
110
Kutuzov, Russian ship in North Pacific
(1817), 108
Kwangchow-wan (Guangzhouwan),
coastal area in southern China leased
to French, 169, 185, 212
Kwantung Army, Japanese forces in
Manchukuo, 212–17, 222, 225
Kyrgyzstan, 9, 235
Kyzyl, capital of Tuvinian Republic, 200
Kzyl-Arvat (now Gyzylarbat), town in
Turkmenistan, 150
Kzyl Orda. *See* Ak-Masdjid

Ladyzhensky, Nikolai, Russian minister
to China (late 19th c.), 163–64
Lange, Lorents, important figure in Sino-
Russian relations (early 18th c.), 63–
65, 118
La Pérouse, Jean François de Galaup,
Comte de, French Pacific explorer (late
18th c.), 87, 99, 120
Laptev, Dmitri, Arctic explorer (1739–
1742), 95, 98
Laptev, Khariton, cousin of Dmitri and
also an arctic explorer (1739–1740),
94–95
Laxman, Adam, leader of mission to
Japan (late 18th c.), 79–83
Lazarev, Mikhail, naval explorer (early
19th c.), 104, 109
Lebedev-Lastochkin, Pavel, merchant
who attempted to colonize Kuril
Islands (late 18th c.), 76
Lend-Lease, xvii, 223
Legnica. *See* Liegnitz
Lenin (real name Ulianov), Vladimir,

About the Author

G. PATRICK MARCH pursued a 30-year career in cryptology with the U.S. Navy which involved duty in Asia, Europe, and Africa. After final tours with the National Security Agency and the office of the Chief of Naval Operations, he retired with the rank of Rear Admiral. He has been a lecturer of history at the University of Hawaii and is the author of *Cossacks of the Brotherhood* (1990) and of articles appearing in *Pacific Historical Review* and *Sibirica*.

ISBN 0-275-95566-4

90000>

EAN

9 780275 955663

HARDCOVER BAR CODE